THOMAS VOGEL

BREAKTHROUGH THINKING

A GUIDE TO CREATIVE THINKING AND IDEA GENERATION

Cincinnati, Ohio
www.howdesign.com

 Published by HOW Books, an imprint of F+W Media, Inc., 10151 Carver Road, Suite 200, Blue Ash, Ohio 45242. (800) 289-0963. First edition.

For more excellent books and resources for designers, visit www.howdesign.com.

18 17 16 15 14   5 4 3 2 1

ISBN-13: 978-1-4403-3326-2

Distributed in Canada by Fraser Direct
100 Armstrong Avenue
Georgetown, Ontario, Canada L7G 5S4
Tel: (905) 877-4411

Distributed in the U.K. and Europe by F&W Media International, LTD
Brunel House, Forde Close, Newton Abbot, TQ12 4PU, UK
Tel: (+44) 1626 323200, Fax: (+44) 1626 323319
Email: enquiries@fwmedia.com

Distributed in Australia by Capricorn Link
P.O. Box 704, Windsor, NSW 2756 Australia
Tel: (02) 4560-1600

Edited by Scott Francis
Designed by Claudean Wheeler
Illustrations by Harini Chandrasekar
Icon illustrations © fotolia.com/bloomua
Cover photograph © fotolia.com/roberaten
Production coordinated by Greg Nock

DEDICATION

To my wife Ilene and my daughters Jessica and Alexandra for being my biggest supporters.

To my parents for having encouraged me to dream, practice my own creativity and take risks.

ACKNOWLEDGMENTS

This book would not have been possible without the help of many collaborators, contributors and helping hands. My deepest gratitude goes to: my research assistants Gillian Barbieri, Erica Olmstead and Kristina Shigaeva; Brenna McCormick, who was my former student, became my colleague at Emerson College, my mediaman, and who helped shape the project in its initial phase; my research partner Dr. Jorge Villegas at the University of Illinois in Springfield for his collaboration and support analyzing the data and presenting our first results at the American Academy of Advertising conference in Mesa, AZ; Harini Chandrasekar for helping organize and create the many visuals and reworking several illustrations and exercises; my former student Siobhan O'Shaughnessy for reviewing the manuscript; my colleague Dr. David Emblidge at Emerson College for his editorial insights and constructive feedback; my business partners Armin Bieser and Stefan von den Driesch for supporting my visions and challenging me in many aspects of my work; the HOW Books staff; and the faculty and administrators at Emerson College for supporting my work with a sabbatical semester.

I would like to thank my former students Noreen Arora, Lorelei Bandrovschi, Harini Chandrasekar, Kimberly Crunden, Alyse Dunn, Usen Esebiet, Matthew Fiorentino, Marissa (Missy) Goldstein, Milena Guzman, Samantha Gutglass, Sarah Hamilton, Rebecca Hempen Schäfer and Dan Higgins, who also helped connect me with some of the creative executives; and Dylan Klymenko, Summer Lambert, who helped me interview Margaret Johnson and Rich Silverstein; Veronica Marquez, Brenna McCormick, Shannon McGurrin, Michael Miller, Celia Nissen, Amanda Mooney, Siobhan O'Shaughnessy, Trang Phan, Eric Rosatti, Christiane Schaefer, Kristina Shigaeva, Michael Shek, Andrew (Andy) Staub, Cyril Urbano and Sara Wynkoop for sharing their personal experiences with every reader of this book and for illustrating that creativity can be taught, practiced and turned into one of the most powerful muscles we can have.

My sincerest appreciation goes out to the creative masterminds and thought leaders: Alex Bogusky, Edward Boches, Susan Credle, Andrew Deitchman, David Droga, Blake Ebel, Chris Foster, Mark Hunter, Roger Hurni, Margaret Johnson, Lance Jensen, Woody Kay, Tim Leake, Michael Lebowitz, Tom Moudry, Tom Ortega, Marshall Ross, Robert Sherlock, Norman Shearer, Rich Silverstein, Rob Schwartz, Doug Spong, Lynn Teo and Johnny Vulkan for donating their time, participating in the interviews and sharing their wisdom.

I would also like to acknowledge Dr. Joanne Montepare for her collaboration, feedback and encouragement of my early creativity research, which provided the foundation for the bonus chapter (available online at www.breakthroughthinkingguide.com); Dr. Donald Hurwitz, who helped me stay on track and encouraged me to finish the book project instead of starting a completely new research agenda; Glenn Griffin for having published *The Creative Process Illustrated* with Debra Morrison and for being an inspiration, for encouraging my research and for recommending me to HOW Books.

Last but not least, many thanks go to: my former research assistants Sebastien Klein, Tracy Hwong, Suchismita Mohapatra, Orlindes Perez and Amy Yen for their help and support with my creativity research several years ago; Jodi Burrel, Jacqueline Holland, Dr. Kristin Lieb and Dr. Paul Mihailidis at Emerson College for their encouragement and constructive feedback with my book proposal.

CONTENTS

Introduction.....1

CHAPTER ONE:
New Truths About Creativity.....6

CHAPTER TWO:
What Is Creativity?.....14

CHAPTER THREE:
Creative Thinking.....23

CHAPTER FOUR:
The Creative [Problem-Solving] Process.....39

CHAPTER FIVE:
Creative Thinking Methods and Techniques.....52

CHAPTER SIX:
Evaluation of Ideas.....61

CHAPTER SEVEN:
The Importance of Communicating Ideas Effectively.....73

CHAPTER EIGHT:
Creativity and Place.....87

CHAPTER NINE:
Creativity and Philosophy.....105

CHAPTER TEN:
Maintaining a Flexible Mind.....124

Student Case Studies.....135
Creative Executive Profiles.....164

ENDNOTES.....188
REFERENCES.....189
INDEX.....196
PERMISSIONS.....202

INTRODUCTION

Right now, at this very moment, this book is changing your brain.

It is a small change, but as you continue to read, it will become a larger and lasting one.

Creativity is the quality that enables us to generate novel approaches to situations and to discover new and improved solutions to problems. Throughout history, creativity has been a powerful force for change. Compared to previous centuries, the pace of change has rapidly accelerated in the twenty-first century. Creative thinking provides us with the tools and skills needed to adapt and thrive in this fast-paced environment. Through creative thinking, we have the ability not only to understand change, but also to learn how to make it work for us. Better yet, we can even learn how to create the change that benefits us personally and professionally. When put into practice, creativity allows us to move beyond our accepted patterns of thinking and into the uncharted territory of new and innovative ideas. Creative thinking allows us to find solutions to problems—from what to serve for dinner at in impromptu get-together to how to eliminate abject poverty around the world. And, like any skill, the more it is used, the more exceptional, valuable and (dare we say) fun it becomes.

While creativity helps us individually, it also helps companies in the business environment. Simply maintaining a business is not enough to survive anymore—companies need to become more productive and, at the same time, stay competitive. Companies must embrace an active strategy to build and grow creativity, fostering it as an essential ingredient for obtaining success. For many companies, creative thinking has become not only a tool for strategy but also a key factor in discovering new ideas that will differentiate them from the competition, be it through product design, new services offered or something beyond.

The emphasis on creativity within industries such as film, entertainment, advertising, music, performing arts and architecture has allowed several experts to become leaders in creative thinking, and many are seeing a renaissance that has enabled them to weather economic turbulence. In recent years magazines have started to highlight creativity. Major trade publications, like *Advertising Age* and *Creativity*, as well as business magazines like *Fast Company* and *INC*, feature annual rankings of the most creative individuals and innovative organizations.

The advertising industry, in particular, has been the source of many research findings about creativity. Not exclusive to advertising, the growing need for applied creativity in all business environments makes the characteristics of creativity relevant to all forms of communication, from traditional marketing to interactive and social media. As a communication discipline, creativity has long been considered the driving force of the advertising industry. According to researchers, creativity is "arguably the most important aspect of advertising,"[1] with some claiming that creativity is the mission of the entire advertising industry, its raison d'être. Industry magazines and conferences focusing on the practitioner's point of view agree that creativity is a power that can save a whole industry from ruin (Iezzi, 2006). Creativity in advertising has been defined as "being new and relevant with your ideas." Some argue that advertising creativity is a form of creativity different from the concept of creativity. Creativity in advertising is also regarded as creative problem solving, constrained by marketing objectives, competition and the organizational hierarchy, among other things.

This book is the result of a significant paradigm shift in the marketing and advertising industries. Creativity is no longer under the sole proprietorship of copywriters, art directors and designers. Susan Credle, chief creative officer at Leo Burnett in Chicago, describes this change by saying "if you're going to do great creative [work], you can't be a creative department. You have to be a creative agency. I think that's asking every single person to do their job creatively." Based on interviews conducted with top creative executives, every employee is expected to be visionary, brave, generous, confident and curious, independent of job description and discipline.

Thanks to rapid advances in technology and a liberated understanding of the benefits of how and where creativity can be applied, creativity has transcended the form of a quality applied to individuals or industries to become a highly sought-after skill, a corporate value and way of thinking that is driving innovation and businesses today. Within the marketing, communication and advertising industries, traditionally considered to be creative industries, the conversation regarding the need for creativity at all corporate levels has intensified. David Droga, founder of Droga5 knows that without creativity, society would lack innovation. "Creative intelligence is crucial ... it's the creative people who instigate everything," says Droga. This innovation is becoming increasingly difficult. Mark Hunter former creative executive at Deutsch LA expressed the need for his agency to remain revolutionary instead of reactionary: "Everything needs to be interactive. Whether we like it or not, all other forms of communication are becoming two-way."

Additional industry experts describe another shift. Edward Boches of Mullen in Boston says, "We're not in the words-and-pictures business anymore; we're in the business of building our client's business, and creativity is the strongest asset you can have to do that." The leading creative agencies in advertising and marketing in the United States are acknowledging that they are not just creating advertising anymore but are actively helping their clients to solve their business problems and create value through product development. According to Marshall Ross, chief creative officer at Cramer-Krasselt in Chicago, it is important for agencies to recognize that the definition of creativity needs to be very open. "It isn't just how you are putting words and pictures together. It is about how you are thinking about strategy; how you are thinking about measurement; it's how you are thinking about where the intersections between this idea and audience lie." He adds that it is also about influencing the client's ability to develop products. "If we don't bring creativity, we don't bring surprise or novelty to readjust the positioning or product development."

Changes in technology and advances in scientific research in the past decade have not increased our creativity per se, but rather have provided additional insights into how creativity can be improved. One of the most important findings of the past half century is that creative thinking is a skill. Like any skill, creativity is ours to possess, practice and master. Like any ability, it can be neglected or, through dedication and work, strengthened and honed into a powerful skill. This book is designed to help you do just that.

As the knowledge and benefits of how to enhance creativity have grown, the myths surrounding the creative process have been deconstructed. The democratization of technology and the fact that creativity can be learned and practiced have created a shift for creative thinking. It has moved from the domain of industries such as advertising or the fine arts to become a core discipline within mainstream education that can enhance both the learning process and the practitioner's ability to think in new directions. With both industry and education converging and modernizing the concept of creative thinking, creativity has become known as a skill that is highly beneficial to all people and gives practitioners a competitive edge.

> **"Like any skill, creativity is ours to possess, practice and master."**

Compared to other academic disciplines, creative thinking has a relatively short documented history. From Alex Osborn's initial exploration of the creative thinking process at the advertising agency BBDO in the early 1940s, to the current breadth and scope of academic courses, conferences and even dedicated higher education programs focused on creative thinking, our societal perceptions of creative thinking have undergone a very important change. The ability to think creatively, to develop ideas and to find solutions is beginning to receive universal recognition as a required skill that will make world economies more competitive and students brighter and provide humankind with the answers for the challenges of the future.

While creativity, and the creative thinking that inspires it, is on a trajectory to become the quintessential component of success and customer connection in the future, the threat still exists that creative thinking is too playful to be taken seriously, too risky and too time-consuming to be invested in—especially in the minds of busy students, overwhelmed educators and cash-strapped companies. Hopefully together we can change their minds.

This book is a testament to the importance of creative thinking as a skill and as an investment in future economic and personal success. The goal of this book is to provide not only a complete understanding of creative thinking as a core discipline within the context of the current changes to the advertising, marketing and business industries, but also to connect academic knowledge and professional practice. The book will help readers to better understand and evaluate the quality of creative thinking as well as the creative process of transforming creative ideas and thoughts into effective business solutions. This book also teaches creative thinking habits and ways to communicate your ideas that strengthen your ability to succeed in competitive environments.

The market needs a holistic approach and a fresh perspective. While I understand that creativity is a broad and complex topic, twenty years of teaching creativity has confirmed that it is possible to study it, learn it and look at it holistically. Even though creativity is highly complex and influenced by many factors, this book uses a structured conceptual model called "The 4Ps of Creativity." Based on extensive academic research, this model provides a lens with which we can look at the interconnected aspects of creativity, develop creative thinking techniques and habits, and apply them. When creativity is viewed through the multiple dimensions of the 4Ps—person, process, place and product—this complex subject, which cannot be understood via one dimension alone, can be addressed in a systematic way.

The book consists of three main parts. The first, and arguably the core of the work, represents theoretical frameworks and insights that examine what creativity is, how it works and how we can apply it in our daily lives. The second part represents the insights of experienced professionals; in most cases chief creative officers, founders and partners in some of the premier creative advertising agencies in the United States. These agency executives have won numerous awards for their outstanding creative work and are respected experts within the domain of advertising, marketing and communication. These award-winning agency executives share their knowledge, expertise and experience related to managing for creativity and mastering creativity in their respective organizations. The insights of these professionals help add a perspective we can apply in many situations and industries beyond advertising. Lastly, the third part of this book offers real-world cases from numerous former students who have taken an undergraduate or graduate course in creativity, creative thinking and problem solving. Through personal essays they share their opinions and experiences concerning how they have developed the thinking and problem-solving skills they practice regularly and how they use those skills in their personal lives and professional careers.

However, how you use this book and the knowledge in it is most important. Creativity is a broad and complex topic that cannot be achieved through one-time workshops or quick fixes. Mastering the skill of creative thinking takes time, dedication and practice. It involves an active mind that will become more and more open to fresh ideas and seeing new ways of doing things. One can achieve better creativity and creative thinking only by making behavioral changes within oneself and the organizations one works in regularly. The perspectives of advertising executives and former students illustrate how everyone can use and practice the various topics of this book in different and very individual ways. Since not only one path to success exists, the interviews with agency professionals, as well as the cases of former students, invite you to read the book in a nonlinear way. I invite you to jump from one topic to another based on its connectedness to each testimonial featured in the book or as it feels most appropriate to your individual situation. Each interview and case includes cross-references that connect to the 4Ps of Creativity. Hopefully, you will be inspired by the framework of the 4Ps as well as by the many examples you can apply to your own personal journey. Use this book as a framework to begin building one of the most valuable life and business skills there is. When applied, creative skills will take you much further than the classroom or the boardroom and into a world of infinite possibilities and opportunities. It is time to develop thinking habits that lead to breakthrough thinking!

CHAPTER ONE

NEW TRUTHS ABOUT CREATIVITY

Since humanity's early beginnings, creativity has come in many different shapes and forms. Not long ago, the concept of creativity was not a defined or explored entity as it is today, but rather was something that simply existed. While creativity has always played an important role in human lives, in today's world the concept of creativity is becoming increasingly important. People are realizing the impact it can have in a variety of fields and organizations. For example, when searching the word *creativity* in one of the popular search engines on the internet, roughly 159,000,000 results pages appear within less than a second.

CREATIVITY: THE TRADITIONAL DEFINITION

The traditional dictionary definition describes creativity as, "the state or quality of being creative." But what does that mean? To be less elusive and to get to the meat of the definition, creativity is further defined as: "the ability to transcend traditional ideas, rules, patterns, relationships, or the like and to create meaningful new ideas, forms, methods, interpretations, etc.;

originality, progressiveness, or imagination." Ultimately it also means the act of being creative, as in, "the process by which one utilizes creative ability." (Dictionary.com[1])

Numerous dictionaries define creativity and all its etymological offspring—creative, creative thinking, etc., through similar words—an act of fresh, independent and unique expression, which includes originality and imagination. To the traditional definition, *The Macquarie Dictionary* goes so far as to add the additional description of "groundbreaking" and "innovative." At its core, creativity means to take action on an idea; sometimes that includes moving the idea from imagination into reality, or it can simply mean evolving an idea to a new level. Action and creativity go hand-in-hand—otherwise, human beings would not live in the world that they do. People taking action on the ideas that come into their imaginations have given us everything from the Notre Dame Cathedral in Paris to the iPhone.

One of history's greatest thinkers went a bit further with the exploration of creativity and its importance; William Shakespeare described creativity as "seeing something new when you look at something old." Others have described creativity as the breaking down of barriers and ignoring preconceived notions and fears. Creativity, in a casual context, is associated with "fiddling around" and "having fun with ideas," embracing the belief that playfulness and tinkering will lead us to possible solutions.[2] Within the music industry, creativity can be defined as hearing a rhythm or pattern that has not yet been put together. For example, Ray Charles combined gospel and blues to create a unique sound in his songs.

Others hold to a more extreme view, believing that creativity requires an innate ability to suspend rationality, even sanity. This comes from the fact that the nature of creativity is not strictly characterized by birthing new concepts, but also by making unusual connections. Processes that result in innovation may look rational in hindsight. However, the vast majority of creative breakthroughs come from people who have dissented from accepted thinking patterns (DeBono). From Edison's radical idea to use electricity rather than whale oil to provide light, to placing paint on a blank canvas in a very unique style like Van Gogh, creativity involves change in order to truly fulfill the definition of the word. In the art world, Picasso expressed this shift to creativity by saying, "every act of creativity is first an act of destruction."

While creativity involves both the creation of new ideas and sometimes the destruction of existing concepts, it's important to note that the act of combining existing ideas in a new and foreign way is also creativity. Some of history's greatest inventors have found new combinations of existing objects, harnessing them for new purposes. For example, wine presses inspired Johannes Gutenberg to adapt the concept to printing. Gutenberg's printing press is a powerful example of taking existing elements and creating not only a functional tool, but one that accelerated the sharing of information.

Creativity is a complex topic and can be viewed from many different perspectives. One way of looking at creativity is through the premise of the 4Ps: person, place, process and product. The *person* component refers to the actual characteristics and personality traits that make an individual creative and that are responsible for our very personal creativity. The *place* refers to the physical space and the organizational environment in which creativity happens. *Process* concerns the way the final goal is reached and what steps and thinking techniques might lead to the creative product. The *product* relates to a final creative production, work, service or invention that comes from the creative process and creative ideas.

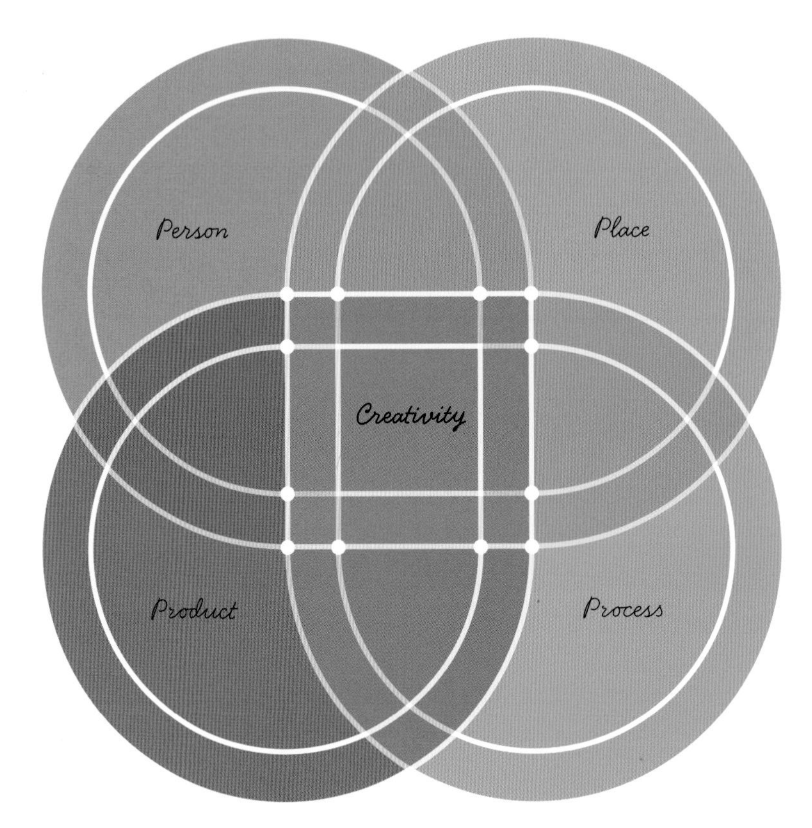

One way of looking at creativity is through the premise of the 4Ps.

Throughout history, there have been certain peaks in thought and creativity, including in ancient Greece, the Renaissance, the mid-1800s in Vienna, Austria, and the current technological revolution. Though creativity was not always defined or examined during these earlier times, it still persisted and flourished. In fact, taking a retrospective look at these periods of time allows for analysis and definition of the elements of creativity that were employed, using the premise of the 4P framework.

The extremely advanced ancient Greeks influenced language, politics, philosophy and the arts for future civilizations. A large aspect of culture in ancient Greece revolved around philosophy, which focused on the role of reason and introspective thinking. Plato and Aristotle were two of the most well-known and influential philosophers of the time. This period of history was also known for its contributions to music, literature, art, science and architecture. Despite all of these contributions and innovations, the ancient Greeks did not believe in the concept of creativity. They did not have a concept that meant "creator" or "to create," although they had the term *poiein*, meaning "to make." They believed that the concept of creativity meant the freedom of action. This did not align with the concept of art. To them, art was defined as *techne*, meaning "the making of things, according to the rules." Therefore the entire premise of art was to adhere to rules as opposed to experimentation and thinking outside the box, as we often associate with art today. According to the ancient Greeks, nature was perfect and subject to laws. Humans were supposed to discover the laws of nature and be subject to them rather than look for freedom. The poet was the only individual who was an exception to this rule and was believed to be truly creative because he or she was not bound by laws and actually created something genuinely

What is the next shape in this sequence?

Credited to Wujec, Tom (1995), *Five Star Mind, Games & Puzzles to Stimulate Your Creativity & Imagination*, Doubleday, New York.
Find answers and solutions to exercises and puzzles at www.breakthroughthinkingguide.com.

new. Looking back at ancient Greece with today's understanding of creativity, it is clear to see that the ancient Greeks did, in fact, employ many of the same principles that people do today. Supported by a strong governmental and political structure, which gave way to freedom and resources in terms of art and culture, ancient Greece was a place in which creativity was born and thrived.

During the medieval period and under medieval Christianity, an increase in the power of the church greatly influenced and diminished creativity. The Latin word *creatio* came to designate God's act of "creatio ex nihilo," which meant creation from nothing. Therefore, *creatio* did not apply to human activities. Human creativity, a secular pursuit, was tolerated but not necessarily celebrated or promoted.

The Renaissance was a cultural movement that began in Florence, Italy, in the fourteenth century. Florence possessed certain characteristics and peculiarities that allowed for this sudden proliferation of ideas and creativity. The Italian city-state had a unique political structure, a large migration of Greek scholars and texts due to the fall of Constantinople and the patronage of the Medicis, one of the wealthiest families in Italy at the time. When considering the 4Ps, Florence was an ideal place for this reawakening of creative thought. The Medici family, who were leading patrons of the arts, commissioned works from Leonardo da Vinci, Botticelli and Michelangelo, among other Renaissance greats. While this movement began in Italy, it gradually moved across Europe by the end of the sixteenth century. The actual word *renaissance* is a literal translation from French to English, meaning *rebirth*. This was in reference to the flourishing activity in the areas of literature, philosophy, art, music, politics and science. It was a time of revival of the secular; an inquiring and introspective way of thinking that had characterized the life and culture of the classical period. While the Medieval period lacked freedom and naturalness, the Renaissance was a time of creative flourish and awakening that allowed for more individualism and the abandonment of the austere ways of the Medieval era. Looking at the Renaissance through the lens of the modern concept of creativity, one can see that the personal aspect was crucial when it came to creative endeavors. The Renaissance allowed for individuals to use their abilities for innovation and creation and encouraged them to have many different skills and talents, untethering

Morning Pages

Morning pages help tap into a nonjudgmental creative space by capturing ideas, thoughts or feelings before you become self-conscious. Julia Cameron, author of *The Artist's Way* advises to set your morning alarm a half-hour early. "Wake-up and immediately write at least three paragraphs of longhand, 'stream-of-consciousness' writing," she says. By keeping a pen and paper by your bedside, you can describe a dream, an activity from the previous day, or even an emotion. Whatever crosses your mind, capture it on paper.

Cameron advises not to read the pages or share them with anyone; she calls them a "blurt." They are simply meant to guide your creative development. "You will find that your ability to create will be greatly affected by this activity. It may be slow going at first, but stick with it," she says. The change will surprise you.

The Morning Pages exercise is credited to Julia Cameron. *The Artist's Way: A Spiritual Path to Higher Creativity*; 1996. Penguin Putnam Inc; San Francisco, CA.

them from just one craft. This gave way to the concept of the "Renaissance Man," an individual who possesses broad intellectual interests and pursuits. Throughout this important historical period, we see the 4Ps exercised. The Renaissance generated some of the world's most celebrated art, literature and philosophy that continue to be influential to this day.

In 1804, Vienna became the capital of the Austro-Hungarian Empire, playing an increased role in world politics, as well as culture and art, serving at the center of classical music and art. The European city became the home to an abundance of theaters and opera houses and was home to some of the most eminent musical composers, including Wolfgang Amadeus Mozart, Joseph Haydn, Ludwig van Beethoven, Franz Schubert and Johannes Brahms. Additionally there was a surge in the coffeehouse culture in Vienna, becoming a popular place for intellectual, artistic, scientific and political debate. Much like Florence during the Renaissance, Vienna served as an ideal place for creative revival and resurgence.

THE PERFECT STORM

The advent of the internet has ushered in a new era of creativity. Not since Johannes Gutenberg began the printing revolution in the fifteenth century has humankind been poised on the brink of such extraordinary changes and progress in thinking. The democratization of technologies and availability of outlets in recent years have altered the concept of creativity, allowing more people than ever to pursue creative careers. Independent of any formal training or education, low-cost or free online tools have encouraged many to engage in creative activities. The internet has provided the world with a wealth of ideas and images that jump-start thinking processes and show new perspectives. This has added to the perception and understanding of creativity as a skill rather than only a talent. While our brains may have not changed significantly, the internet has shown us new things about our minds' inner workings and has allowed creative communities to foster and share ideas. The rise of crowdsourcing and accessibility of software has metaphorically pulled the rug out from under the concept of creativity. Much of what we understand now about creativity and ways to nurture it can be attributed to advances in technology. Advances in scientific and psychological understanding of the human brain, the deconstruction of the myth and preconceptions of a "creative person," the democratization of technology and the realization that creativity can be learned, cultivated and improved by practice, are all blending together to create the perfect storm for the development of creative thinking as a skill.

Truth #1: Technology is a mirror for creativity

The internet is helping people discover new truths about creativity. Technology grants access to people who want to share ideas or learn ways to share them better. Younger generations, such as Generation Y or the Millennials, have been primarily—if not completely—brought up in this technology-influenced world. The way in which this generation thinks, processes and shares information is unlike the way any other generation does the same. As part of the John D. and Catherine T. MacArthur Foundation Series on Digital Media and Learning, Patricia G. Lange and Mizuko Ito researched how technology is impacting and empowering children and young adults aged twelve to eighteen. Lange and Ito found that "the growing availability of digital media-production tools, combined with sites where young people can post and discuss media works, has created a new media ecology that supports everyday media creation and sharing for kids engaged in creative production." [3]

In their documentary *PressPausePlay*, creators Victor Köhler and David Dworsky illustrate through various interviews how technology has enabled children, as well as individuals in their twenties and thirties, to unleash their own creative potential and to engage in endeavors that result in creative products such as film, photography, books, blogs, music or even complex media productions. Many of the featured creatives have learned their trade by picking up tools available on the internet rather than through a formal education in film, photography or writing. Creative expression is no longer bound to a teacher and a classroom. Anyone with internet access has been enabled to engage in creative production.

Technology is also changing the rules of how ideas have developed and turned into innovative products and services in the past, making it difficult to predict what will be the next new thing a month from now, let alone a year or a decade from now. Individuals and organizations are becoming increasingly aware of this trend. Constant rapid change provides the perfect environment for creative thinking to flourish as it enables practitioners of creative thinking to continue to grow and expand their skills, and it establishes a training ground for new thinkers who want to continue to push the limits of their ability to generate and share ideas. As a skill, creativity is now sought after more than ever before. The need to become better creative thinkers, problem solvers and opportunity explorers is a key component of success that is not limited to business, but also has a striking impact on the quality and fulfillment of one's personal life.

Truth #2: Creativity can be learned and practiced

Independent of different cultural frameworks and societies around the world, the belief that an individual is either creative or not creative is still widely represented. Many people still believe that

Creativity Self-Perception

Are you creative? Take a few minutes and think about what you associate with creativity. Write down if you consider yourself creative and to what degree. Then explore how your self-image has been formed. Do you connect creativity with arts and crafts and/or with thinking and problem solving skills?

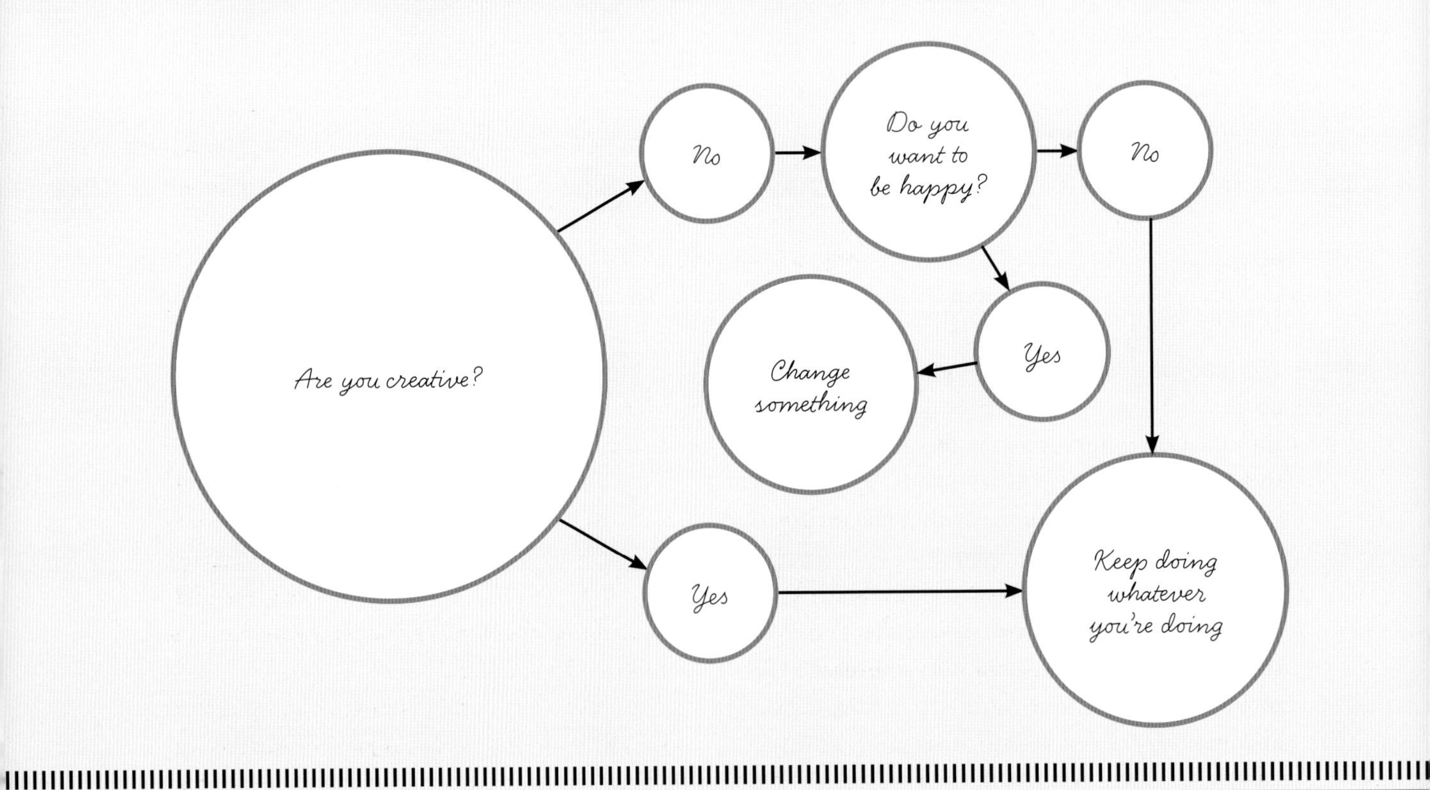

only certain people are creative and that creativity is a special or elite skill that only some possess. But this misconception is now changing. In recent years more evidence that creativity and creative thinking skills can be taught, learned and practiced has appeared. Tina Seelig, executive director of the Stanford Technology Ventures Program and author of *inGENIUS: A Crash Course on Creativity*, confirms that "everyone can increase his or her creativity, just as everyone can increase his or her musical or athletic ability, with appropriate training and focused practice."

Based on my work with students and professionals in the area of creativity and creative thinking, I have been able to observe several trends. First, there are always those who consider themselves creative and typically associate their creativity with creative expression in performance, art, photography, poetry and other artistic media. For example, a former student, Cyril Urbano, says he has always known that he had a creative streak: "My creative expression was always seen onstage—whether dancing to some familiar tune, belting out a song in front of crowds or portraying a role in a stage play. Back then, that was all the creativity I knew—artistic self expression."

The second group has a self-image that they are not creative. Former student Kristina Shigaeva says, "I remember on the very first day [of the Creative Thinking course], my professor asked for a show of hands of those individuals who thought that they were creative. I was one of the few people that didn't raise their hand. At that point in time, I didn't quite understand the concept of creativity the way in which I understand it now. Before [the course], I was convinced that creativity was something that you were born with; you either had it or you didn't, and I was positive that I was in the latter category. It was reserved for those elite few that had a special skill like painting or composing music."

Third, after completing a course in creativity and creative thinking, many students have gained a better understanding about their own creativity and the concept of creative thinking, which allows them to better evaluate creativity expressed and produced by others. Through increased awareness and practice, their own creative thinking not only has improved over time, but also has turned into a skill they can apply in their personal and professional lives (Cross-reference to student case studies, page 135 and to www.breakthroughthinkingguide.com). While individuals may differ in their levels of creative abilities, according to many scientists all are born creative.[4] All young children have the ability to think divergently, a key attribute of creativity. However, over time they lose their creative abilities as a result of formalized training, socialization and self-inhibition, whereby they begin to assess and judge their own creative abilities by comparing themselves to others.

The fact that a person's creative abilities can easily diminish over time means only that you need to rediscover your own creativity and creative abilities and practice them on a regular basis. Former student Rebecca Schaefer Hempen says, "I never really saw myself as a creative person, but [through the creative thinking course], I realized that anybody—including me—can be creative." Former student Trang Phan adds, "When I started [the course], I was skeptical because like most people, I believed that one is either creative or they are not. What I discovered was that creativity is an innate skill that we all possess. Whether or not we practice this skill determines our creative intake and offerings. In addition to creativity coming from within, I also quickly discovered that we could build our creativity through our environment and collaboration."

It seems that there has never been a better time to embark on a personal journey of creative exploration and discovery. Regardless of your creative experience, there is always an opportunity to bolster your creative abilities by increasing your knowledge and by exercising your brain muscle on a regular basis.

CHAPTER TWO

WHAT IS CREATIVITY?

Creativity is a complex topic that involves many different elements and factors, from originality to destruction to combining existing elements in a way that makes something new. However, at its most fundamental level, creativity means to create. Creation, the root of creativity, takes place when something is brought into being. To create means to give rise to, bring about, produce, form, originate, introduce, invent, conceive, compose, author, initiate—you get the inspiring point.

However, if creativity was that forthright and simple, this book would not have been developed. It is important to go beyond the dictionary definition of creativity in an effort to embrace the many perspectives and elements that are part of the inherent nature of the topic.

Defining creativity is just one facet of this complex and broad topic. Creativity takes place on many levels, both within your personal skill level and your environmental knowledge. From an act of imaginative creation to the

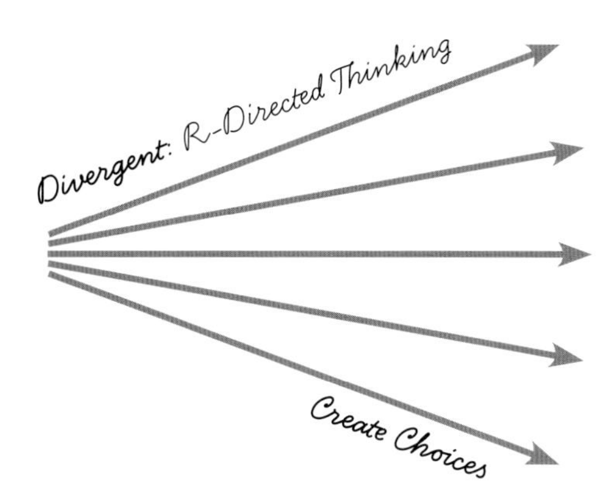

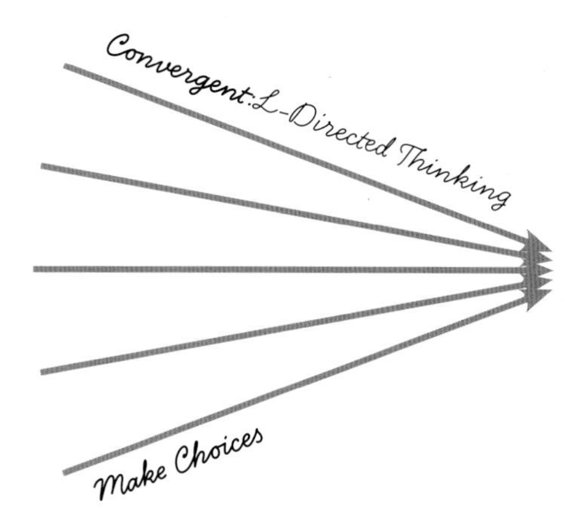

act of making unique connections, creativity is at its best where action meets an idea that has taken a new an unusual direction.

While it has been stressed that creativity is closely linked to action, it is important to reiterate that the result does not always have to be tangible. Creativity is also represented by one's ability to generate fresh ideas and solutions to current problems or challenges.

In looking at the many angles from which creativity can be described, the following two definitions provide a good foundation for this book:

> *Creativity is redefining old ideas in new ways, breaking through conceptual barriers.*[1]

This definition incorporates two important aspects related to creativity: the first part involves adding new perspectives when thinking about a problem, assignment or challenge; the second involves taking risks and moving away from previously established opinions and thought patterns. These are two important topics that will be explored further in chapters four and five.

Po Bronson and Ashley Merryman define creativity in their article "The Creativity Crisis" as:

> *The production of something original and useful, and that's what's reflected in the Torrance tests. There is never one right answer. To be creative requires divergent thinking (generating many unique ideas) and then convergent thinking (combining those ideas into the best result).*[2]

Thinking facilitates creativity and creative thinking is the process of being creative. Therefore, the terms "creativity" and "creative thinking" will be used interchangeably. Although, when I speak of creative thinking, references will be made to the act of the creative process and the ways to enhance it. Specific thought processes can improve the ability to be creative, such as being in an optimal state of mind for generating new ideas, deliberately thinking in ways that improve the likelihood of new thoughts occurring and maximizing mental ability to create original, diverse and elaborate ideas.

Within these thought processes you can apply different methods of thinking when you solve problems. Among several options, the most widely known methods are: convergent thinking, divergent thinking and lateral thinking.

- **CONVERGENT THINKING:** When the thought process is focused on finding a single correct answer to a problem, convergent thinking is used. Ideas are generated, weighed and discarded until the correct solution is found.
- **DIVERGENT THINKING:** Highly associated with creativity, divergent thinking happens when

ideas and thoughts are followed and explored in many directions.

- **LATERAL THINKING:** Often a tactical method for problem solving, lateral thinking involves looking at the identified challenge from multiple angles. Lateral thinking typically is applied during a phase of divergent thinking.

I will delve deeper into these thinking methods in subsequent chapters, but for now they are important to understand when you look at the findings of creativity research and even the methods that some companies are using to stimulate creative thinking.

DEFINING CREATIVITY IN THE BUSINESS ENVIRONMENT

In addition to the traditional definition of creativity, it is important to look at creativity within the context of the business environment. A study on creativity within the advertising industry revealed that there are three main concepts associated with advertising creativity: divergence, relevance and effectiveness (Smith and Yang). These three factors can be helpful for applying the definition of creativity within any industry field and will become even more important when you learn about the evaluation of ideas.

- **DIVERGENCE:** In order to qualify as creative, an idea must be unusual, new, innovative, novel, divergent and/or imaginative; specifically it must go beyond the current environment's level of ideas.
- **RELEVANCE:** The relevance factor describes the degree to which an idea is relevant to a specific audience. In order to be creative, an idea must be appropriate and within the correct context, as well as useful, valuable and meaningful.
- **EFFECTIVENESS:** This dimension relates to the aspect that the creative idea helps the audience see the product or service in a new way, possibly even changing the audience's perspective of reality. According to the study's authors, an effective creative idea must also have impact or be productive, connecting with and/or being useful in the consumer's life.

WHO IS CREATIVE?

Beyond the definition of creativity is the very important question of whether creativity is innate, meaning present from birth, or whether it can be taught, nurtured and ultimately honed. While there are different academic and psychological trains of thought, current research shows that creativity is possessed by more than a select few. Creativity is a perception

Nine Dots

Connect the dots with 4 straight lines without lifting your pencil or pen from the paper, once you have started.

Credited to Evans, James R. (1991), Creative Thinking – In the decision and management sciences, South-Western, and Michalko, Michael (1991), *Thinkertoys: A Handbook of Creative-Thinking Techniques*. Berkeley, Calif.: Ten Speed Press.

influenced by personal actions and environments and it is a skill that can be developed.

During the interviews with industry experts featured in this book, the creative directors noted several characteristic traits in their employees that they believe make them creative. Even though the number of employees, the educational background and the individual areas of expertise at the agencies varied, many creative directors pointed out similar traits that they believe their staff demonstrate and embody. Several mentioned that creative people are always willing to try again and are not discouraged if something does not work out right away. "The best trait you have as a creative person is your ability to try again. You think of an idea and it gets killed or it gets changed, or it doesn't work or whatever and try again" says Tim Leake, formerly of Hyper Island (see profile on page 181).

The employees at the agencies featured in this book also have an inclination towards original thinking and solving problems in unexpected ways. The executives of some of the most creative marketing, communication and advertising agencies are looking to hire as many inspiring, interesting and authentic creative people as possible. Often those people come from different backgrounds. According to David Droga of Droga5 this manifests itself in many different ways. "I'm not looking for one type of creative person or one type of creative thinker; I look at problem solvers," says Droga. Such people do not conform to a specified set of rules but rather bring unusual ways of thinking to the table. The majority of creative directors mentioned that the most creative people in their agencies are those who are willing to work with others and are open to collaboration because, oftentimes, creativity is a collective effort. Creative people must have respect for other people's opinions and are always open and curious about the world.

Lynn Teo formerly of McCann Erickson (see profile on page 179) in New York and formerly of AKQA is looking for people who demonstrate a lot of curiosity, a genuine want to explore, a genuine want to understand and, in particular, have a genuine want to understand human behavior. Teo adds, "I think that personality traits would be openness and receptivity, because the day of creativity now, is one that is very competitive. The creativity doesn't just come from one individual locked up in a room thinking of something, but the creativity is collective. And I think, in this modern day, if the individual is unable to build on someone else's idea and help to make the emerging idea a collective, [that idea] will not have the promise that it could have. So it's this idea of building on top of each other's ideas and having the discussion be a vehicle for thinking."

CREATIVITY AND SELF-PERCEPTION

Another component of creativity in individuals is the self-perception of being creative. Despite multiple mediums of communication, increased competition and a dynamic marketplace environment, many people do not consider themselves creative. Unless an individual has been trained in creativity or creative fields such as performing arts, creative writing, advertising, film, media or visual design, the self-perception of one's level of creative ability is relatively low.

During my years of teaching creative thinking, I found that at the beginning of almost every semester when students were asked to raise their hand if they considered themselves creative, many hesitated. The same held true for corporate creativity workshops I conducted for companies. In many companies creativity is still associated with the work of artists, not of a typical office worker.

This lack of self-confidence associated with creative thinking skills reflects the understanding and knowledge of psychologists of the early twentieth century, when experts believed that creativity was an inherent ability. Psychologists believed that one is either born with creative thinking skills or not. Much of the early research was conducted by studying highly creative individuals. The test subjects demonstrated similarities in several personality dimensions, which led to their establishing specific creative traits such as playfulness, intelligence, originality, nonconformity, self-confidence, skepticism, memory, humor, flexibility and adaptability.

During the last few decades, additional traits have been identified that demonstrate the flexibility and empathy characteristics of creative thinkers. Identified abilities include thinking outside the box, being energetic and passionate, as well as having the yin and yang balance of being both introverted and extroverted, masculine and feminine, and rebellious and traditional.

Everyone's life circumstances surrounding creativity and self-perception of creative ability are unique. Some people have the advantage of environments and relationships that nurture creative thinking. Others may have shed the inherent skills of creative thinking for more traditional and structured social behaviors due to circumstances that did not support or value creativity. The good news is that not being born into an environment that hones creative thinking skills

Enemies & Champions

In this chapter, I discussed that believing that you are creative is one of the most important factors of being creative. As we grow and mature, we often suppress many of our creative tendencies due to judgment from others. Spend a few minutes thinking back to your childhood and adolescence and the relationships, events or encounters that impacted your creativity, both negatively and positively. In your sketchbook divide a page into four quarters. Make a list of the people who inhibited or impaired your creative growth in the first box and the reason or memory that caused the negative association. In the next box, make a list of people who supported and encouraged your creative growth and the reason or memory that makes it a positive association. In the remaining two boxes, write a response to the memory or the person regarding your creativity.

ENEMIES	
Mrs. Chydochyck, 1st grade teacher:	
After using show-and-tell to tell the class a fictitious and wildly embellished story about fighting monsters in the basement with my brother, Mrs. Chydochyck called my mother in to tell her that I had an overactive imagination and that I would not be allowed to participate in show-and-tell if I was wasting the other students' time with imaginary stories.	Mrs. Chydochyck, rather than being overactive, my imagination has provided me with a great source of creative ideas. When I began writing, I turned these ideas into short stories.
CHAMPIONS	
Mrs. Beal, 5th grade teacher:	
Encouraged me to submit my creative stories to local school district contests.	Thank you, Mrs. Beal, for realizing that English was my favorite subject because I loved to read and write (not because I liked sentence diagrams) and for encouraging me to share my writing.

Adapted from and credited to Cameron, Julia (2002); *The Artist's Way: A Spiritual Path to Higher Creativity.* Penguin Putnam Inc, San Francisco, CA.

In My Room

Your childhood holds many insights into your self-perception of your personal creativity. The following exercise is a great jumping-off point for getting back in touch with some of the key characteristics of creativity that come naturally during childhood, such as curiosity or playfulness. In your sketchbook, draw a picture or make a list about your childhood bedroom. What were the objects in the room? The colors? What do you remember most? What was your favorite toy, book, or item in the room? Why? As you work, begin to look for themes that represent areas of interest to you. Are you still pursuing them? Are there any areas that you may have forgotten about that you would like to introduce to your life now?

Adapted from and credited to Cameron, Julia (2002); *The Artist's Way: A Spiritual Path to Higher Creativity.* Penguin Putnam Inc, San Francisco, CA.

does not automatically make one a less effective creative thinker. It just means that the skill may be less natural or intuitive, buried under layers of inhibited self-perception and social and environmental habits.

One of the most important findings I have experienced in my own creativity teaching is this:

> *The major factor that distinguishes creative from noncreative individuals is that creative individuals believe they are creative!*

The mind is a powerful tool, but it is also a tool that needs training. The perception toward being creative or not being creative can be controlled by personal habits and self-perception. By giving yourself the freedom and opportunity to create, one becomes creative.

Former student Sarah Hamilton is quick to acknowledge that she did not consider herself creative or a creative thinker prior to the course. According to Sarah, creativity was the antithesis of what she thought she was or could ever be. She considered herself analytical, skeptical and realistic. Yet during the course she realized that she wanted to be creative. After numerous exercises, assignments and sometimes-frustrating experiences, Sarah discovered that her creativity started to flow and that her skills became more honed. Succeeding more frequently at assignments and receiving very positive feedback on her work from the professor and her peers, Sarah's self-esteem increased. She played with ideas more often and jotted them down, carried an idea book with her everywhere she went and began to draw after sitting in on a drawing class. With this new confidence, Sarah began to believe that she could, in fact, be creative.

Former student Veronica Marquez points out that she "used to cringe at the word *creative*." According to Marquez, *creativity* was word she associated with the unattainable world of artists, designers and photographers—not business people. Taking a course in creative thinking changed all of that. Veronica learned several skills that allowed her to build creative confidence. The ability to think expansively, to discover many possible routes to tackle the same challenge, and to be connected to what she loves has fundamentally contributed to her development and growth, both personally and professionally. These newly gained skills helped Veronica land a job at a creative agency in New York, where she now includes creative thinking and problem solving as part of her daily routine.

To better understand why individuals may not have enough confidence in their own creative thinking skills, it helps to look back into the childhood years. As a person matures and becomes more socially conscious, one adopts behaviors that feel appropriate for one's environment and will be accepted by peers. For example, if you ask a kindergarten class how many of them are artists, they will all raise their hands. Ask the same question of sixth graders and maybe one-third will respond. Ask a group of high school seniors and only a few will admit to it.

What happens to people as they grow up? They become more self-conscious and develop social awareness of others, key factors that inhibit creativity. Rather than express curiosity, they censor their questions (see the exercise on page 19). They learn to fear criticism and tend to keep ideas and creativity to themselves. While some creative habits may still be explored, they are usually personal and not shared. For instance, many people keep journals for writing or sketching, but they never share them with others. When was the last time you invited a friend to read your diary?

This leads to a very important tenet of this book. There is no judgment here: Only encouragement and tools that will help reintroduce you to important and life-enhancing skills so that you may embark on your own creative journey. If you are reading this book in a class, you will have company on your exploration. It is important to remain open-minded, not only toward your own creativity, but also towards the exploration of others. This mindfulness will become a benefit to you, as you will begin to see that your own openness connects you to new and fresh ideas.

PRACTICE MAKES A BETTER BRAIN

Many psychologists agree that humans generally have the capacity to think creatively. I agree with this and believe that creativity is a skill—and like any skill, creativity needs to be practiced. In order to become experienced in creative thinking and for creativity to come naturally, one needs to first rediscover her own creativity, then practice, nurture and refine it on an ongoing basis. That is the good news. The challenge is that this is not as easy as it sounds.

Like putting any muscle to use in a new way, your brain will give you similar resistance as you practice honing your creative thinking skills.

Other than keeping your body functioning, the brain does not want to exert itself and waste energy. Gregory Berns, author of *Iconoclast,* summed it up when he called the brain "a fundamentally lazy piece of meat."[3]

According to Berns, in order to think creatively, one must develop new neural pathways and break out of the cycle of how his past experiences are categorized. For most people, this does not come naturally. Often the harder you think differently, the more rigid the categories become. Ultimately though, the networks that govern both perception and imagination can be reprogrammed. Berns explains that "by deploying our attention differently, the frontal cortex, which contains rules for decision making, can reconfigure neural networks so that we can see things that we did not see before. You need a novel stimulus, a trigger, such as a new piece of information or an unfamiliar environment, to jolt the attentional systems awake. The more radical the change, the greater the likelihood of fresh insights."[4]

Like any skill, enhancing your creativity requires discipline, devotion and practice. Having worked with graduate and undergraduate students for more than fifteen years, it has become clear that creativity and creative thinking is a skill not gained by reading and processing information, but by exploring, trying and doing. The following chapters provide you with more information for understanding creativity. But, more importantly, they aim to inspire you beyond mere comprehension through points of action that create actual change. The exercises in this book are designed to help you increase your skill level. As with a physical fitness routine, this is a program that requires discipline. Sometimes it will feel fun, other times it will feel a lot like a lot of work. Stick to it. The results will inspire you.

CHAPTER THREE

CREATIVE THINKING

What is Creative Thinking?

Even though collaboration, teamwork and crowdsourcing have been on the rise, an individual's thinking skills—specifically, his creative thinking skills—are arguably the most valuable skills one can own and market. "Individual creativity is absolutely critical ... Without our individual employees, quite frankly, this agency doesn't exist. It is really the combination of the brainpower of everybody that really makes this place tick," says Roger Hurni, founder and chief creative officer of Off Madison Avenue in Phoenix. Hurni relates the brainpower of his employees to their ability to think creatively, as well as to the fact that they do not stop thinking after they leave work. "They're the kind of people who are thinking about it, sort of letting ideas and issues percolate, even if they're driving down the road, or they're doing other kinds of things. So nobody here turns that off. [If] they have an idea at three o'clock in the morning, they're going to get up and they're going to get it figured out," says Hurni. According to Margaret Johnson, executive creative director and

Alphabet Sequence

Determine how you could complete the following sequence:

A				E	F	
	B	C	D			G

How would you place the remaining letters of the alphabet above and below the line to make some kind of sense?

The alphabet exercise illustrates how we can come up with different options to answer a problem that can be explained with more than one solution.

Exercises like the above allow us to use our imagination and apply our "divergent thinking" skills. Based on how we interpret the pattern of the letters we see, we can come up with multiple new ways to complete the sequence by using every letter of the alphabet.

Once we have come up with various ideas and options to complete the sequence we then have to ask ourselves if our solutions make sense and if our newly created patterns appear to fit the task.

Credited to Adams, James L. (1986), *The Care and Feeding of Ideas: A Guide to Encouraging Creativity.* Reading, Mass.: Addison-Wesley.

partner at Goodby, Silverstein & Partners (GS&P) in San Francisco, the people who work at GS&P "are absolutely the most creative people in the industry." Johnson points out that the employees are creative to begin with and that otherwise they would not end up at GS&P. This highlights the importance of harnessing one's creativity to get jobs at certain agencies. As more companies in creative industries, specifically in marketing, advertising and communication are looking to hire creative problem solvers, more than just the so-called creative designers, art directors and writers need to demonstrate their creative thinking skills. Anyone interested in getting a job should be prepared to demonstrate some aspects of her creative skills.

According to Alexandra Bruell of *Advertising Age*, "creative executives are a hot commodity at a time when every marketer is looking for big ideas that can boost sales." Individual agencies, as well as the advertising industry as a whole, are paying more money for people with creative skills. According to an Adage.com poll, creativity and creative thinking skills are sought to improve strategy and media and to generate big ideas. Evidence of this is found in the increased salary within the creative suite. For example, in 2013, more creative executives have seen a greater increase in salary than during the previous year. Thinking is a highly individualistic and complex activity that facilitates creativity and represents the process of being creative. As creative thinking can be learned and improved, it helps to understand some basic concepts.

American psychologists J.P. Guilford and E. Paul Torrance, among other researchers and creativity specialists, established a clear way to describe and assess thinking. Guilford developed a framework featuring two different modes of thinking: convergent thinking and divergent thinking. He was a strong proponent of the idea that creativity is inherent in all individuals.

According to Vincent Ryan Ruggiero, author of *The Art of Thinking*, the mind works predomi-

How Many Triangles Can You Count in the Picture?

Credited to Wujec, Tom (1995), *Five Star Mind, Games & Puzzles to Stimulate Your Creativity & Imagination*, Doubleday, New York, and Evans, James R. (1991), Creative Thinking – In the decision and management sciences, South-Western.

nantly in two ways: the production phase and the judgment phase. The production phase is responsible for the mind's ability to produce a variety of possible solutions to problems or challenges and to look at problems from various perspectives. This phase also includes abilities associated with creative thinking and imagination, specifically one's ability to apply divergent and convergent thinking. During the judgment phase a person examines and evaluates creative production and applies critical thinking. The judgment phase is also associated with the fact that the mind makes judgments. Ruggiero defines thinking as "any mental activity that helps formulate or solve a problem, make a decision or fulfill a desire to understand. It is a searching for answers, a reaching for meaning." Human beings are all born with the ability to think and are trained in developing thinking skills further through education. During high school and college, we learn how to apply different kinds of thinking in subjects like mathematics, sciences, languages, literature, history and art. Many have been trained to develop specific thinking skills related to critical thinking, analytical thinking and deductive reasoning.

Creative thinking is also described as a mental process in which past experiences are combined and recombined, frequently with some distortion, in such a way that new patterns, new configurations and new arrangements are created. These are then applied to a given problem, ultimately creating solutions that can range from fairly common and seen before to more unusual, creative and original. Consequently this enables a person to come up with new and innovative approaches when solving a problem.

The two main kinds of thinking that facilitate creativity can be divided into conscious thinking, also called vertical thinking, and unconscious thinking. Conscious thinking is applied when one incorporates the information gained through the sensory system and consciously applies that knowledge to a certain situation. It can be a powerful way of thinking, since we can actively influence the direction we want to think or determine the perspective from which we look at specific problems. During conscious thinking we can play a more active role when making mental connections between two thoughts or ideas. In our minds we can draw from our knowledge, bringing together random thoughts from different disciplines and experiences where no obvious connection might exist.

Yet this conscious thinking happens at a slower rate than unconscious thinking does. Unconscious thinking represents an integral part of the creative process and typically happens at a faster rate than conscious thinking. It also occurs nonsequentially. When a mind is thinking unconsciously, it can go in numerous directions. However, this happens within a very short time frame, and you may not be aware of the connections your mind makes.

While forming the "structure of intellect model," Guilford established the concept of convergent and divergent thinking. Convergent thinking assumes that the logical imperative is to go down a path in order to arrive at a specific solution that has previously been determined. Convergent thinking applies when the thinking process is focused on finding a single correct answer to a problem. Ideas are generated, weighed and discarded until the correct solution is found. For example, multiple-choice tests apply specific knowledge. During a test, your mind sifts through your knowledge, then decides if it matches a question and applies it accordingly. Convergent thinking describes a systematic approach to sifting through information and finding the most appropriate solution for a problem, challenge or task.

Alternatively divergent thinking, initially is not focused on arriving at a specific solution but is focused around trying to come up with as many possibilities as possible. Divergent thinking happens when ideas and thoughts are followed and explored in many directions. This type of thinking can be used to consciously increase the total number of possible solutions without being concerned about whether these solutions will ultimately solve the problem. This allows you to better push yourself to come up with as many different ideas and concepts as possible without expecting those ideas to relate to one another. Divergent thinking is a process that moves away from finding only one specific solution to a problem or answer to a challenge. Instead the mind tries to see as many different possibilities as one can imagine.

CREATIVE THINKING

While creative thinking has historically not been considered a strong component of the American education system, educators, psychologists and politicians in recent years have identified the need to place greater emphasis on the topic. Undergraduate students in American colleges and universities are already or will soon be educated in the areas of creative thinking. The Association of American Colleges and Universities

DIVERGENT AND CONVERGENT THINKING

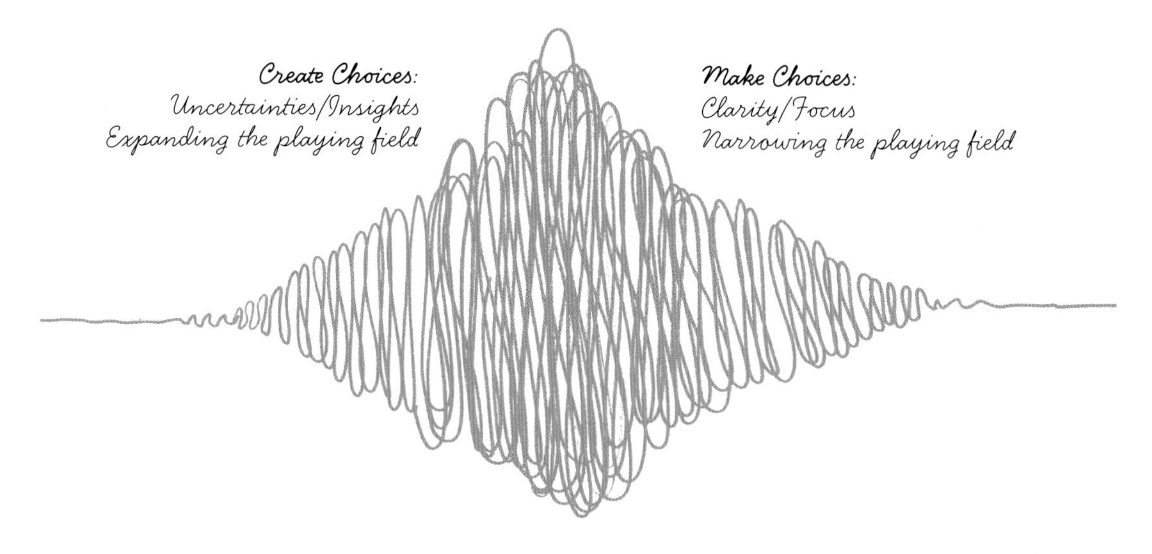

(AACU) developed a tool for Valid Assessment of Learning in Undergraduate Education (VALUE) and created a creative thinking value rubric to help educators teach creative thinking. This rubric helps to assess the learning outcome associated with specific skills like risk taking, problem solving, embracing contradictions and innovative thinking as well as connecting, synthesizing and transforming. According to AACU, "creative thinking is both the capacity to combine or synthesize existing ideas, images or expertise in original ways—it is the experience of thinking, reacting and working in an imaginative way that is characterized by a high degree of innovation, divergent thinking and risk taking."[2]

E. Paul Torrance, the famous creativity researcher and creator of the Torrance Test of Creative Thinking (TTCT), a standardized test that assesses our creative abilities and thinking skills, defined creativity as "a process of becoming sensitive to problems, deficiencies, gaps in knowledge, missing elements, disharmonies, and so on; identifying the difficulty; searching for solutions, making guesses, or formulating hypotheses about the deficiencies; testing and retesting these hypotheses and possibly modifying and retesting them; and finally communicating the results."[3] Influenced by Guilford, American psychologist and creativity researcher, Torrance decided to use four main components that he considered important to divergent thinking and creative thinking skills.

Fluency

Fluency refers to the ability to produce a large number of ideas or alternative solutions when working on a problem. Two dimensions easily measure fluency: time and number of ideas. Testers can set an idea quota and measure how long it will take to come up with a certain number of ideas. Additionally they can define a time limit and measure the number of ideas developed during that period. Fluency represents the ability to access previous knowledge and make as many associations as possible related to the problem. In the case of the Twenty Circles exercise (see page 29), the task consists of filling the circles with meaningful shapes. The faster you can complete the task, the more fluid your thinking skills are. During this exercise it is helpful to scan your knowledge/memory and remember anything you have seen or associate with a circle or round shape. Circles appear everywhere in the world. During the many circle exercises conducted over the years, professionals and students have typically drawn a manhole, a ball, a ring (e.g., wedding, engagement or diamond), an orange, a plate, a coin, an earth, a moon, a cup or symbols like yin and yang.

Flexibility

Flexibility refers to the production of many kinds of ideas—and the concept behind those ideas must be different from each other. Similarly to fluency, you tap into your memory and knowledge and sift through anything that connects (such as circular shapes and roundness for the circle exercise). Additionally, while coming up with many ideas, you also are aware that every idea you come up with is different from the other. During the many circles exercises conducted during creativity courses, students and practitioners often draw items of similar concepts, such as baseball, soccer ball, golf ball, basketball and beach ball or moon, faces with different facial expressions such as happy and sad during the first round. Yet, when drawing symbols of similar or same concepts, like different types of balls or round fruits, our thinking is limited and less flexible. The most flexible thinking can be demonstrated when drawing shapes that represent many different concepts and meanings. Within the context of the circle exercise, flexible thinking is expressed not only by how many different circles we are all familiar with but also by drawing objects that are not circular or round at first glance. For example, everyone is familiar with a pen or pencil, yet few look at a pen from the top or bottom perspective. Or see the holes in Swiss cheese. Or combine two circles to draw a bicycle or car. Or a pair of glasses. Or a pig's snout. Compared to the more easily seen examples (such as an orange or moon), the pen, Swiss cheese, pair of glasses, bicycle and pig's snout require the ability to switch thinking modes more quickly. This includes the ability to look at details while also being able to see the big picture. Roger Hurni highlights the importance of this ability in a business context: "We want people to look at our client's problem and be able to solve them from a different perspective and not just rely on [the] tried-and-true or best practices kind of techniques."

Elaboration

Elaboration is the ability to apply more details and enhance an idea. This includes adding several other ideas that might expand an existing idea or fine-tuning an idea and improving it by making it more beautiful or adding more detail. Elaboration also relates to the ability to see details that other people overlook, to add information and to look for a better way when others might stop. For example, I can think of an egg and see it not only as an oval shaped object but as a round object when looking at it from above. Then I can expand the idea of the egg and relate it to the circle exercise and come up with a hard boiled egg cut open and exposing the round egg yolk enclosed by the egg white. Depending on how I look at the egg its shape will differ. Elaborating further I can also see an egg sunny side up where the egg yolk takes up the shape of the circle and the egg white expands beyond the circle outline. Imagination comes into place and can push an idea further. Questions like *What if we did this?* or *What if we did such and such?* could expand

Twenty Circles Exercise

Add drawings to all the circles to turn them into recognizable pictures. For example, you could draw a peace sign, a face, an eyeball, a wheel. Complete twenty different pictures. The circle exercise provides an excellent framework to illustrate the key concepts Torrance has developed (see page 38 for part 2).

Adapted from Wujec, Tom (1995), *Five Star Mind, Games & Puzzles to Stimulate Your Creativity & Imagination*, Doubleday, New York.

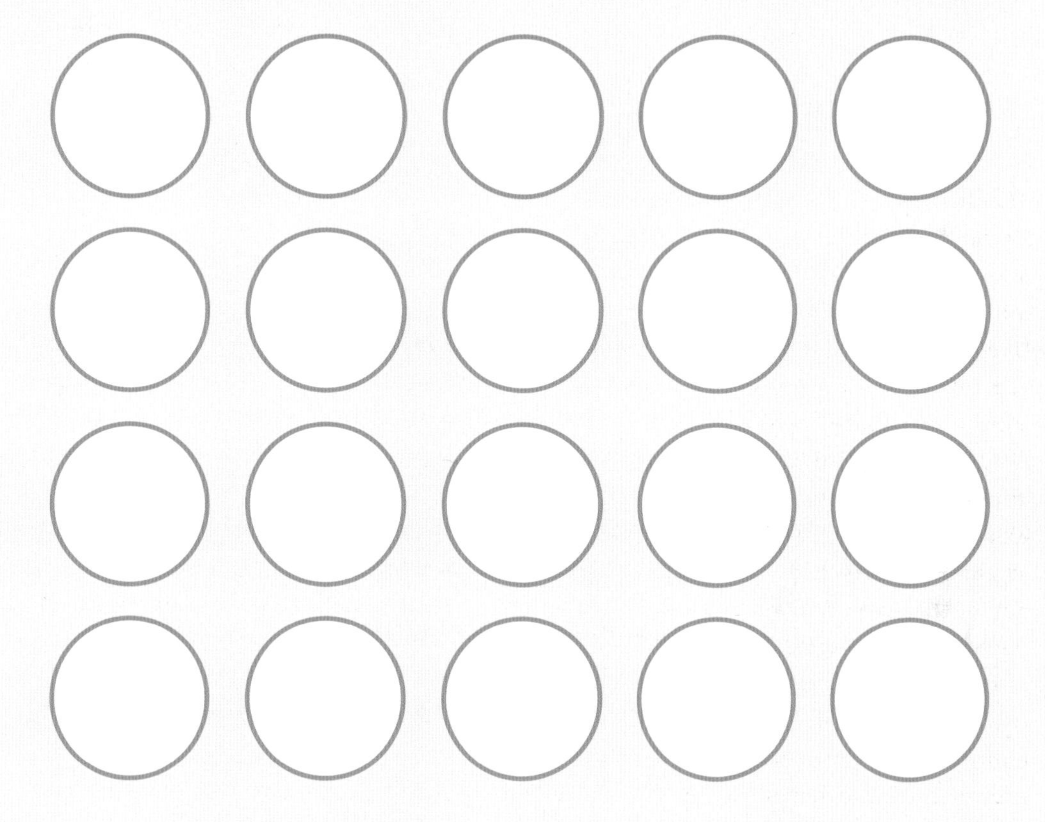

an idea. "It's not just about killing ideas, it's about making the ones that exist better," says Tim Leake, global creative innovation and partnership director at Hyper Island.

Originality

Originality relates to the ability to develop unique or unusual ideas, as well as putting things or situations in a new or unusual context.[4] In a classroom setting, originality is usually typified by a single

Divergent Thinking Exercise

Now that you understand the different ways that we solve problems, use your sketchbook to identify three activities or recent experiences in which you have used one of the two different methods of creative thinking. 1. Convergent Thinking: the gas tank was on empty, so I went to the gas station and filled up the car. 2. Divergent Thinking: What can I do with a shoe?

Adapted from RSA Animate - Changing Education Paradigms, http://www.youtube.com/watch?v=zDZFcDGpL4U

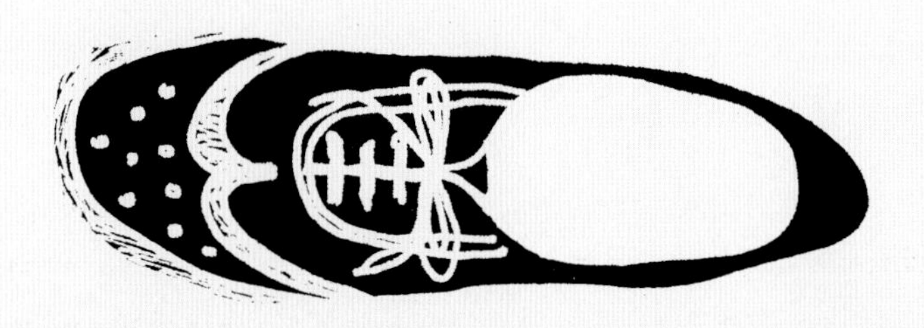

student developing a specific solution to a problem that no one is seemingly able to do. In a business setting, originality is a highly sought factor. "I think the qualities that really good creatives have, natural or taught, is a kind of natural inclination towards original thinking," says Mark Hunter, former chief creative officer at Deutsch LA. He argues, "The really great creatives solve the problem in a different way, bring a very original solution to the table. And I think, in the same way, great creatives are probably the central component in making good work alongside a good brief and all those other things, but [the creatives themselves] are the dominant force ... For me, I think originality is the dominant force." Tom Moudry, president and chief creative officer at Martin Williams in Minneapolis is looking for interesting things that have not been seen before and for new ways of looking at something.

The increased focus on developing creative thinking skills during college represents an important step toward building valuable skills beyond a special degree in a core discipline. In addition to looking for industry-specific specialists, employers are looking for prospective employees with creative thinking and problem-solving skills. In creative industries, like architecture, performing arts, film, media, advertising, visual design and product design, individual thinking skills are considered even more important. According to Norm Shearer, chief creative officer at the agency Cactus Marketing Communications in Denver, the aim is to hire creative people, whether they are an assistant at the front desk, the CEO, an account person, or a media person. He believes that it is not just the creatives that are creative. "I think everyone has to be creative," Shearer says. Lance Jensen, co-founder of the former agency Modernista and chief creative officer at Hill Holiday in Boston, says "In our agency, our value walks out the door every night. [It's] all we have, other than some chairs, some

Macs and a keg. So, if we don't have good people, you don't get good work." According to Edward Boches, former chief creative and innovation officer at Mullen, the output of any company heavily relies on the individual part of each employee. "Even though we live in the 'wisdom of the crowd,' where crowdsourcing has become more and more important, it is the individual ability to create, design, invent, inspire and think that makes a company successful," says Boches.

David Droga, founder and chief creative officer at Droga5 says, "I try to hire as many inspiring, interesting, authentic creative people as possible and that manifests itself in many different ways. I'm not looking for one type of creative person or one type of creative thinker. I look at problem solvers. I look for people with disparate backgrounds and give them the canvas and the freedom to express themselves."

Doug Spong, president at Carmichael Lynch Spong in Minneapolis, believes that "Highly creative people have an enormous attention to detail. I don't mean typos and grammar. What I am talking about is they tend to notice things in personalities, characteristics and behaviors of the people around them. They tend to notice very minute details."

Understanding how people think and how one can improve thinking skills provides you the opportunity to practice your thinking on a regular basis and improve your divergent and convergent thinking skills. Since many people learn from practical experiences as well as theoretical cases, this book includes several examples of how young professionals, who have studied creativity during a college course, have improved their thinking.

Former student Alyse Dunn describes her situation. "I entered my Creative Thinking course at Emerson [College, in Boston] as any ideal student would. I sat there thinking, 'What will this class really teach me? I am already creative. What more could I learn?' I quickly realized that there was a lot to learn and that the creativity that was so inherent had been slowly wilting away, and I hadn't even noticed. As we were given creative thinking tasks, I found it challenging to think quickly and really pull unique thoughts. My mind felt rusty, which it never had before. I didn't like the feeling, but it also wakened me to a stark reality: If creativity is inherent, then how can it be slipping away? I took the rustiness as a sign that I needed to challenge my mind more. I read each book hungrily in order to shake my mind of the proverbial cobwebs. I pushed myself to actively engage in the classroom activities and not default to the easy answer. It was a challenge, which was new to me. I wasn't used to working so hard at being creative, but I am so thankful that I did. I could see the change in the way I thought and looked at problems. I could think faster, look at problems from many different angles and truly arrive at solutions that I would not have been able to originally. I really enjoyed this change. I began to pursue creative avenues in my everyday life.

In the past, I had always been actively involved in anything creative, but when I left college and moved, I lost that part of myself. I never realized how much I missed it until I began retraining my mind. I began taking card making classes and crepe making classes. I began dancing again and exploring different museums and historical landmarks. I read books that I enjoyed and started writing creatively again. I took back that part of my life. My creative course taught me how to hold on to my creativity and how to hone my creative skills. Whenever I am feeling mundane, I do something that sparks creativity. It is something I truly enjoy, and it is eye-opening. You can really see the world differently and that has translated well into my career."

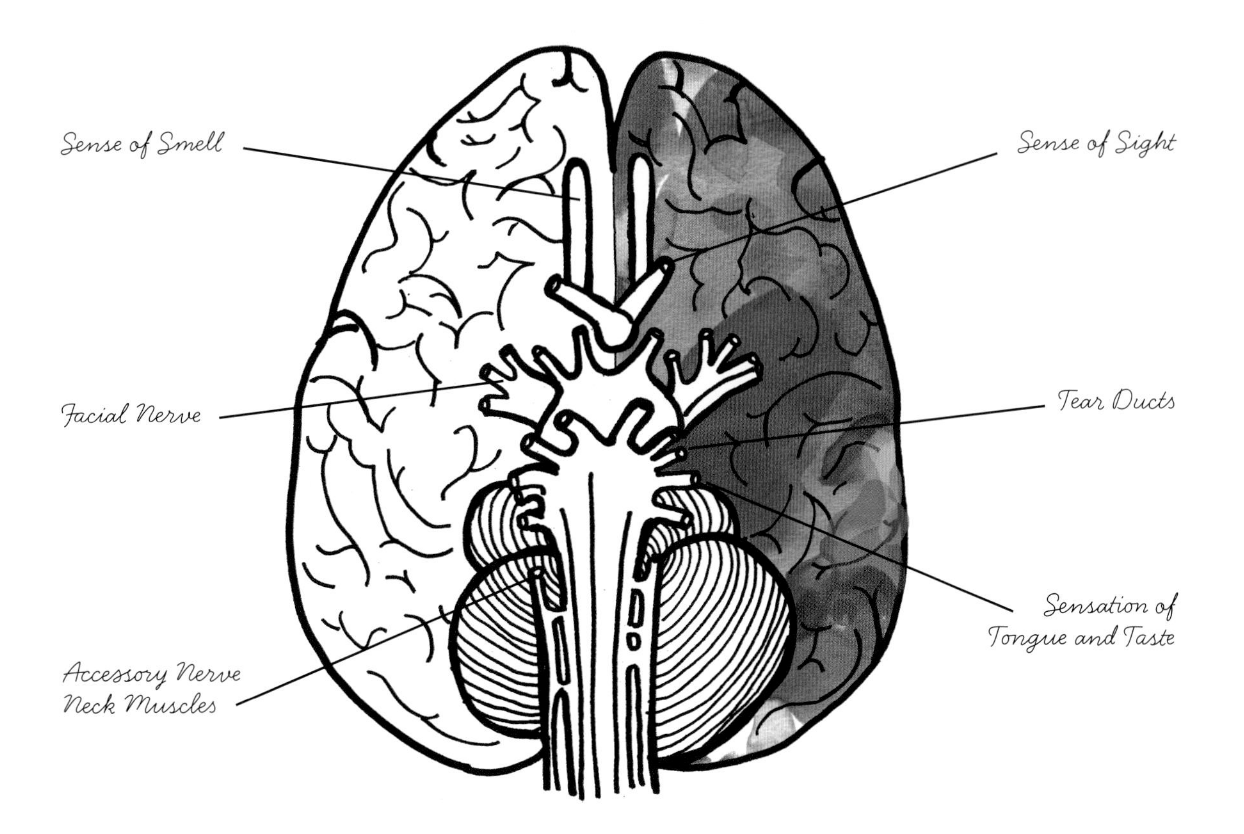

CREATIVE THINKING AND THE BRAIN

The way the human brain works has not changed much over time. Fortunately technological advances in medicine, psychology and neurosciences have brought new information to light, allowing humans to better understand what is going on in our brains when creativity is at work. This new scientific insight might not make us better or more creative thinkers. However, new studies may help us understand what happens when we practice our thinking and further develop our creative skills.

You probably have heard that an individual's thinking falls into two categories: left-brained or right-brained. According to this theory, each hemisphere controls different types of thinking. Left-brained people are said to be more logical, analytical and objective. Some of the abilities that are often associated with this side of the brain are logic, critical thinking, numbers, reasoning and language. Right-brained people are said to be creative and expressive. They are more intuitive, objective and thoughtful. Some abilities that are typically associated with this side of the brain are facial recognition, emotional expression, emotional reading, music, color, images, intuition and greater creative ability.

This theory grew out of work that was conducted by Nobel Prize–winning psychologist Roger W. Sperry. While working with patients suffering from epilepsy, Sperry discovered that by cutting the corpus callosum—the structure that connects the two hemispheres of the brain—the number of seizures were reduced and, in some cases, eliminated. However, this was not the only thing that occurred when this communication pathway was cut. Some split-brained patients that were unable to name objects that were processed by the right side of the brain but were able to name objects that were processed by the left side of the brain. With this finding, Sperry concluded that the left side of the brain controls language. Through extensive research, he believed that the two sides of the brain acted independently and had different processing styles. This eventually led to the left-brain, right-brain theory that is widely referenced today.

According to Rex E. Jung, the concept of left-brain and right-brain thinking and the distinct brain activities associated is part of "folk psychologies." The concept that creativity is related to stronger right-brain activities has been promoted by popular media rather than supported scientifically. More recent studies have shown that in healthy individuals, these two sides of the brain are very much connected and have evolved to operate together in most everything a person does. In his own neuroscientific studies, Jung and his colleagues discovered that creativity takes more than just the right part of the brain. "If you didn't have your left hemisphere, I guarantee you wouldn't be creative," Jung claims.

Although there are some tasks that the two hemispheres tackle independently, the integration of the two sides yields some of the most uniquely human characteristics. For example, when humans make mistakes, the realization and ability to correct a mistake is a result of both the left and right hemispheres working together. Individuals with damage to their corpus callosum have a more difficult time correcting their errors than people with healthy brains. Both hemispheres must work together to solve these problems. While there are certain tasks that occur primarily on one side of the brain, in certain circumstances, it is possible for the other side to take control of the process. For example, if someone experiences damage to his Broca's area, a region located on the left side of the brain linked to speech production, there is an increased amount of activity in the right inferior frontal gyrus on the opposite side. This demonstrates that our brains, even as adults, have enough plasticity to adapt to change and damage.

You may think that your strengths are more left-brained or more right-brained in nature. However, the truth is that you can train your brain to think with *both* hemispheres. In fact, creativity flourishes the most when you are able to integrate both sides of the brain. You may think that your brain does not have the capability of being creative, but this simply is not true. Anyone can train her brain to be creative. It just takes practice.

The brain is an organ that can evolve. Much like regular exercise can help develop and strengthen muscles, the brain can be trained in a similar manner. The more exercise you do to engage your brain creatively, the more creative your brain will become. However, just like with physical exercise, you must train it regularly not intermittently. Many people feel like they are not creative because they are not actively engaging their brain in activities that trigger creation. Rather, many of the activities that we do on a day-to-day basis are training the brain to be passive not active. For example, many people spend hours watching television or browsing the Internet. These activities do not actively engage the brain in activities that train it to create. Furthermore, not many of us permit ourselves to do nothing—allowing our minds just wander and daydream. Think about your typical day; how much of that time is spent on passive activities rather than active ones?

The brain wants to be as efficient as possible and is always looking for the easy way out. This means that it seeks straightforward, familiar answers that are based on past experiences. This is why it may be difficult at first to break these habits and to force the brain to move from old thinking patterns to new ideas generated instinctively and on command. Neuroscientists once believed that the brain was fully developed by early adulthood

Minds at Work

Here is an interesting exercise that illustrates our minds at work: A man has married twenty women in a small town. All of the women are still alive and none of them are divorced. The man has broken no laws. Who is the man?

This exercise appears in numerous sources: *The Malleability of Implicit Beliefs of Creativity and Creative Production*, page 81, 2008, by Matthew C. Makel; *Imagine: How Creativity Works*, by Jonah Lehrer, 2012; and at www.indiana.edu/-bobweb/Handout/insightproblems.doc by Curtis J. Bonk.

and that there was nothing to be done after a certain time in a person's life to change its chemistry. The fact that your brain can only be changed and developed during your formative years, in your childhood and adolescence, has been widely accepted. However, this belief has been overturned in recent years. Studies have demonstrated that the brain can, in fact, be changed and developed throughout your life by engaging it in various activities. Our brain is much more flexible than we think! In fact, the brain is neuroplastic, which means that it can learn new ways of thinking and create new neural connections. This can be done well into old age, which means that you can start changing your brain at anytime. It just takes practice and dedication.

In recent years several new methods have been built to aid in training our brains and strengthening our thinking muscle. Nintendo adopted brainteaser games for their Game Boy and numerous magazines publish puzzles and brain exercises. For example, the leading newspaper in Germany, *Frankfurter Allgemeine Zeitung*,[5] devotes a special section to brain training. And there are plenty of web-based services that provide exercises. These activities are all built on new findings in neuroscience that claim the human brain is not merely a preformatted computer with limited computing power but an apparatus that is flexible and can be trained.

Two brain researchers offer additional insight on how our brain works. The first, Joydeep Bhattacharya, a psychologist at Goldsmiths, University of London, found some interesting results when researching the influence of alpha waves. Specifically he discovered why it is so important to rely on taking showers, taking walks on the beach or doing something completely unrelated to the problem you are working on. These activities allow the brain to defocus. Our conscious and unconscious minds appear to be playing an important game of tennis, firing neurons back and forth along the alpha waves at high speeds and in increasing quantity—until the conscious mind reaches game point. According to Bhattacharya, the alpha waves stem from the right hemisphere.

The second brain researcher, Mark Beeman, a psychologist from the University of Chicago, also gained some new insight when looking at the neural source of insight. He gave a group of individuals specific brainteasers and observed how they solved them. Beeman found a strong connection between left-brain thought process and right-brain thought process. When we are given problems to solve, we apply knowledge that we have gained over time and try to solve those problems consciously through analytical thinking. Yet with many problems, we require new insight and perspective in order to solve a problem creatively. Rather than rely exclusively on associations we are familiar with, we need to shift our perspective. According to Beeman, unexpected associations occur when we step away from the given problem. He considers the "stepping away" a mental shift. By removing our focus from the problem, we can allow our brains to make connections that we are not consciously aware of. This shift can give us the insight and new perspective to solve what seems impossible and to see new connections.

In his article "Neuroscience Sheds New Light on Creativity," Gregory Berns discusses how MRIs have shed light on how people develop new ideas. Berns argues that there are certain people, like Walt Disney and Steve Jobs, who belong to a certain class of people he calls Iconoclasts. In simple terms, they have the ability to see things differently. Some of these Iconoclasts are born this way. However, those of us not naturally blessed with these abilities can learn from Iconoclasts. According to Berns, "We all can learn how to see things not for what they are, but for what they might be." The brain uses the same neural circuits for perception and imagination. "Imagination is like running perception in reverse," says Berns.

Many people have a hard time thinking of truly original ideas, which is in large part due to the way in which the brain interprets signals from the eyes. Your brain explains ambiguous visual signals by basing it on past experiences and things that it has been exposed to in the past. "Experience modifies the connections between neurons so that they become more efficient at processing information," claims Berns. When you are exposed to something for the very first time, your brain uses an entire network of neurons to interpret it. However, by the time you are exposed to that same thing, say a sixth time, a much smaller number of neurons are at work because your brain has become much more efficient at interpreting this stimulus. Therefore, if people have been exposed to something multiple times and are asked to describe it, they are much less likely to use their imagination. But if they are asked to describe something less familiar to them, they provide more original and novel explanations. This is because they have fewer past experiences to rely on. Therefore, Berns claims that in order to think more creatively, a person needs to develop "new neural pathways and break out of the cycle of experience-dependent categorization." If the brain has a hard time predicting what is to come next, the individual is more likely to use her imagination and think more creatively. This research is encouraging as it demonstrates that anyone can trigger novel thinking by exposing themselves to new environments and experiences. The more radical the change, the more likely it is that a person will have novel insights. Berns believes that "the surest way to provoke the imagination [is] to seek out environments you have no experience with."

Anyone can be a creative type. It is just a matter of getting your brain to think in new ways and exposing yourself to new experiences and situations. A big aspect of creativity is allowing your brain to make associations and connections in places that you never thought possible. The likelihood that you will make unique connections is increased if you have more diverse information stored in your brain. Steve Jobs said that the best inventors are those people that seek out "diverse experiences." This could mean a number of things. For example, you could take up something completely unknown to you, like playing the banjo. Or it could mean interacting with people from a different discipline than you and gleaning information from them to use in your own line of work.

Many companies are beginning to realize how important it is for people to be exposed to diverse experiences. The belief is that these activities will translate to better overall work for the company. In our interviews with the creative directors of various advertising agencies, many emphasized the importance of having interests outside of work. Marshall Ross of Cramer Krasselt says, "I think the people who are good, or who are successful, within creative organizations are people who are learning constantly from lots of different resources. They learn from their friends; they learn from their peers." David Droga of Droga5 in New York engages in many activities that lie outside the realm of advertising. "I like being open to the world and seeing [things] because it sometimes can inspire in the most unlikely places. And I would say the majority of the work that I've done or the work that other people have done that I love, comes from something that is back to real life." Of his employees, Droga believes that "they are more interesting people and more interesting creative thinkers if they have a real life out there and interests far beyond [the office]. So we certainly promote and celebrate any other interests, whether they are aligned with our business or not."

R/GA, the digital agency responsible for Nike+ and many other innovative technology-based platforms, campaigns and products, fully understands the power and special interests of their employees, knowing that many of those interests lie outside the core business. Former student Sara Wynkoop's research on R/GA's culture (see her creativity essay at www.breakthroughthinkingguide.com) points out that the agency lets its employees explore activities like knitting, sketching, painting or creative writing through various employee special interest clubs. These activities provide great opportunities to defocus from daily problems and they expose the brain to activities in completely different fields and topics, sparking new insight.

Children arrive at original ideas more often because their thoughts are less inhibiting, allowing their brains to wander. They do not have a fear of failure that often paralyzes and inhibits an adult's thinking. As children, humans are equipped with the ability to dream and be imaginative. They are less experienced and are still attempting to make sense of the world around them. Therefore, they have a greater propensity to imagine things. I invite you to take a brief moment and remember your own childhood or think of children that you know. Try to recall when you have asked your parents or relatives any "What If?" questions. In my experience, my youngest daughter, during her elementary school years, frequently asked questions like, "What if we lived for one day in a house that is upside down?" Or "What if I could fly like a balloon to the moon and touch it and my hair is so long that you can hold on to me?"

An excellent way to expose yourself to new experiences is the "Artist Date," an exercise developed by Julia Cameron, which she describes in her book *The Artist's Way*. I use this exercise in my course on a weekly basis and find that my students have explored new topics and areas, and gained new experiences. One student, who is not from Boston, believed that Bostonians seem to be rather cold and unapproachable. She realized that this was quite judgmental and began approaching a stranger once a week. Whether it was during a walk in the park or on the subway, she introduced herself and started conversations that allowed her to see people and the world around her through a new lens. Emboldened by her new insight, the student decided to take the bus, which she had never done before, and experienced new neighborhoods and areas in the city.

You can engage in simple things on a regular basis in order to boost your own creativity. It could be taking a new street to walk to your house or trying a new dish at your favorite restaurant. (See the sidebar on page 37 for ideas.)

SIMPLE WAYS TO BOOST YOUR CREATIVITY

1. Always carry a notebook or a pen because you never know where or when inspiration may hit you.
2. Limit the amount of time you spend watching television, which causes your brain to go into a neutral, passive mode. In one study, people who watched television had an increased amount of alpha waves, which are waves that are triggered when the brain is in a passive state. In other words, the brain has the same reaction to watching television as it does if you are just sitting in a dark room. Remember, keep your brain active, not passive. This is the key to creativity.
3. Find reasons to laugh. In one study done, subjects were better at solving exercises that were designed to measure creative thinking right after they were exposed to something funny. Also, consider a quote by advertising man David Ogilvy, who said, "Where people aren't having any fun, they seldom produce good work."
4. Read as much as possible and expose yourself to the creations of creative people.
5. Step out of your comfort zone by doing something unusual. Or do something in a way that you do not usually do it. Take a new route to work. Do a task that you are used to doing on a regular basis in a particular order, but in a different sequence. A simple example is to prepare your cereal in the morning by putting in your milk first, then toppings, and finally the cereal (as opposed to cereal, milk, then toppings).

6. Learn a new language, master a new hobby or engage in debate. Engaging your brain in these kinds of activities stimulates blood flow and strengthens the connections (synapses) between nerve cells in the brain. Do a puzzle or even do something as simple as brushing your teeth with a different hand.
7. When you hit a roadblock in your thinking, distract yourself and go back to it later. This is especially effective when you distract yourself with a completely unrelated task. For example, rather than switching to a different math problem, get up and water your plants as a method of distraction.
8. Think of a problem as if it is physically farther away. This may help you come up with more innovative solutions because you are thinking of the issue in more abstract terms.
9. Think of yourself as further away from the problem in terms of time. Research has shown that people tend to solve more when they were told to imagine themselves solving a problem in a year rather than the next day.
10. Break out of the barrier of thinking of objects in a conventional way. Challenge their purpose and their use. What else could a shopping bag be used for? Play with different ideas.
11. Interact with people that come from different backgrounds than your own.

Twenty Circles Exercise Part 2

Add drawings to all the circles to turn them into recognizable pictures. Since you have completed the first set of twenty pictures previously you can start all over again by drawing twenty completely new pictures. Try completing several sets of 20 circles and come up with a total of 150 pictures.

Adapted from Wujec, Tom (1995), *Five Star Mind, Games & Puzzles to Stimulate Your Creativity & Imagination*, Doubleday, New York.

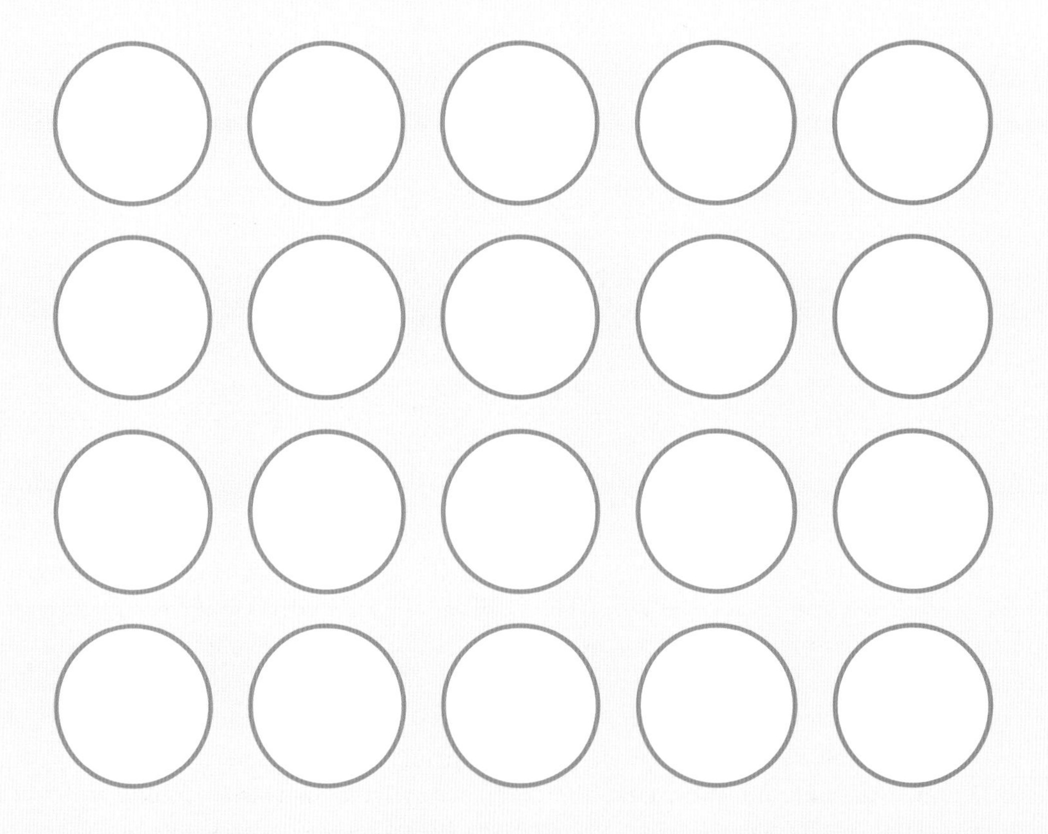

CHAPTER FOUR

THE CREATIVE [PROBLEM-SOLVING] PROCESS

Since an individual's decision-making process is influenced by the knowledge he has acquired over the years, the brain often makes decisions the individual might not be fully aware of. As discussed in chapter three, it can be helpful to better understand how thinking works and how you can apply different types of thinking when solving problems. Having a creative thinking or problem-solving process can lead to even better problem-solving skills. Several exercises, like the Nine Dots (on page 17), demonstrate that people often get stuck in the way they think because they are unable to shift their thinking mode. For example, when approaching the Nine Dots exercise, your brain processes the information by subconsciously making assumptions. Therefore, it is helpful to learn how you can think about the ways in which you process information and be aware of the kind of thinking you are applying at any given time. Psychologists call this process metacognition. This term, coined by John Flavell, professor of developmental psychology at Stanford University, refers to how people leverage their understanding of

Two Riders and Horses Puzzle

1. Download and print a copy of this puzzle at www.breakthroughthinkingguide.com and carefully cut out the three pieces along the dotted lines.
2. Without folding or tearing put a rider on each horse.
3. No trick riding allowed!
4. Think out of the box!

The two riders and horses puzzle was provided during a leadership course in creative problem solving at Creative Problem Solving Institute (CPSI) 1994, Creative Education Foundation, Buffalo, NY. Source unknown.

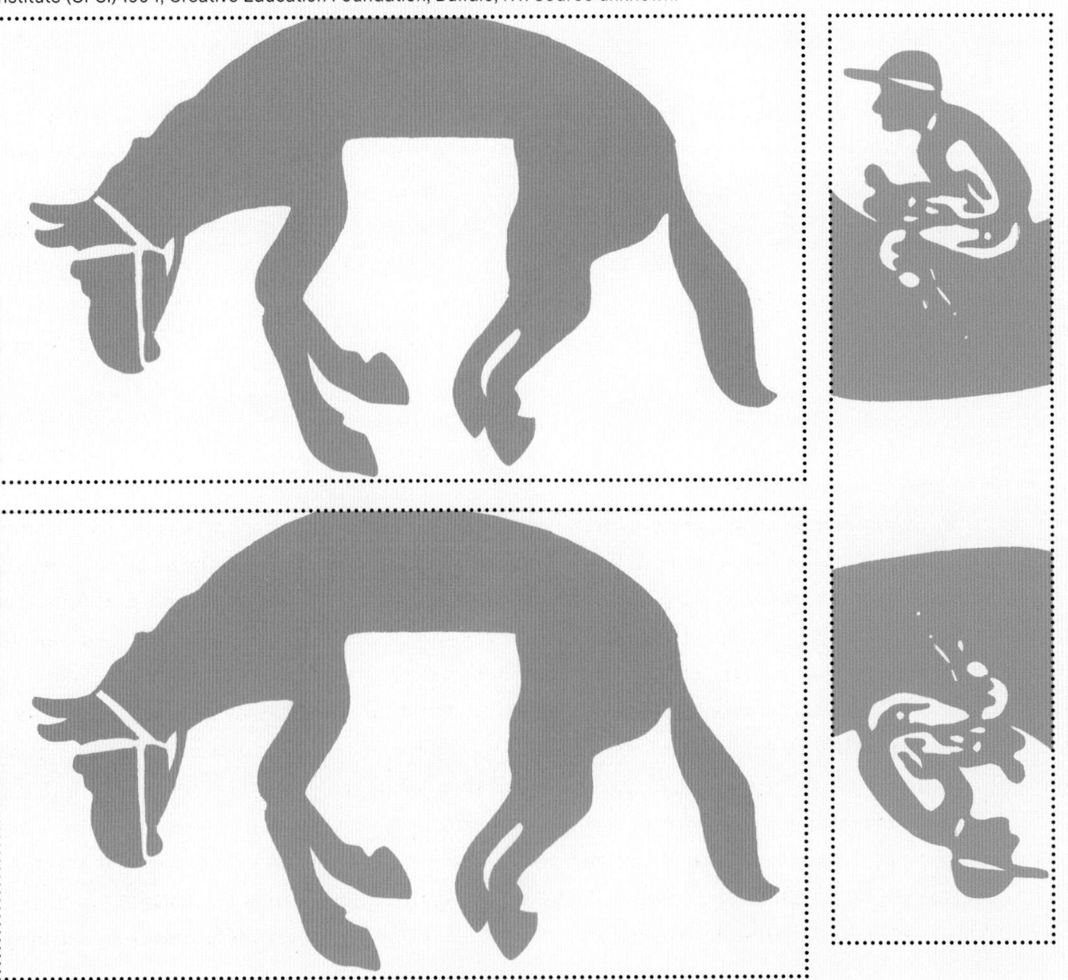

how they think and what goes on in their brains when they are trying to achieve a certain cognitive goal.[1] Flavell worked with young children ranging in age from preschool to elementary and studied how they handled cognitive tasks based on their ability to gauge their memorization skills. He discovered that the older children were better able to understand their capacity to perform a memory task. With age, the recognition of our cognitive abilities improves. Being able to identify your own mental abilities is important, especially during a problem-solving or creative thinking process. Understanding how you think when considering a specific topic can help you shift gears and guide your thinking in different directions.

During the last six decades, several creativity researchers have developed different models of thinking processes, and these models help us to see the thinking process as a set of different stages. Some of those processes aid us in gaining a better understanding of how we think and when to apply the different kinds of thinking, such as divergent and convergent thinking when solving problems or generating new ideas for campaigns, products or services. In any creative problem solving process, divergent thinking should be applied during the Generation Phase in order to come up with as many ideas as possible. During this phase it is important to defer judgment, strive for quantity and freewheel, which means that you should capture and record every solution that comes to mind, no matter how crazy or out there it may seem. Finally, you should seek combinations, building on your ideas or other people's ideas in order to go into new, unexplored directions. Divergent thinking allows us to push ourselves to come up with as many different ideas and concepts as possible without expecting those ideas to relate to one another. This type of thinking is used to consciously increase the total number of possible solutions without being concerned about whether or not these solutions will ultimately solve the problem.

Once a predetermined number of ideas has been generated or an allotted amount of time for generating ideas has passed, convergent thinking is then applied as the next step in the creative problem-solving process. During the convergent thinking phase, all ideas are evaluated and measured against the initial problem (see table of creative processes on page 43). The separation between divergent and convergent thinking forces the mind to take a nonjudgmental tack.

In the 1980s, advertising executive Alex Osborn and psychologist Sidney Parnes developed the Creative Problem-Solving Process. The Osborn-Parnes Creative Problem-Solving Process (CPS) provides a widely applicable framework for solving problems and generating as many solutions as possible. The CPS encourages thinking that is unusual and varied in nature, then evaluating and streamlining ideas into something worth implementing.

In chapter two, creativity is defined as the production of something original and useful and reflected in the Torrance tests—but there is never one right answer. Creativity requires divergent thinking (generating many unique ideas) and convergent thinking (combining those ideas into the best results). This definition of creativity supports the notion that one divides thinking and actions into several steps when trying to solve a problem.

Graham Wallace, a British political scientist and sociologist who wrote the book *The Art of Thought* (1926), developed a four-stage model. This creative process uses four steps to apply creative thinking in order to come up with original, worthwhile and applicable ideas. The four steps are preparation, incubation, illumination and verification. By dividing problem solving into several steps, an individual can consciously apply various thinking

Visual Self-Presentation

Companies are increasingly interested in learning new things about people during an interview process. Let's assume you have 10 minutes during which you can present yourself and make an impression. Present yourself with 9-12 images/visuals. The presentation can be produced in an abstract, concrete, symbolic, descriptive way aor can also make use of analogies. The key visuals can be in relationship with each other or can be independent from each other. This exercise should encourage you to think in abstract ways, develop core concepts and ideas, be playful, take risks and experiment. The key visuals should have an appropriate size of 8 ½" x 11" to present to an audience of 6-10 people. You can use any visual design tools or elements available to you (photography, painting, drawing, collage and objects).

Below are table and list views that point out some basic similarities of various processes.

OVERVIEW OF DIFFERENT PROBLEM-SOLVING PROCESSES:

Wallace Four-Step Process

PREPARATION: preliminary analysis
INCUBATION: making associations, ideas not yet being generated
ILLUMINATION: ideas are making their way out
VERIFICATION: testing out the ideas

Amabile Process

PROBLEM: task identification
PREPARATION: situation analysis, gather information
RESPONSE GENERATION: generate as many ideas as possible
RESPONSE VALIDATION AND COMMUNICATION PHASE: evaluate ideas and analyze which will work

Five Stage Process of Creativity by James Webb Young

PREPARATION
DIGESTION
INCUBATION
ILLUMINATION
APPLICATION

The Osborne-Parnes CPS Process

MESS FINDING: establish clear statement of the objectives
FACT FINDING: gather as much information about the problem as possible
PROBLEM FINDING: reexamine the initial problem and see if it's still the same after the fact-finding
IDEA FINDING: generate as many ideas as possible
SOLUTION FINDING: pick the best ideas
ACCEPTANCE FINDING: actually testing the idea

Design Thinking

DISCOVERY: research the problem, gather as much info as you can, define the problem
INTERPRETATION: look at all of your research from various angles and interpret it
IDEATION: create as many ideas as possible
EXPERIMENTATION: build prototypes, test the ideas
EVOLUTION: refuse and further developed

Phase	Wallace 4-step Process	Amabile Process	5 Stage Model of Creativity by James Webb Young	The Osborn/ Parnes CPS Model	Design Thinking
Determine the task/ problem on hand, situation analysis	Preparation	Preparation	Preparation	Mess finding	Discovery
Research the topic and gather as much information as possible (no idea generation yet)	Incubation	Preparation	Digestion	Fact finding	Discovery
Re-examine the problem at hand with new information				Problem finding	Interpretation
Generate as many ideas as possible	Illumination	Response generation	Incubation	Idea Finding	Ideation
Choose the best ideas out of the ideas that were generated		Response validation and communication	Illumination	Solution finding	Experimentation
Test the idea, build prototypes, and make changes as needed	Verification		Application	Acceptance finding	Evolution

Coffeehouse Exercise: Day One

Go to a public place such as a coffee shop and spend one hour observing a person. Describe the person, and what he or she is doing. (See Day Two on page 54).

The coffeehouse exercise is credited to Shelley Berc and Alejandro Fogel's, The Creativity Workshop, New York. http://www.creativityworkshop.com/

styles in order to change the outcome of his or her thinking. As demonstrated by the Nine Dots exercise, these steps help us to view information in a way that differs from what our brains normally do by default. Wallace claimed that these steps were experienced in order and did not overlap. However, he believed that the four stages are recursive and that each stage could be revisited. This model continues to influence and inform the development of later models in thinking.

During the preparation phase, the preliminary analysis begins. The general situation is analyzed and we define what we are about to do and the kind of information we are looking for. We also determine what kind of research will be applied in order to find the necessary information. During this first phase, we will look at the problem and connect it to the bigger picture. It is acceptable to start collecting ideas as they arise during the preparation phase. But at the same time, it is important to delay the real concepting and ideation thinking.

During the second phase, our mind continues to work on the problem, unconsciously forming trains of associations. We might come up with several ideas and our mind will wander, connecting ideas and looking into different areas, while drawing from past experiences.

During the third phase, we can expect some promising ideas to break through and to move into our consciousness. Ideas emerge, and we compare them to our existing knowledge. We start thinking about which idea might be the most appropriate solution to solve our problem.

During the last phase, which is the verification phase, the ideas we chose as potential solutions are further developed, evaluated and refined.

Since the 1970s, American researcher and Harvard professor Teresa Amabile has been exploring how creativity works, how the creative place and environmental aspects influences the creative output (see chapter 9 and 10) and how creativity can be increased. In 1983, Amabile provided a model for a creative process that includes four steps and is similar to the Wallace model. The first step is problem or task identification. This step is arguably the most crucial. I would like to stress the importance of clearly defining the problem before offering any solutions. In my extensive experience, I have often seen problems poorly defined at the outset. In turn, solutions are developed without fully understanding the real problem. It is important to clearly identify the focus of the problem and to question whether the initial problem is truly the real issue at hand. Problems frequently need to be redefined or broken into smaller subsets.

The second step of Amabile's model is preparation. During the preparation stage, a situation analysis is conducted and as much information as possible is gathered. Thereafter, during the third step, called response generation, as many ideas as possible are generated. Finally, in the fourth step, the response validation and communication phase, ideas that have been developed are evaluated and analyzed to determine which best solve the problem.

The most important takeaway from this chapter is that a clear problem-solving process or creative process can increase the likelihood of coming up with the best possible solution. As we have learned, creativity is a complex topic. There is not just one way that explains how creativity happens or what happens when creativity is at work. The same is true for the creative process. Several problem-solving processes and creative processes have been developed—and new research and knowledge is added to the discipline every year.

In addition to the processes described here, many individuals have developed their own unique thinking process. As you read this chapter, you may want to think about your own work and any processes that you are applying. In some cases you may have already developed your own personal creative process that works well for you.

Rob Schwartz at TBWA\Chiat\Day believes that "the process of disruption is one of the smartest ways to get great ideas fast, consistently." A concept like disruption can provide important information during any step of the thinking process. Everyone in the agency knows that disruption is a key outcome of the agency and that any idea has to be good enough to measure up to this goal. People involved in research will have to look at the marketplace and target audiences in order to understand where norms might exist and where the concept disruption might fit. Understanding human behavior and competitive environments will help us evaluate whether or not an idea has the potential to be disruptive in the first place. Knowing that an idea must be disruptive becomes an evaluation criterion that helps identify the best idea suited to solve the challenge.

The ideation process plays an important role at Cramer Krasselt in Chicago. Marshall Ross points out that "there is no embarrassment. It's a bad idea, a good idea. Pin it up. And the idea there is to share that thinking. That's one level of show-and-tell. It was literally a daily, hourly, minute-by minute process. And what happens is that people walk around and provide feedback or get inspiration."

This approach focuses on two main components. First, a key objective is the development of as many ideas as possible. The second is that ideas must be shared and viewed by many people in order to increase the overall quantity and the quality of ideas developed that solve a client's challenge in new and appropriate ways. Tom Moudry of Martin Williams puts special emphasis on situation analysis and research at the beginning of the process, a stage at which it is important to discover the norms within the industry his clients are competing in. "We have a sequential process that we call creative habits. It starts with just challenging assumptions. In every single category there are conventions and assumptions," says Moudry.

There are several other creative problem-solving processes available that have been developed by various individuals or teams. Some of those processes were developed as part of creativity research and others come from more applied fields, such as IDEO's process of "design thinking." I personally have worked with the Osborn-Parnes Creative Problem Solving Process for more than twenty years and have participated in many CPS training sessions and leadership programs at the Creative Education Foundation (CEF) at SUNY Buffalo in New York. Based on my personal and professional experience, both the Osborn-Parnes model and the IDEO Design Thinking Process provide two frameworks that are highly applicable in real-world situations. Any of the processes mentioned in this chapter can also be helpful when writing a research paper, reviewing and working on a case analysis, or developing new marketing solutions, communication plans and products.

The Osborn-Parnes Creative Problem Solving Process (CPS) model consists of six individual steps. The first phase, *mess finding*, consists of a clear statement of the deductive objectives that are being developed. Instead of accepting any problem or challenge as initially presented, this phase provides the opportunity to include different perspectives and to determine some key objectives that may help identify the problem or subproblems, and describe the expected outcome at the beginning of the process. Typically, during the mess finding stage, a general research plan, or situation analysis with a big picture perspective, is developed. During this step, it can be helpful to apply some creative thinking techniques—for example, look at the problem through the perspectives of various company stakeholders.

Based on my experience with various agencies, dedicating a certain amount of time to this phase can make a huge difference between finding expected results and arriving at ideas that are more unusual and original. Many students, as well as practitioners, tend to focus on what the client asks for rather than taking that information into consideration but focusing on a more diverse perspective. By basing the resolution on a client's brief (or problem), you may easily miss out on opportunities that go beyond the scope of the client's problem or fail to develop solutions that are original, unusual and innovative.

The average problem solver is focused on identifying the obvious and most common facts about a problem or task. But allotting more time and resources to discovering unusual facts and insights, as well as looking at a problem from various different perspectives, problem solvers can uncover powerful information that will increase the potential of developing more innovative solutions. In my own teaching experience and agency practice, I have pushed the idea of "let's find the most unusual facts, uncover new information and try to educate our clients" by adding not only a new perspective, but also more value. This goes hand-in-hand with postponing the ideation phase until we know what the real problem is and then applying our unusual insights and perspectives to it.

The second step in the process is fact finding. During this step, it is important to look at all the facts related to the assignment, including the ones that you may initially assume are not relevant or important. Our minds often process information unconsciously and direct our thinking in very specific directions. Such unconscious guidance can be helpful in some cases but detrimental in others.

Clearly allocating resources and spending as much time as possible identifying facts provides a nurturing ground to create more ideas during the ideation phase.

Before starting the idea finding phase, the Osborn-Parnes process recommends a separate phase, called the *problem finding* step. During the problem finding step, one should reexamine the initial problem and determine if it is still the same problem after all of the facts have been considered. The problem may need to be broken down into smaller or simpler problems because it is possible that the problem is too big to be solved in one step.

REAL-WORLD EXAMPLE: A few years ago, several of my graduate students at Emerson College participated in InterAd, an international student competition organized by the International Advertising Association (IAA) in New York, which was sponsored by the international advertising agency network Dentsu. The United Nations (the client) required competition participants to develop a marketing strategy and communication campaign that would help the organization in its eight Millennium Development Goals (MDG) for improving world prosperity by 2015. The UN's MDG were as follows:

1. Eradicate extreme poverty and hunger
2. Ensure all boys and girls complete primary school
3. Promote gender equality and empower women
4. Reduce the mortality rate of children under five by two-thirds
5. Reduce the ratio of women dying in childbirth by three-fourths
6. Halt and reverse the spread of HIV/AIDS and malaria and other major diseases
7. Ensure environmental sustainability
8. Create a global partnership for development; ensuring developed countries play their part to help developing countries end poverty

You will likely agree that this is a huge communication task. Solving this problem may require dividing the problem into smaller chunks and applying a different thinking process. Rather than trying to address each of these millennium goals as a

Artist Date

Julia Cameron offers this advice: "Every week, take time out of your busy schedule to explore something new. Take yourself on an 'artist's date.'" This can be anything, from a trip to a dollar store to attending your first opera. Perhaps you simply allow yourself to get lost in a different neighborhood. By just keeping these artist's dates in mind, you'll find yourself noticing and appreciating curiosities you may have previously ignored!

Try going to a hardware store to buy silly things you normally wouldn't use. What can you make out of your treasure? A sculpture; an interesting contraption? You decide.

The Artist Date exercise is adapted from and credited to Cameron, Julie. *The Artist's Way: A Spiritual Path to Higher Creativity*, 1996. Penguin Putnam Inc, San Francisco, CA.

CREATIVE PROBLEM SOLVING PROCESS: OSBORN & PARNES

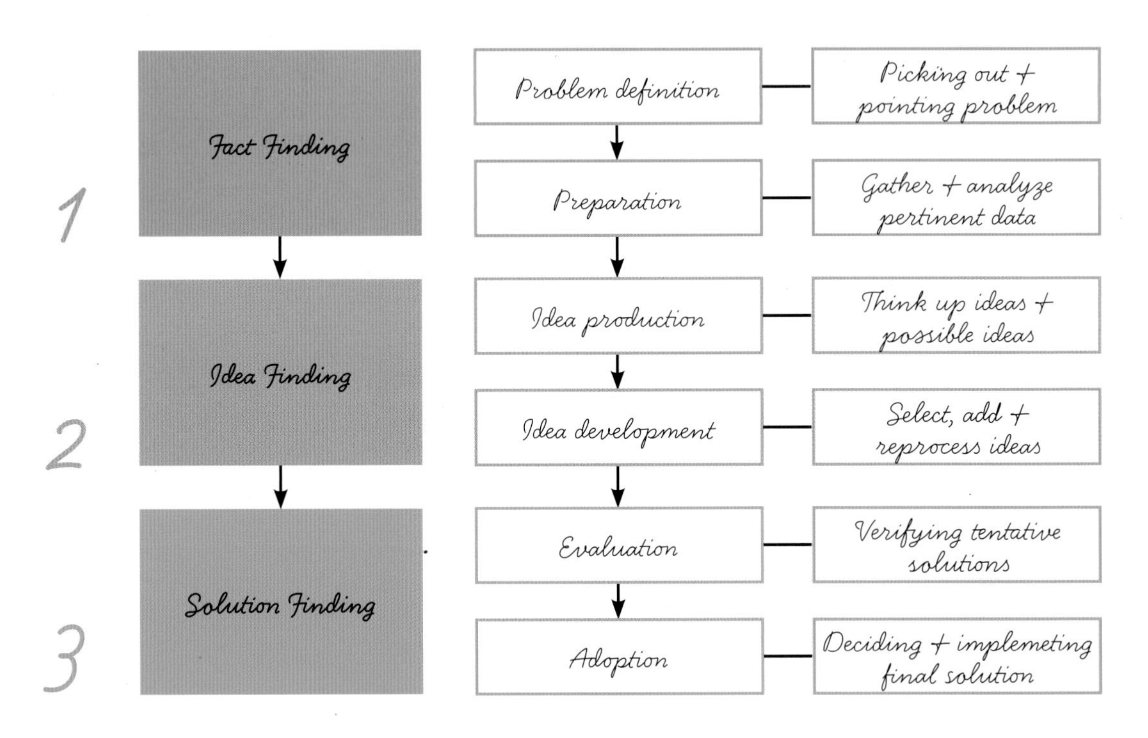

Adopted from Paul Williams, Idea Sandbox, Alexandria, VA2

whole, our student team, Half Glass Full, tried to break down the problem into smaller units. They conducted consumer research and identified ways to expose audiences to smaller issues. Building on the insight that most people feel overwhelmed when exposed to complex problems, they decided to reach consumers' ability and willingness to get involved. The theme "StopW8ting" emerged and served as an umbrella message for the various goals of the UN. Each of the eight challenges was addressed individually within an overall integrated marketing campaign.

It can be helpful to analyze a problem against the setting in which it is situated, using many different perspectives and then ask: Does the problem still appear to be the real problem within the context we need to solve or has a different problem arisen? Redefining the problem can be one of the most powerful first steps towards developing creative solutions. This requires in-depth knowledge within a specific domain, as well as the ability to marginalize anything known and accepted within that domain.

Phase four is called *idea finding*. During this phase, it is important to generate as many ideas as possible, be it individually or as a group. Being aware of the dimensions fluency, flexibility, originality and elaboration can improve the total number of ideas developed. This phase is when divergent thinking skills are applied best. Judgment, assumptions and criticism are the enemies of this phase. Several different thinking techniques, which are described in more detail in the next chapter, can and should be applied in order to increase the likelihood and possibility of coming up with the best solutions. These include brainstorming, lateral thinking, mindmapping, six thinking hats, chain of associations, brainwriting, brainfloating, visual synectics, provocation, concept fan, random input, morphological analysis, among many others.

Once you have generated a sufficient number of ideas during the idea finding phase, it is time to select the best ones. During the fifth phase, *solution finding*, it is important to establish some specific checklists or evaluation criteria, which will help narrow down the solutions and identify the best ideas that will solve the problem in the most unusual, relevant and effective way. This phase is also considered the convergent phase, since convergent thinking is required in order to narrow down ideas. As soon as one or several winning ideas emerge, users of this process move into the next phase: *acceptance finding*.

During the acceptance finding stage, thinkers explore and apply a proof of concept. The winning idea(s) must be tested against the problem. The model, which consists of the attributes needed to meet the expected outcome, can be applied when determining the best idea or ideas.

Design thinking provides another very interesting and applicable problem-solving process. Initially developed by engineers at Stanford University, the philosophy of design thinking was advanced and publicized by the design firm IDEO. David Kelley, a cofounder of IDEO, and Tim Brown, president of IDEO, have presented their methodology in numerous outlets, such as TED Talks, *60 Minutes* and the *Harvard Business Review*. Design thinking centers around the understanding and observation of what people want and need in their life, as well as what they like and dislike about existing products in terms of packaging, marketing and how the products are supported. The designer then can match these needs with what is technologically feasible and create a product or service that will have customer value and market opportunity.

Design thinking represents an additional problem-solving process that takes advantage of divergent and convergent thinking. Design thinking is based on the combination of analytical thinking and intuitive thinking. The process applies visual thinking to analytical thinking. When the process was developed at Stanford in the 1960s, the engineers were looking for additional perspectives for approaching problems. They decided to take into consideration the perspective of the end user of any given product or process that they were developing at the time. IDEO and Riverdale Country School in New York have developed an online toolkit called *Design Thinking for Educators*. The e-book is intended as an "invitation to experiment with the design process"[3] and available for download. According to *Design Thinking for Educators*, design thinking provides a mind-set that includes four different dimensions that are human centered: empathic, collaborative, experimental and optimistic.

The *discovery* phase represents the research portion of the process during which the situation is analyzed and facts are compiled. This phase provides a deep understanding of the task or problem at hand. During the discovery phase, it is important to understand and define the challenge and audiences, to build teams and to share the knowledge that is gained. This phase is also about research that involves making a research plan, identifying sources of inspiration and inviting research participants. During this first phase, it is also important to be open and inspired by what you are learning as you gain a deeper understanding of the context. In addition to gaining personal knowledge about the challenge, you should also incorporate what

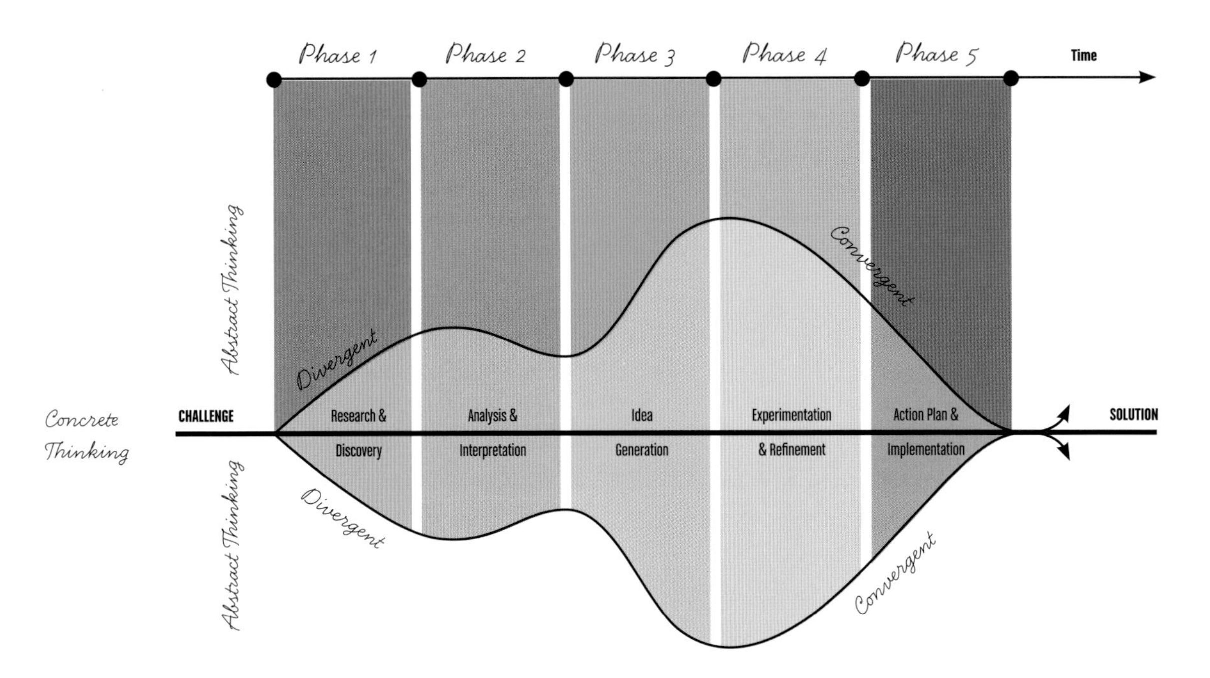

Visual overview of a creative [problem-solving] process.

you learn from others, whether it be from collaborators, experts or peer reviewers. The discovery phase is all about fully immersing yourself in the subject at hand in order to successfully complete the job.

Interpretation is the second step in the design process. In this stage, the knowledge that was gained during the first phase is looked at from different angles and then interpreted. The creators of design thinking suggest that users of this process share observations and create meaning from the facts they have found. Based on all the information gathered, themes will begin to emerge through clustering, organizing and synthesizing of the data. In addition to looking at and connecting your facts and insights, you should also tell stories that might have appeared during the discovery phase. Since design thinking relies heavily on the human perspective and the ability to apply empathy, it is important to connect any research findings back to humans and the stories they represent. Developing narratives will help research data become meaningful and connect at the human level.

The next phase is called *ideation*. The goal during this phase is the development of as many ideas as possible. As described earlier, divergent thinking should be applied and the maximization of ideas is the goal. IDEO focuses exclusively on the brainstorming technique, but many other thinking techniques may prove useful to you. (Brainstorming and other techniques will be discussed in the next chapter.) After generating a sufficient number of ideas, users of this process should refine and compare those ideas against their objectives. In short, check to see which idea best solves your problem.

After the ideation phase is completed, it is time to start the *experimentation* phase, the fourth step in the design process. According to IDEO, it is important to build upon the idea that has been developed during the ideation phase. This translates into building prototypes, making the ideas tangible and learning and gaining even more information by applying the solution at an early stage. Prototypes provide an excellent opportunity to gain feedback. It is important to define what kind of feedback you are looking for and how you can learn from it and make improvements.

Evolution is the last phase in the design process. In this phase, the winning ideas are being applied and further developed. According to *Design Thinking for Educators* it is important to insure an idea's success over time.[4] This might include looking ahead and considering how ideas might have to adjust in changing environments, thinking about how ideas should be communicated to audiences and stakeholders. During this phase it is also important to document any process and progress. In today's fast-moving business environment, a solution's life span may be shortened based on change that happens down the road. A solution requires constant review and further development in order to maintain an innovative mind-set. A solution that may have worked at one point in time may become outdated and useless. It is crucial to constantly learn more about and improve upon that solution.

All of these processes help problem solvers become more aware of the kind of thinking they may want to apply when solving problems. Having the skill to consciously know when to use divergent and convergent thinking can help individuals achieve the optimal state of mind when generating the best ideas to solve problems. All of the creative processes mentioned above allow us to think more deliberately and improve the likelihood of generating new and original thoughts. Even though the various creative processes consist of different elements, they also possess commonalities. Each includes a clear problem definition phase during which users dedicate time toward analyzing the situation. Additionally, all processes separate idea generation (divergent thinking) and the analysis and evaluation of ideas (convergent thinking). All processes include a decision-making process, during which users determine the next steps that need to be taken in order to introduce the best solution. It is important to note that problem-solving processes provide a framework to come up with solutions, but they are not decision makers. Decision making comes at the end of the problem-solving process. These various creative processes provide us with the tools necessary to circumnavigate the decision-making process our mind often unconsciously jumps to. By applying the creative process and separating problem definition, situation analysis, idea finding and solution finding in a more conscious way, we can dedicate more time to the specific kinds of thinking and activities necessary for each phase. This allows us to come up with truly imaginative, original, innovative and unique ideas that are relevant to the target audiences and ultimately can be more effective at solving a task.

CHAPTER FIVE

CREATIVE THINKING METHODS AND TECHNIQUES

Like it does for many other disciplines, developing good technique will help you become a better creative thinker over time. Eventually you will be able to use any thinking technique more effectively and efficiently. An athlete can improve her game not just by maintaining a rigorous training program, but also by fine-tuning technique, whether she be a runner taking better advantage of her arms, a swimmer cutting through the water more ergonomically or a cyclist optimizing pedal stroke in relationship to cadence. Just as an athlete can apply and improve technique within a certain sport, a musician can learn and apply technique when playing an instrument, whether it entails learning how to breathe in the most efficient way or how to hold a bow when playing a violin or bass. Like a conductor working with an orchestra, one can employ different thinking tools and techniques to guide our thinking in many differing directions. Orchestras are made up of many musicians playing different musical instruments and a conductor can use those musicians to emphasize certain portions of a score in order to evoke feelings and engage the audience.

During the ideation phase, you can choose from a wide array of thinking techniques and devote a specific amount of time to a particular technique. As you learned in chapter four, you can improve your creative output by applying a creative process in order to guide your thinking in a more directed and effective way. Though several different frameworks for creative process are available, each clearly devotes one phase to the development of ideas. Depending on the particular process, this phase can also be called ideation, idea development, idea finding or divergent thinking. Developing as many ideas and solutions as possible is the main focus during the idea-generating phase.

The ideation phase is crucial to developing original and unique solutions. During this phase there are many thinking techniques that can increase the number of ideas developed as well as elevate the quality of those ideas. With the help of certain thinking techniques, you can maximize your brain power and push the total number of ideas way beyond what an average person comes up with. One of the biggest hurdles during any ideation phase is judgment. This refers not only to the conscious judgment of ideas, but also the subconscious or unconscious evaluation your brain practices. In order to maximize and improve your creative ideas, you must set a certain amount of time aside during which your only concern is the production of ideas. Guilford and Torrance introduced and further developed the concept of divergent thinking and the generation of many ideas. As mentioned in chapter three of this book, it is important to focus on four main aspects during this specific phase of idea finding: *developing fluency* and focusing on *flexibility*, while achieving *originality* and applying *elaboration*.[1]

In the following pages, you will find a list of effective thinking techniques that may help you during the ideation phase—some you may already employ without even realizing it. These methods may

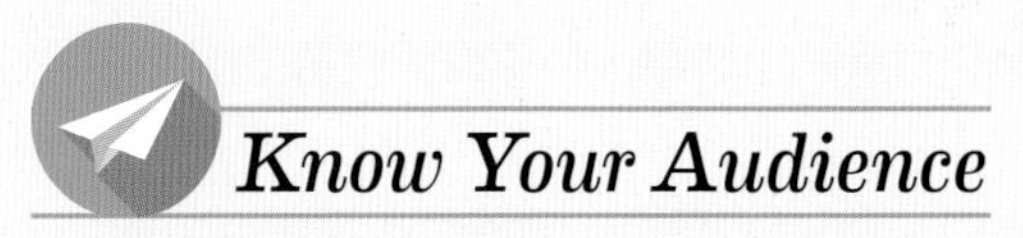

Know Your Audience

Invent a product that every teenager in America would buy.

Credited to an advertisement run by J Walter Thompson in the *New York Times* in 1989.

even introduce you to some new ways of thinking not covered in this book. In fact, the interviews I conducted with various advertising agencies suggest that most employees have unique ways of approaching a problem that vary from person to person. "It would be a reach for me to say that they have specific techniques. They might that I don't know of ... I think it's quite varied on how they solve things and I don't think there's a specific technique to it," says Tom Ortega of his employees' thinking strategies, while Norm Shearer of Cactus Marketing Communications suggests that "maybe people have their own [strategies] that they've picked up along the way." Similarly, Robert Sherlock says "everybody has their own way of doing things. And I don't think we force or even promote a certain way of thinking or anything." This was echoed by Edward Boches of Mullen, who says, "We don't have any thinking techniques per se, and I think a lot of people have their own approaches to things." These insights help us arrive at the conclusion that there really is no right way of thinking up new ideas; the process will vary from individual to individual, but it is helpful to consider a few thinking techniques in order to get you started.

The following techniques may help you jumpstart your thinking and guide your thoughts toward new directions that you may have not previously considered.

Coffeehouse Exercise: Day Two

Go back to your favorite coffee shop (or other public place), and spend one hour observing a person.

Describe the person. This time describe only his/her inner life. (See Day One on page 44).

The coffeehouse exercise is credited to Shelley Berc and Alejandro Fogel's, The Creativity Workshop, New York http://www.creativityworkshop.com/

BRAINSTORMING

Brainstorming is probably one of the most widely used thinking techniques in marketing communication and advertising, and possibly in other disciplines as well. Alex Osborn, one of the co-founders of the advertising agency BBDO, created brainstorming as a conference technique by which a group attempts to find a solution for a specific problem by amassing all ideas. Osborn developed this technique in order to allow the members of his creative department the ability to manipulate their thinking modes and to put their minds into an optimal state for idea generation. As the process is designed to obtain the maximum number of ideas related to a specific topic or area, one of its main goals is to suspend judgment and to allow participants to add any ideas that come to mind, regardless of the initial worth of that idea. It is important for participants to put aside rules and social inhibitions during the brainstorming process.

In recent years, several researchers have explored and tested the brainstorming technique in more detail and have concluded that even though brainstorming has been a popular technique for decades, it is no longer considered the most effective way to generate ideas. According to *Fast Company*[2] several experts provide different perspectives on the effectiveness of brainstorming. Some argue that if left to work individually, the total amount of ideas generated by several individuals would be greater than the number of ideas developed by the same people in a brainstorming session. Several hypothesize that the group setting and the free flow of ideas during brainstorming sessions seem to be influencing ideas the members generate due to a priming effect of what was said before one comes up with a new idea. Others argue that during brainstorming sessions, the more extroverted participants tend to provide more ideas compared to the ones who tend to be more introverted. The article concludes that brainstorming is simply not as effective as some people may perceive it to be, and the brain might not be meant to come up with ideas in such a rigid atmosphere. On the contrary, the brain might come up with the most ideas when it is relaxed and engaged in something that has nothing to do with the problem at hand.

LATERAL THINKING

Several other thinking techniques can be considered part of *lateral thinking*, a concept developed by creativity expert Edward de Bono. He introduced the concept of lateral thinking in his book *Lateral Thinking: Creativity Step by Step* in 1970.[3] Lateral thinking seeks to problem solve and develop ideas by using an unorthodox or apparently illogical method of thinking.

Human evolution, socialization, education and cultural environments have influenced our thinking. As psychologists like Sigmund Freud and Abraham Maslow have pointed out, much of human thinking takes place without 100 percent

consciousness. Lateral thinking allows a person to manipulate and direct his or her thinking into a very specific direction. For example, based on upbringing, many have learned over a long period of time that a door is a door, which is essentially a movable structure that separates rooms from one another, allowing movement from one room into the other. The knobs or hinges of a door might make each door unique, but the basic concept and functionality of a door remains the same. Opening or closing a door allows entry or exit from a room or building. A table is a piece furniture with one or more legs, has a flat surface on which objects may be placed, and provides space around which one can sit and work or do other activities. We know a chair to be a piece of furniture upon which we can sit, and a glass to be a container that can hold liquid. Because such thinking has been so ingrained, in order to truly think creatively, we have to let go of all of these notions associated with our learned systems; we have to open our minds to look at the world a little bit differently.

Lateral thinking can be used as a powerful tool to change your concepts and perceptions, and also to generate new concepts and perceptions. Lateral thinking allows you to deliberately forget what you have learned and know about a door, a table, a glass, a bottle or anything else. It gives you permission to unthink what you know and to take your thoughts into unknown and undefined territory. The main advantage of lateral thinking is the exploration of multiple possibilities and approaches instead of pursuing the standard approach—the one the brain automatically falls back on. The end result of lateral thinking, as with any thinking technique, is a huge number of ideas. These ideas may not be the final answer, but they at least allow the chance to create many more possibilities. Here are several lateral thinking techniques to try.

SIX THINKING HATS

In his book, *Six Thinking Hats: An Essential Approach to Business Management*[4], Edward de Bono devised the Six Thinking Hats as a simple tool kit that allows thinkers to direct their thinking in different directions. Each hat is associated with a different color and represents a specific think-

Based on your personal experience, can you remember a meeting during which someone mentioned some facts or possibly something negative, and another group member responded with emotion positive or negative?

ing mode that encourages an active mental switch to take place. As a thinking technique, the Six Thinking Hats provides a concrete framework for exploration which provides a means for moving from one way of thinking to another. Since we are often not aware of our mode of thinking at any given moment, our mind might come up with emotions, intuitions, facts and judgments all at the same time. The Six Thinking Hats can help you to become more aware of your own thinking, and this awareness allows you to change the course of your thinking in a conscious way.

The first hat, the *white hat*, represents information-based thinking; that is, the kind of thinking that is influenced by knowledge, facts and details. When we are thinking with a white hat perspective, we try to access as many details as possible related to a problem, challenge or task in order to guide our thinking. All judgment and interpretation is deferred when applying the white hat.

The second hat, the *red hat*, represents intuition, emotions, desires and feelings. While thinking in the red hat mode, we specifically listen to intuition, feelings, hunches and the emotions associated with the problem or task we are trying to tackle.

The next hat is the *black hat*, which represents judgment. When thinking with the black hat, the mind is in a cautious and logically negative mode, consciously thinking of what might not work and what hurdles might stop us from achieving our goal.

The fourth hat, the *yellow hat* represents optimism and promotes logical and positive thinking. With the yellow hat, we are looking at a challenge, assignment or problem and trying to come up with as many positive associations and ideas as possible. Those ideas are guided by the rational belief that something is going to work out.

Hat number five is the *green hat*, which represents possibilities. The green hat encourages us to think in the most creative and imaginative way possible. When thinking with the green hat, one really pushes oneself to think of things we otherwise might never have dreamed. This conscious, out of the box thinking encourages imagination and the formation of ideas that might seem outrageous and unrealistic. The overall goal is to come up with as many ideas as possible without judging (lack of judgment is common to all of the thinking techniques).

The last hat is the *blue hat*, and unlike the other hats, it does not represent any specific direction of thinking. Instead the blue hat represents the control of the thinking process itself. The blue hat is responsible for managing the process of using the six thinking hats as a tool. The person who is moderating the meeting or thinking session wears the blue hat. The blue hat wearer acts as a referee and calls out participants who might be thinking outside of a specific color hat. The blue hat is also responsible for timekeeping and for moving from one hat to another.

De Bono's Six Thinking Hats is one of the most simple yet powerful thinking techniques in existence. Having used this technique in group settings, as well as during my own personal thinking sessions for more than two decades, I believe the Six Thinking Hats allows for an easy transition between thinking styles, duly separating them so they don't interfere with each other.

Like many other thinking techniques that are applied specifically during the ideation or idea development phase, the Six Thinking Hats technique does not necessarily lead to one final solution. Rather it allows the user to create infinite ideas while also allowing for divergent thinking. One of the key advantages of this technique is that it helps us to deliberately direct our thoughts in a certain direction. It's a great tool to use for generating a large number of ideas and is also excellent for managing and moderating group meetings.

RANDOM INPUT

Random input, also called *forced relationships*, is a lateral thinking technique that forces your mind to go outside of its established thinking patterns in order to generate ideas. Developed by Edward de Bono in 1968, this technique was later published in the book *Serious Creativity*. Oftentimes when we problem solve, we recognize patterns and apply certain solutions that have been effective in the past. But doing so can be constricting; these established patterns and solutions might not be helpful for the task at hand. Random input is a thinking technique that allows thinkers to come up with new patterns and associations to solve problems. With this technique, you can use random words, pictures or even sounds to help you think of new connections. Some of the new thoughts might not directly solve the problem but rather allow the mind to venture in new directions.

One example of a way to do this is to simply open up the dictionary to a random page and point to a random word. Then use this word as a springboard for new thoughts and ideas. The same can be done with music by putting your iTunes on shuffle and listening to a random song. Some of the ideas that you come up with may be completely peculiar and out there, possibly even eccentric, but that is the whole point of the ideation phase. You are trying to come up with as many ideas as possible, and though they may not be the final solution, they will at least direct your thoughts into new and innova-

You Are a Cartoon/ Comic Author

Buy a local Sunday newspaper and go to the cartoon/comic section. Pick a cartoon/comic and white out the text in the word balloons. Now write your own copy for the cartoon/comic of your choice.

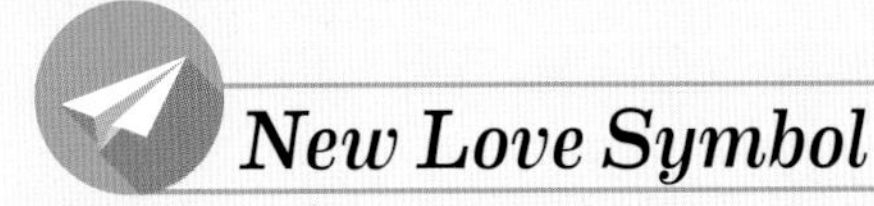

New Love Symbol

For centuries, the heart has represented love. But love has changed. Develop a new symbol.

The "new love symbol" exercise is credited to an advertisement run by J Walter Thompson in the New York Times in 1989.

tive directions that might not have occurred to you otherwise.

REVERSAL

Especially good for improving a product or service, reversal is another technique that forces the brain to think in a way that it is not accustomed to. It involves asking the opposite of the question at hand and then taking those results and reversing them so that they suit the original question at hand. For example, let us assume that you are trying to figure out how to improve customer service. In order to apply the reversal thinking technique, you would ask, "How would I reduce customer satisfaction?" You would then consider the times you were in situations involving customer service that made you experience negative emotions. Some possible ideas could be not answering the phone when a customer calls, not returning a customer's call, having customer service employees that have no product knowledge, having rude staff or giving the wrong advice to customers. This list could probably go on for some time, but the point is that you then can use these ideas in reverse order to solve your original problem. To continue this example, to improve customer service, you would make sure that calls are always returned and answered and that the staff is cordial and understands the products or services you sell.

Sometimes it helps to look at a problem from another, or even opposite, direction.

SCAMPER

SCAMPER is a thinking technique that allows for the generation of ideas by considering ways that might improve and change existing products or services. The mnemonic SCAMPER stands for Substitute, Combine, Adapt, Modify, Put to another use, Eliminate, and Reverse. Alex Osborn, who also developed brainstorming, developed many of the questions that are used in this technique; however, it was Bob Eberle, an educational administrator, who actually developed these questions into the SCAMPER mnemonic. For this technique, you start off by considering a certain existing product or service that you want to improve, that you're having problems with or that you think that has potential for further development. You can also apply SCAMPER to any of your ideas in order to develop them further. Each one of the SCAMPER words has a set of questions associated with it that you can ask yourself and answer in order to develop ideas.

For *Substitute*, some example questions would be, "What materials or resources can you substitute in order to improve the product?" or "Can this product be used somewhere else or in a different way?" For example, using tofu instead of meat would be a method of substitution in order to create a vegetarian hot dog. The next element to consider is the idea of *Combining*, and some questions you can ask yourself are "What could you combine in order to maximize the uses of the product?" or "How can you combine this product with another one in order create something new and possibly

TRASH CAN—MORPHOLOGICAL BOX					
1	Rubber	Cylindrical	Collapsible	Outdoor	Stain-Resistant
2	Plastic	Rectangular	Foldable	Office Space	Odor-Lock
3	Metal	Cube	Industrial-Strength	Kitchen	Painted
4	Paper	Irregular	Modular	Basement	Glow-In-The-Dark
5	Bamboo	Hexagonal	Stackable	Garage	Wheels

even better?" An example of this could be a musical greeting card, through which music and the conventional card are combined in order to come up with something innovative and creative. Next is the idea of *Adaptation* and two questions you could ask are "What else is like this product?" and "What other contexts could this product be put into?" An example of this would be snow tires, which are regular tires that have been adapted in order to fit a certain environment. *Modify* is about how the product could be changed, and some sample questions include "What could you add to modify the product?" or "How could you change the shape or look of the product in order to improve it?" Miniature Snickers are a good example of taking something in its normal form and changing its size to create something new and innovative. *Put to another use* refers to the idea of how your product or service can be used differently or by different people or a new setting. For example, a newspaper is not for reading only and could also be used as interesting wrapping paper for presents. *Eliminate* is all about streamlining the product and those elements that can be removed in order to maximize its effectiveness and efficiency. An example of this is the cordless telephone, which is much more practical and functional than its plugged in counterpart. *Reverse* is all about thinking in the opposite direction of what you're used to. You can ask yourself "What if you did the exact opposite of what you're trying to currently do?" and "How could you reorganize this product?"

The SCAMPER tool will allow you to develop ideas, concepts, new products and services by asking yourself important questions and leading your mind in different but specific directions. Some of the ideas you generate using the SCAMPER tool may not be feasible or may be completely impractical, but that is okay. Just like with any other thinking technique, it is important not to judge your ideas but rather to allow your mind to roam free in order to think of as many ideas as possible.

METHODS OF ANALYSIS

Several different ways to analyze a problem exist, and each way allows thinkers to generate ideas. *Attribute Listing* involves writing out all the properties, qualities or design elements of the product or service that you are examining or trying to improve. For example, you are taking on the task of improving pizza at a pizzeria or a food manufacturer. Many properties and elements go into making a pizza what it is, including the shape, size, sauce, topping, the type of cheese and the actual experience of eating it. Again, this list could go on and on, but the point is that it allows you to break down a broad object into more specific elements that are easier to manipulate and improve. Once you have this list, you can alter any one of these attributes in order to improve the overall product.

Morphological Analysis is a method developed by Swiss astronomer Fritz Zwicky that is similar to attribute listing, but its aim is to create new products by combining different attributes. With this method, for example, you would make a list of the materials that can be used to make the product, the shape it could be, the size it could be, etc., and then make different combinations of those elements in order to come up with the best possible solution. Morphological analysis is often used in combination with the so-called morphological box, a tool that allows you to collect and analyze multidimensional aspect such as attributes, lists, options, variations and items in a visual matrix, chart or table. The morphological box can be used during the morphological analysis.

Matrix Analysis is exactly like morphological analysis except that it is applied to business practices. So instead of listing the physical attributes, you would examine market sectors, customer needs or promotional methods and then make different combinations of these elements in order to come up with the best possible solution.

10 STEPS TO BOOSTING YOUR CREATIVITY

1. Read, listen or view the creations of creative people.
2. Brainstorm regularly, whether you do it alone or in group settings.
3. Always carry a notebook and a pen in case a great idea pops into your head.
4. If you're stuck on a problem, open up a dictionary and select a random word and then randomly combine words in order to help your mind move into new unexplored directions.
5. Make sure you define your problem since this will make it much easier to come up with ideas and solutions.
6. Take a walk or a shower.
7. If you are looking for relaxation, consider taking a walk, listening to relaxing music or observing natural beauty (e.g., ocean, sea, mountain or trees) while contemplating. If you want to activate your creative thinking consider reading books, solving puzzles and engaging in creative activities that stimulate your mind. Create your own entertainment.
8. Do something new every day that you have not done yet (e.g. eat new food, dress differently, drive a different route to work, take a different mode of transportation, introduce yourself to a stranger).
9. Read, read, read.
10. Exercise your brain by doodling, writing, solving puzzles, debating or doing anything that allows you to form new mental connections, and by completing the exercises below and throughout the different chapters.

CHAPTER SIX

EVALUATION OF IDEAS

For Marshall Ross, president and chief creative officer at Cramer Krasselt Chicago, creativity solves business problems. And everything begins with strategy. He describes his evaluation process as one that requires asking key questions. "First and foremost, [I ask] is the idea illuminating strategy? We all agree to it. So that's number one. It's our strategy. Is the idea magnetic? Do you want to spend time with the idea? Do we think that the idea feels surprising? And is the idea worth sharing? What about this idea makes me tell my friend more about it? What about this idea makes more participate? And if the idea doesn't have participation, somehow build into it. If the idea doesn't have shareability, built into it, it's not a good idea."

As I progressed through the interviews with the creative advertising executives, a trend began to emerge. When I asked: How do you evaluate your ideas, and what filtering mechanisms does your agency employ? The majority of creative directors described a more intuitive and gut-feeling process when evaluating ideas. Here's what some of them had to say:

> I feel like I've got a good nose for what's right for that and stuff, not always right. It's a gut really. —David Droga of Droga5.

Insight & Intuition

Based on your personal experience, think of a time you had to evaluate an idea. Ask yourself: How did I get that insight and intuition? Where did it come from—was it education, experience or instinct? What do I need to do to become good at developing that instinct?

> I think for me, when I look at an idea most of the time, it's a gut thing. You just have to trust your gut. And you watch a commercial, or you look at a digital idea or someone describes a stunt, you immediately feel like it's something groundbreaking, and something that you've never seen before, you just know it. Intuitively, you just know it. So for me, I just go with my gut. And if I'm still questioning, then I think it's probably not a great idea. —Margaret Johnson of Goodby, Silverstein & Partners

> Well, step number one is gut instinct. If you've been doing this a long time, you have a frame of reference for everything that's ever been done. You have this repository of executions and ideas and headlines and platforms and digital experiences that you've seen or heard about or been involved with. —Edward Boches of Mullen

But what exactly does it mean to have a gut feeling?

Creativity researchers define the frame of reference and repository that Boches speaks of above as domain knowledge and expertise. According to psychologists and creativity researchers certain people are capable of judging the creative product. Numerous studies confirm that experts within a specific domain, industry or field are highly qualified and make accurate decisions when evaluating ideas and concepts within their domain. Therefore, it does not come as a surprise when these highly successful creative agency executives in the advertising industry speak of gut, instinct, intuition and innate ability to judge the work their agencies produce. They all have completed ten thousand hours or more within their respective field, have won numerous awards and qualify as industry experts. Each of them possesses a repository of domain knowledge and expertise that allows them to decide which ideas are extraordinary, just good or simply not worth further pursuit.

As industries mature, more expertise and experience is shared among the members. Professional organizations form and industry-wide guidelines and standards develop. Therefore it is important to learn and study the ways individual experts as well as whole organizations judge professional work and evaluate ideas. In this chapter you will look at several frameworks and perspectives from which ideas can be evaluated. In addition to instinct and gut reaction, several creative directors provide very specific criteria for filtering out bad or not-so-great ideas in order to allow the best ideas to emerge.

Once you have developed a sufficient number of ideas, which in an agency environment can easily reach one thousand on any given client assignment, it is important to narrow them down and identify what makes one idea stand out over another. It is crucial to have a system through which to sort the ideas in order to figure out which one best fulfills the task. You probably already have some informal process that you go through in order to evaluate your ideas. In previous chapters, I emphasized how important it is to come up with as many ideas as possible by avoiding the filtration and judgment of your thoughts in the early stages of the ideation process. Once you have settled on some ideas though, you have to figure out which one will best tackle the task. What makes a certain idea truly stand out?

Different people and organizations have various ways of evaluating ideas, but some of the core concepts overlap. First of all, an idea needs to somehow stand out. People are constantly bombarded with messages and advertisements, so it is crucial to get the attention of your audience. You may have a truly brilliant and original idea, but if this does not come through in the messaging, it will just go unnoticed. The idea, along with its execution, has to be interesting enough to break through all of the other messages that your target audience sees and hears on an everyday basis.

But an idea, campaign, platform or simple advertisement cannot merely be flashy or beautiful for the sake of getting the audience's attention. Once a person actually does take notice of the idea, they must be able to recognize the core benefits of that product or service. An important element of the evaluation process is determining whether or not your idea truly adds value to the life of your target audience or brings out the true value of a product or service. Communicating those aspects has become more important as consumers have become better informed and more critical toward marketing.

Many of the agency executives represented in the book are putting more emphasis on finding the truth and honesty. Johnny Vulkan of Anomaly goes even as far as to challenge marketers about the products they market to consumers and asks these fundamental questions: "Is this a good product or service? Does it have a right in society? Has it been built well? Is it well priced? Is it going to the right places?" He believes that the real battleground is identifying the most appropriate modern tools we have today and combining those to deliver "pure old-fashioned marketing" of authentic goods and services.

Attention-grabbing ideas are simply not enough. The idea not only must hold the attention of the viewer, but also encourage the viewer to act; otherwise the viewer will move on to something else that captures their eye. For example, a commercial could be beautifully made but that does not mean the viewer will be intrigued enough to take the time to understand what the product is about. There must be a reason for them to want to continue to pay attention to the idea. As a marketer, agency or someone who develops marketing and communication messages for specific audiences, it is important to research and gain insights in order to better understand what might encourage interaction among audiences, organizations and brands. Those insights then lead to better creative ideas that increase the potential for audiences taking action on messages they are exposed to.

Since breakthrough ideas often involve some kind of interaction between the consumer and a digital platform, device or application, Michael Lebowitz, founder and chief creative officer at Big Spaceship adds a behavioral component when evaluating ideas. "Is anybody going to interact with this? Or is it only good in a vacuum? It's the 'If you build it, then they will come' question. Because they won't. 'What is somebody's incentive?' is a pretty fundamental question to ask. We try not to ask it too early in the process—bad ideas quickly can become good ideas so you want to be as open as possible. But I would ask: 'Is there a real behavioral opportunity here?' Because if there isn't, then we need to simplify or change our approach. There's a value exchange question that we should be asking: 'Is this giving more than it expects in return?' Lebowitz believes that in the digital world the users must experience something positive and should be rewarded for their click. He knows that offering a utility, humor and/or entertainment can add an

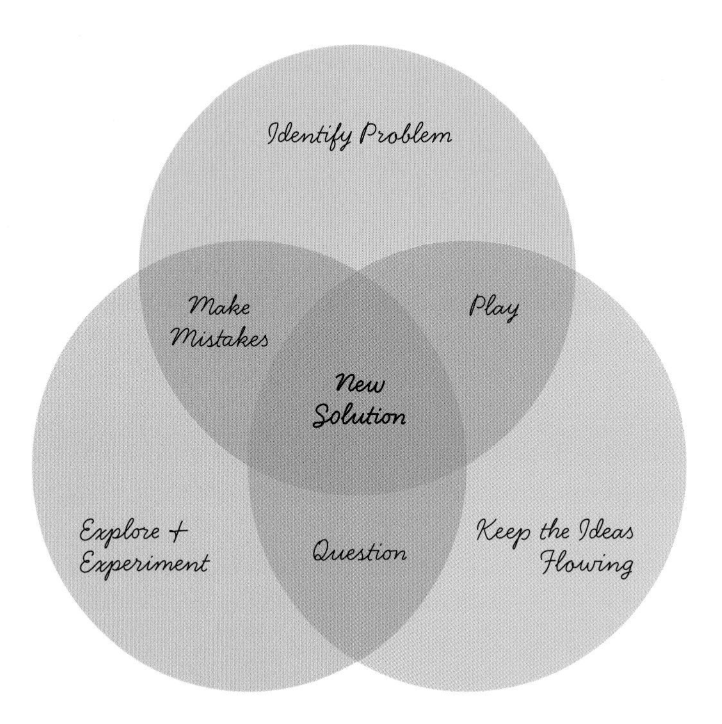

equilibrium." According to Lebowitz digital does not work without establishing such a balance or win-win situation between users and marketers.

Clients approach advertising and marketing agencies with a need to fulfill a certain task or to best market a product or service. Based on the needs of the client, the agency puts together a creative brief that reflects the kind of messaging needed to reach the target consumer. In the interviews that I conducted with some of the top advertising agencies around the world, I asked about the ways in which creative directors evaluate ideas.

Creativity in applied fields is different from pure art or personal artistic endeavors. In many cases, creativity is constrained by specific business, marketing, advertising or communication objectives associated within an industry or domain. Therefore evaluating ideas in advertising differs from judging your own personal and individual creative projects. According to Roger Hurni, partner and creative director at Off Madison Ave, "Any failure is something that does not meet the client's overall business goals ... We should be able to learn from the things we experiment with in order to make sure that we reinvest money in the proper channels and the proper kinds of ideas." Robert Sherlock, creative director at Draftfcb Chicago echoes this idea. He says that the filtering and evaluation process for him involves "using the brief as a sort of epicenter of everything. Does [our idea] meet the brief?" He continues asking questions like "Is it differentiating? Does it separate us from the competition? Is it relevant? Is it unexpected? Is it sustainable? Does it allow us to proliferate and to expand into the relevant touch points for the consumer?"

While it is important to keep in mind the needs and requests of the clients, sometimes it is important for advertising agencies to trust their own instincts and expertise. For example, based on the interview with Robert Sherlock, it is sometimes not enough to do what the client wants. The idea also has to stand out from all of the other competition out there. It must be unexpected as well as sustainable. Sometimes the client may have one thing in mind and does not realize the potential things that could be even better. Rob Schwartz, the global creative president of TBWA\Chiat\Day, believes that "particularly in advertising, you always show the client what they ask for, but then show them what they never dreamed possible. That's the secret right there." There are times when the client may think they understand the solution to their problem, and they may have a certain vision. But an advertising agency can elevate solutions to a place the client never previously envisioned or thought possible.

A handful of agencies are taking a different approach altogether when evaluating ideas. For Johnny Vulkan, the judging of ideas starts by asking the right questions at the beginning of every project. "It puts pressure on the front end, because if the question is clearly articulated, then it's pretty easy to judge whether the work answers that question or not," Vulkan says.

Many of the evaluation criteria expressed by the agency executives can be applied to any kind of evaluation process, not just those established in advertising agencies. As mentioned earlier, people are constantly bombarded with messages and advertising, and they have learned to tune most of it out. Therefore it is important to be able to capture their attention and hold it. One element to consider when evaluating an idea is its novelty. Is it something new and original? This goes back to the idea of convergent and divergent thinking. By employing divergent thinking during the ideation process, you can produce many more ideas and increase the likelihood that you come up with ideas that are unique and innovative.

There are many different ways in which an idea can be novel. An idea that is novel for one individual or a group may not be novel and original to a different individual or group. An idea can be novel on a personal level, meaning that a certain idea is original and new for one individual but may not be novel to another. An additional form of novelty is societal novelty, meaning that a certain idea is original to a certain society. Historical novelty also needs to be considered. Some ideas are recycled and slightly modified over time. A certain idea may have already been used in the past, but if it is updated and made relevant, it can be considered novel for a new period in history.

The work of Australian film director Baz Luhrmann illustrates this well. In several of his movies, Luhrmann has worked with classic themes of such stories as *Romeo and Juliet* and *The Great Gatsby*, retelling them in novel ways. David Droga describes the challenge of constantly adding fresh light and newness to our world. "Sometimes we have to tell familiar things in interesting ways, and sometimes we have to tell interesting [unfamiliar] things in familiar ways." Droga is aware that people might not like advertising or might even use technologies that block advertising and adds, "So we try and create advertising in that narrow band that people actually want to engage in, and creativity is our secret weapon."

Another element to consider when evaluating an idea is whether or not it is sustainable. Ideas need to be evaluated based on their long-term usefulness and their potential harmful side effects once implemented. An idea can be completely novel and original, but if it is impossible to produce, then it may not be a good idea. Every environment has certain constraints and restrictions and these are important to keep in mind during the evaluation stage. If an idea cannot be produced, it should be replaced in favor of an idea that is workable. The idea should be sustainable over time. This means the solution will continue to work over time with a high degree of reliability, consistency and effectiveness.

Another important consideration of the evaluation process is whether the idea is relevant to the task at hand. As discussed in the previous chapter, it is very important to establish what the task is as well as the problem that needs to be solved. Many times people lose sight of the actual problem, do not fully understand it or do not fully define it. These problems lead to poor ideas that don't address the real problem. Many advertising agencies use creative briefs to firmly establish the objectives that an idea, concept, service or product should fulfill. A brief also provides everyone involved with a guide so that ideas do not stray and become irrelevant.

While many agencies work with traditional briefs that define marketing and communication objectives, consumer insights and target audiences, creative briefs can be confining. With this shortcoming in mind, Johnny Vulkan and his team at Anomaly New York have dismissed the traditional agency brief for a more iterative process that focuses on asking the right questions. This allows the team a continued debate while they develop a project. Vulkan points out that projects are discussed and iterations continue until the best results are realized. "If we change this, then it answers that question better. So let's work out what we can to make that happen. Ask the right questions, answer the question. That's it," explains Vulkan.

Anomaly's approach works well when it is not possible to immediately know whether a solution or an idea will actually work. In some cases, it may be necessary to allow some time to pass and to evaluate afterward. The solution can be evaluated at intervals and then modified, if needed, for improvement and also to keep it relevant. When evaluating an idea, you may find that the idea was only partially successful. The degree to which the solution works is also an important element of the evaluation phase.

Another element of the evaluation process is to consider an idea's or solution's trade-offs. It is important to establish which of the trade-offs are acceptable and which trade-offs are not. Failure to consider these negative side effects and trade-offs is often a major weakness of problem solving. Considering trade-offs also relates to a trend that many of the interviewed expressed: All agency executives spoke about their agencies becoming more socially responsible and concerned about the impact their creative productions and solutions have while delivering on their clients' expectations to increase business.

Susan Credle describes the work she and her team at Leo Burnett developed for McDonald's and Happy Meals, and the opportunity to educate parents and kids in tandem with increasing the sale of French fries, breakfast cereals and sodas. "Instead of just advertising to kids, I think we are taking a problem and saying: 'Well, how can we help?" Credle acknowledges that too much sugary cereal might not be the best choice for a healthy children's diet and recommends an educational approach to advertising. She realizes that advertising can support parents in telling their kids that cereal can become a breakfast desert and that they have to eat the nutritious stuff first, like fruit or protein. Credle is excited about the possibility to continue the work needed for the [advertising] business in order to make her clients happy, but also to "help make the world, this country—*everything*—smarter."

When evaluating an idea, you should consider the ultimate user or recipient of your solution. The idea should be agreeable and useful to these individuals. Tim Leake, director of growth & innovation at RPA Advertising, articulated this idea. "I tend to try to put myself in a consumer's viewpoint of 'Would I care about this?' For advertising agencies, it is crucial that they do not lose sight of the ultimate consumer of the product or service that they are marketing." Acceptance is a perceptual, emotional and psychological phenomenon, as well as an intellectual and experiential one. It is crucial to think beyond the engineering and technology when deciding whether the solution is or will be successful. You may have invented an antigravity device, but if no one will use it, it is not a successful solution.

Simplicity is also an important criterion in the evaluation of ideas, specifically for those ideas that are used in communication and media arts. A successful idea should be as simple as possible in order to fulfill the desired outcomes and not be overly difficult or complicated for the intended benefits. The solution needs to be useful and understandable. In fact, many successful ideas are those that seem obvious in hindsight. Have you ever said, "Why didn't I think of that?" or "I can't believe I didn't think of that!" That's the kind of reaction these ideas produce.

Another important feature of successful ideas is if they are seminal. This means that the idea is not just a means to the end but rather a way to open new doors. The most successful solutions provide the framework and foundation for further solutions and development. A great idea has the potential to become bigger and has room to develop further and go in new directions. "We have our wall," says Edward Boches, "where the work goes and it lives or dies." He continues, "One day it might be the best thing on the wall, the next day it might be the fifth best thing on the wall, and then it falls off the wall. And the process then is we try to get to that idea. And we try to apply consistent standards to that idea. And we constantly challenge it, up until the last minute. Challenge it, challenge it, challenge it, challenge it, try to beat it, try to beat it, try to beat it, try to beat it, which is also a big part of the process. And then we not only challenge it with how good it is, but we ask if it is more than a message. Is it a platform? Can it live in all of these places? Is it formed by all of these things?"

The aesthetics of the idea is another important factor that needs to be considered. The solution needs to be attractive and appealing to the intended audience. This is especially important to adver-

You Are a Cartoon/ Comic Author (Part 2)

Buy another Sunday paper and pick a new cartoon/ comic. Again, white out the text in the word balloons and write your own copy.

A Man Is Found Dead

A man is found dead in a field with a backpack and no one around him. How'd he die? 150 words max.

"A man is found dead" exercise is credited to The Martin Agency, Richmond, Virginia

* This is one of several assignments given to candidates who are applying for the highly competitive and prestigious annual Martin Agency student workshop. Retrieved from the application on September 29, 2013, http://www.martinagency.com/students.

tisers because they need to be able to capture the attention of the consumers with their marketing. As mentioned earlier, no matter how good an idea is or how many of the criteria are fulfilled, none of it will work if it's not executed properly.

Now that we have explored some of the general ways in which ideas can be evaluated, we can look at some specific examples that incorporate these wider ideas. Specifically the ways clients and agencies evaluate their creative productions. Award shows like the Cannes Lions International Festival of Creativity, Addy Awards, Effie Awards and others regularly evaluate and honor the best work within the marketing communication industry.

As international agency networks and marketers produce large numbers of creative productions around the world that represent a certain quality standard of a brand or an agency, it can be helpful to assess the creative work. Leo Burnett and its Global Product Committee (GPC) have developed the Leo Burnett Humankind GPC scale, which allows the global agency network to evaluate the work that is being produced by its offices around the world. Not only does this instrument help assess the quality of ideas and creative productions; it also serves as a guide for how everyone within Leo Burnett approaches a client problem. In combination with Leo Burnett's overarching theme "Humankind," the Leo Burnett Humankind GPC scale assures that the work fully supports the agency's clients and their brands' purpose, as well as meets the criteria the agency has set as a global standard. Chief creative officers and key agency personnel affecting the creative product from different international offices meet four times a year to look at the work produced worldwide. "It's really looking into all the work and saying: Are we proud of what we are creating?" says Susan Credle.

The instrument also provides a great motivation and learning tool. Meeting and sharing work allows everyone to see the different problems that are being solved for clients, and how they rate on the scale. The Leo Burnett Humankind GPC scale provides a clearly defined framework and scale that makes it easy for employees to understand how the creative product is judged and how they should judge their own work as well as the work of others. "Everybody's internal scale is different, so we have a real scale of how you look at work," Susan Credle explained.

The bar of the scale was designed to motivate everyone to reach high. The scale consists of ten items: 1 being the lowest and 10 the highest value, and the most difficult to reach. 1 represents "This idea is destructive"; 2 is "I don't get it or there is no idea"; 3 is "Invisible"; 4 is "I don't understand the brand's purpose"; 5 is "I understand the brand's purpose"; 6 is "An intelligent idea"; 7 is "An intelligent and inspiring idea beautifully crafted"; 8 is "It changes the way people feel"; 9 is "It changes the way people act"; 10 is "It changes the world."

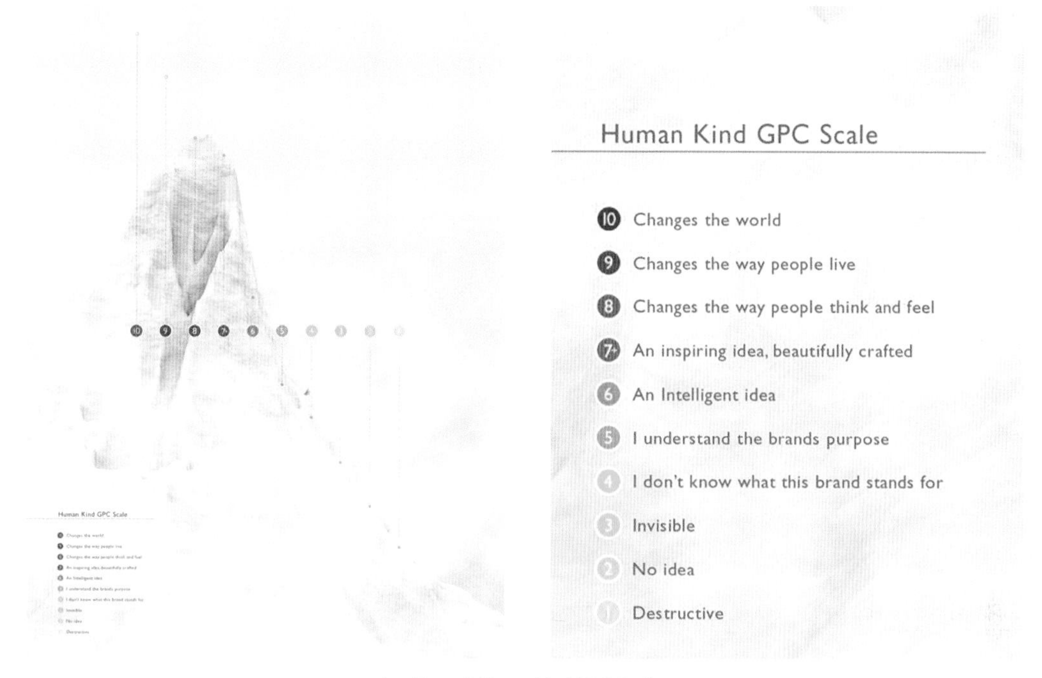

Leo Burnett Humankind GPC Scale

"So suddenly when you are looking at that scale, you are humbled really quickly, because that 'changes the world' is difficult to achieve. We hope we can achieve that one day," says Credle.

Using scales similar to the Leo Burnett Humankind GPC Scale, several marketers have begun to evaluate their work as well. This allows international companies and brands to review the work done by numerous service providers around the world and to assure that a certain level of quality is being met in different markets. The German car manufacturer Audi has used the Audi International Advertising Contest (AIAC) as an instrument to evaluate commercials and other marketing work based on their creative excellence. Audi believes their creative work must be original, with a clear and comprehensive message. But it is not enough to have a novel and clear idea. The execution must be high quality coupled with an intelligent and provocative approach. Finally, it should elicit brand affinity.

TED.com is another organization that has come up with a set of criteria to evaluate ideas. For the last few years, TED.com has held an international competition called Ads Worth Spreading, where the creative merit of commercials and online advertisements are judged based on six elements.

First of all, the ad should have an element of storytelling. As I said earlier, the competition for consumers' attention is at an all-time high. A compelling story is what makes a good commercial stand out. Online videos that incorporate this element are often the advertisements that people want to share because they can connect with them on a deeper, more emotional level. Shareability and social good are only possible when they are supported by a strong and compelling story.

Another key element of a successful commercial is talk, which is the ability to continue the conversation on multiple platforms. The commercial itself should open up the possibility for people to participate with the brand through social media.

Coffeehouse Exercise: Day Three

Go to another public place that will be the setting for this third exercise in this series.

Look for a detailed and richly decorated café or other space. Imagine the two people you have worked on during the previous coffeehouse exercises in this setting. Bring them to life. They are going to meet for the first time and they should share a secret.

The Coffeehouse Exercise is credited to Shelley Berc and Alejandro Fogel's Creativity Workshop, New York

This has become more important in today's world of Twitter, Facebook and Instagram. Brands need to realize that today's conversations take place through these platforms. Advertisers need to enter those conversations in meaningful ways. Doing so encourages loyalty from the consumer to the brand and also becomes a useful tool for the brand to acquire feedback from consumers. People feel much more loyal to a brand that is accessible, helpful and interactive. Not every product or service has to be organized around social media, but it is important for companies to realize that social media will be an essential part of the creative process going forward.

Next is the cultural compass of a brand, and whether it is pointed in the right direction. When brands listen carefully and closely to their customers, they can translate and identify new and innovative ways in which their product can be used. Brands can adapt services and products based on cultural themes or current events in order to be relevant.

The Prudential Day One campaign developed by Droga5 illustrates how marketing of financial services products can be reframed when looking at retirement from a new perspective. Ted Royer, chief creative officer at Droga5 says that most financial advertising is boring and that the agency he works at wants to change that. Most financial advertisers do not talk about the deepest parts of people's lives. Analyzing what is and is not said in financial services and trying to change the topic a whole industry is talking about provided his team with the opportunity to look for deep insights and do something new for the entire category. Using the fact that ten thousand people retire every day in the USA[1], Droga5 created a campaign built on real truths that were captured in various media outlets and constructed with different levels of content. Real people provided testimonials describing their inner feelings about their first day of retirement. Additionally a dedicated website provided scientific research about human behavior related to financial decision making.

Focusing on current events too much can be risky and potentially perceived as chasing a trend. The judges at TED's Ads Worth Spreading recommend assessing the durability of any trends to be aware of their potentially short lifespan and to know that they will most likely soon disappear in favor of a new trend. Companies should also consider which trends and events make sense for them in terms of the image that they are trying to exemplify and whether it goes along with their core values.

Another criterion in the evaluation of creativity is brand bravery and whether it finds success amplifying causes and ideals. Many brands are successful, in large part, due to their ideals and ads that reflect their point of view of issues that matter the most to consumers. If the brand's core values and ideals are not accurately reflected in their ads, they run the risk of losing the audience. The animated online video "Back to the Start," created by the Creative Artist Agency in Los Angeles, illustrates how Chipotle tells the story of a farmer. The video connects well with an audience that is concerned about the environment and mass food production. According to the TED's Ads Worth Spreading report, the ad shows that Chipotle "stands for family farmers and against industrial food processes."[2]

The way in which a brand utilizes and creates social good is another criterion for the evaluation of a successful commercial concept. Online videos can be an effective way for brands and nongovernmental organizations (NGOs) to call attention to a relevant and critical social issue. Social good is likely to be defined in highly subjective terms—it is important to consider whether a video will alienate a large portion of the audience and to carefully consider the medium. Brands need to take care in order to avoid exploiting sensitive topics that could possibly backfire and have negative repercussions.

The final criterion for evaluation is creative wonder. This is highly subjective concept and represents the perspective of many traditional advertising award competitions for which ideas are mainly evaluated based on their professional execution and their originality and unusual ideas. A creative production can be impressive based on its professional level of craftsmanship or because it speaks to a large audience due to its unconventional messaging. Different people may have varying definitions of creative wonder so therefore this is more of a subjective element of evaluation, but an important one nonetheless.

For many decades, the world-famous Cannes Lions International Festival of Creativity has been known as a premier competition to celebrate creativity. To illustrate how creativity can help increase the bottom line, the festival organizers established the Cannes Lions Case for Creative Bravery. Awarded to work that effectively and actively demonstrates brave creativity (work that really pushes the limits and challenges the status quo), the Case for Creative Bravery argues that creative work is the most effective kind of marketing that a company can employ because it has feasible and tangible benefits for their business. For example, not only does creative work look beautiful and emotionally connect with its viewers, it also drives an increased return on Investment (ROI).[3] According to Cannes Lions Case for Creative Bravery 2013, work that demonstrates creativity also drives share price performance—and the market share growth is increasingly significant. Companies that have used creativity as a pivotal point in their work have seen the dramatic benefits that creative work can have. Vice president global advertising and strategy director Jonathan Mildenhall of Coca Cola says that "creativity drives effectiveness" and that he truly believes in "the correlation between creativity and commercial success." This idea is echoed by Marc Pritchard, global marketing brand building officer at Procter and Gamble, who says that "great creative ideas build the business."

Marketers are becoming increasingly aware of the fact that creativity should be an important focal point of advertising and marketing because it produces tangible benefits to the business. The Cannes Lions reward the work that demonstrates the power of creativity. Andy Fennell, the chief marketing officer at Diageo, says that "creative excellence is pivotal to drive brilliant performance." The Cannes Lions demonstrate that creativity is a huge component of the idea evaluation process. Heineken has been one of the most creatively awarded brands at Cannes Lions and provides many examples of creative excellence. Alexis Nasard, president Western Europe & global chief marketing officer at Heineken in Amsterdam explains the importance and effectiveness of creativity in a letter called "Why Cannes Matters." He explains that award-winning work builds the business, provided that the basics of any business, such as on-strategy pricing, competitive marketing spending and right sales focus are firmly in place.[4]

In the book *The Case for Creativity*, James Hurman illustrates that creativity really does have a huge impact on the effectiveness of advertising and business objectives. He draws upon research done in the past, including the "Do Award Winning Commercials Sell?" study conducted by Donald Gunn, which concluded that creatively awarded advertising is more effective and is also more creative than advertising that does not win any awards. Similarly to the Case for Creative Bravery by the Cannes Festival, Hurman concluded that creative advertising resulted in significant improvements in market share, penetration and profitability.

Though this chapter looks at several frameworks and perspectives that specifically evaluate ideas and concepts within the marketing and advertising industry, the core concepts and key factors can be applied in other fields and disciplines when reviewing and evaluating ideas, concepts, products or services. Festivals that judge fine art, films, product design, services, business plans or even technology typically consider the three key aspects:

- The divergence factor that represents newness, innovation, originality and "not seen before."
- The relevance factor that measures the degree to which the idea relates to the problem as well as the audience.
- The effectiveness factor that represents the action that the idea can generate. This factor also includes the ability to engage with audiences and allow them to take the idea further and share or interact with it.

CHAPTER SEVEN

THE IMPORTANCE OF COMMUNICATING IDEAS EFFECTIVELY

A business idea is only as good as its execution.

It's true. There are many ideas in the world and, as you know by this point in the book, they come in all shapes and sizes. Ideas can appear like the quintessential lightbulb with a "ding!" sound effect, or they can materialize in your sketchbook, evolve over a series of walks or even show up in the shower.

On a daily basis we have countless small ideas that we act on, sift through or ignore, depending on our focus. We may have the idea to put strawberries on our cereal in the morning or to color coordinate and improve the communication structure in documents for stakeholders on a project at work.

The arrival of an idea—not the process of generating ideas, which is the subject of the first half of this book—but the actual "aha!" when an idea materializes is still mysterious. Ideas come into our heads in myriad ways, but the arrival of an idea is usually an unexpected moment. That is how we know it is an idea.

Personal Twist: Myth, Legend, Fairy Tale or Fable

Using a personal story that you discovered through your Morning Pages, or of personal choice, write a three-page, double-spaced retelling of your story in the form of a myth, legend, fairy tale, fable, urban legend or conspiracy theory. You can use elements of the above story types to accent your story, or you can add elements of your own story to a classic tale. Utilize strong storytelling elements and "sticky" factors. Make sure to think creatively and mix it up! Present your story to one or several friend(s) or colleague(s) in a five-minute presentation. Include three visual elements of your choice.

Often, the bigger the idea, the greater the moment of sudden recognition. Even for ideas that evolve over time, the initial moment of the idea is usually a moment that has the staying power to be pondered and, in time, acted upon. The way that ideas evolve has even been described as magical or mystical.

Johnny Vulkan of Anomaly thinks that good ideas are only one part of the equation and that for most people in advertising and marketing it is not that hard to come up with interesting ideas.

"Being able to articulate your idea in a way that convinces somebody else it's a good idea is really hard," says Vulkan. "There are many great ideas that do not go anywhere because the creator has not figured out how to tell the story and to see the idea through until the very end of its production. Often ideas have to be resilient. Great ideas rarely just sail through a system with ease, they have to be fought for. And I think a lot of people come in and go 'I've got this amazing idea, and the client didn't buy the amazing idea.' And I say, 'It might take us three years to sell this amazing idea because whilst you think it's amazing and I think it's amazing, we have to convince an organization with various stakeholders that it's amazing. We have to prove it. Are you willing to sit with it for three years, or are you only looking for a quick win?' I think the best stuff has to probably be fought for quite hard to make it a reality."

Compared to the relatively short-term nature of advertising, where schedules typically span over several months, product innovation can be a multiple-year cycle for many organizations where the time from identifying a business opportunity to actually seeing a product marketed in mass scale can be four years. Vulkan notes, "So you've got to sit with ideas and creativity for four years, and that's hard."

In business the transition from idea to a tangible action inherently involves communication. Executing an idea and communication go hand in hand. Whether you are translating the idea into a work of art or into a digital slide show for a presentation, you are communicating that idea to a larger audience. In both of these examples, for instance, you are communicating visually.

Ideas in action attract other ideas. When you watch a movie, you are seeing and experiencing an infinite number of ideas woven together and communicated through visuals and sound. All of these elements combined create a unique experience, at the core of which is an original idea.

BRINGING IDEAS TO MARKET

Ideas are everywhere. At any given moment, companies— advertising agencies specifically—are developing an infinite number of ideas to increase sales, drive industries and change the economy. Many talented creatives are adding to these ideas and generating independent ideas of their own. As you can imagine, there is no lack of ideas being generated in business and industry, yet there is a steep drop-off when it comes to the number of ideas that make it to market.

Marshall Ross agrees: "A lot of agencies are putting out great ideas all the time. Great ideas are not that hard to come by; they are not rare. So I think the big change or difference between agencies that are okay, good and great is that some agencies know how to bring comfort to the unfamiliar. One of the things that we work really hard at, which is: How do you make a really unexpected idea feel okay?"

Based on Ross's experience it helps to be a good listener. He strongly believes that listening is reciprocal and that clients want to work with people who understand and believe their problems and their opportunities. When agencies listen, understand their clients' challenges and gain their clients' trust, it is easier to sell their most innovative and creative ideas. "You have to find clients who get what you are about, who believe that creativity is a tool in your business," he says. "And if you don't have clients who believe that creativity matters, you're dead."

The difficultly of bringing ideas to market does not lie in the development of many creative ideas, it lies in selling the ideas to clients. Three important aspects to consider when executing ideas and bringing them to a new audience are: resistance, simplicity and interactivity.

RESISTANCE TO NEW IDEAS

First, there is a general human aversion toward new things and change. The more radical an idea, the less likely the people involved in the decision-making process will readily buy into the new idea. In his book *Creativity*, Mihaly Csikszentmihalyi discusses why it is always difficult to present a new idea. The key factor is that many companies function the same way the mind does: They have become successful by doing the same things over a long period of time and by holding on to a set of strategies and business processes that have worked in the past.

The presentation of new thoughts and the introduction of new ideas cause companies to consider the threat to their established and proven track records. This can be a good thing—it can keep companies on track in areas where they are competitive. On the other hand, this can present a challenge. Many organizations are accustomed to certain set strategies or processes that make it difficult to accept new directions. In some cases, organizations might be unable to recognize the promise of a new, different idea. The brain works similarly when it comes to accepting change or new ideas on a daily basis. The brain is comprised of high-quality processing power, that enables us to work within the context of the already learned and familiar. When confronted with new ideas or change, however, the brain often goes into autopilot mode and dismisses the newness coming into our life. The more foreign the change or idea, the more resistance we encounter.

When presenting new ideas to decision makers, you must consider the established framework of the system they operate in on a daily basis. One way to sell new ideas is to build bridges and fill the gaps between the known and the unknown. Before introducing or selling a new idea, you can

Musical Time Travel

Music is great for setting a mood and even evoking a certain time period. You can leverage this when working on projects in which you would like to tap into the feel of a certain era or historical moment, for instance the patriotism of the WWII era or the turbulence of the 1960s. With your sketchbook in hand, play a song from a specific era, such as Benny Goodman's *Sing, Sing, Sing with a Swing* to represent the 1940s or Led Zeppelin's *Black Dog* to represent the late 1960s. Create an image or the rough draft of an advertisement that is influenced by or references one of these eras.

develop a framework your audience can relate to so that the new idea does not sound as revolutionary or aggressive. Then you might add a rationale and an explanation as to why the idea works very well. One of the most common ways to do this is to add supporting customer insights and market research data. Tom Moudry of Martin Williams is highly aware of this challenge. "That's why we are hoping to use research and we're hoping to prove to them that taking risk and having original ideas is going to make them more successful," he says.

In today's highly competitive advertising environment, doing things the established way might not lead to the success that is required to survive in the future. When developing communication strategies and campaigns, it is important to build on previous work and to maintain a level of continuity, and by the same token, it's more necessary to be different from the competition to get noticed. Not taking any risks might become the biggest risk to a company in today's challenging markets. As David Droga puts it, "The biggest risk is to be vanilla. The biggest risk is to be one of the herd. That's risky."

IDEAS NEED TO BE SIMPLE AND TRANSLATABLE

In the past, ideas were often created for a specific medium or one channel. The ideation process and concept development phase were relatively easy since one could focus and concentrate on one specific area. Today ideas need to be media neutral and capable of translating across mediums, since customers interact with products and companies via multiple touch points.

An important aspect of developing ideas is the focus on overarching concepts that resonate with some universal aspects that are ingrained in our brains' experience. More than ever before, ideas and concepts that lead to unusual, original and novel products, as well as communication messages, need to connect with people on a holistic level. In other words, the ideas must speak to the emotions of the audience, as well as the minds of the audience, in that the ideas must connect and relate to past experiences. Archetypes and metaphors can provide direction toward finding concepts that many people can relate to. Archetypes and metaphors represent patterns, symbols and images that hold universal meaning for many people and are often processed subconsciously. Based on many exercises conducted with students over the last ten years, I have found that the best ideas are simple and are connected to an overarching theme or concept that we can relate to.

Another important element in the process of executing ideas is the production of numerous ideas. Before the new millennium we saw many one-dimensional ideas that carried just one TV commercial or one print ad. Today's hypercompetitive media environment requires the production of many creative pieces that all fit under an overarching concept but can be applied through a multitude of channels and mediums. This strategy requires the idea to work on multiple levels of engagement with the audience.

Due to the interconnectivity of today's networked society, it has become more important to develop media neutral ideas. Media neutral ideas are of such universal quality that they can be executed across various media channels. The execution style can even differ from media to media as long as the overarching idea remains the same or holds together. For that matter, it is equally important to evaluate the appropriate medium when deciding on the best ideas.

One example of an idea that is applied across mediums is the Dove campaign "Real Beauty" developed by Ogilvy and Mather. The campaign has run for many years. Thanks to its simple concept, the core idea of the campaign can be updated and modified over time. The various videos "Little Girls," "Evolution," "Onslaught," "Sketches" and "Camera Shy" demonstrate how simple ideas can evolve over time and maintain their strength. The project "Real Beauty Sketches," portraying a police artist drawing faces of women based on interviews, illustrates how differently a simple idea can be interpreted and executed. "Camera Shy" takes the concept of real beauty further by reversing the concept real beauty. The idea is built around the concept of women who stop believing they are beautiful and become shy, and therefore do not want to be photographed. The reversal illustrates one of the many thinking techniques discussed in chapter six.

Sight, Seeing and Perception

Go to a museum or art exhibit with a friend and your sketchbook. Decide in advance which selections of the collection you wish to view. As you enter each room, split up and agree to meet at a set time.

Suspend your judgment and look at each painting or sculpture with fresh eyes. Avoid looking at the information labels until after you have had a chance to fully appreciate the piece deeply. Make notes in your sketchbook on what moves you.

Meet back up with your friend and share your impressions of the works that speak most deeply to you and why.[2]

IDEAS NEED TO ALLOW THE AUDIENCE TO INTERACT

Lastly, ideas are no longer developed based on the classic sender-receiver communication model. Today an idea that is supposed to sell a product or service needs to make customers want to engage, participate, embrace or introduce it into their personal lives. When developing ideas, the consumer's reaction and interaction must be incorporated. Similar to a good movie script that pulls the audience completely into the story or the videogame story line that makes the player become part of the game experience, ideas for marketing communication, new products and services need to include similar success factors as those found in good movies and

Musical Interpretation

Select a set of several songs that vary in pace and style. Try some with lyrics, some without and possibly songs that use natural sounds or sound effects. As you listen to the music, use your sketchbook to sketch, draw or write anything you feel inspired to draw or write. Try to work quickly, impulsively and without judgment to interpret the music visually.

video games. Some examples of success factors include a captivating story or a core idea that an audience can relate to, an interesting plot or challenge that gets resolved, some new information that allows the viewer or participant to gain knowledge, something original or innovative that surprises or something just beautifully crafted are only a few elements to consider.

Good ideas spread like wildfire thanks to the use of new technologies. Social media technologies offer a vast opportunity to disseminate ideas quickly among a large audience.

Volkswagen's famous 2011 Super Bowl ad, "The Force," featuring a mini-Darth Vader, illustrates how agencies and clients can use pop culture references to tap into specific audiences that increase the likelihood of an advertisement going viral. Mark Hunter, former chief creative officer at Deutsch LA, the agency responsible for developing the Darth Vader spot, acquired some key insight related to the fact that the most talked-about pop culture topics on the internet seemed to be Star Wars, cats and dogs. Hunter and his team could have come up with just any idea to introduce a new car. Yet, knowing that Star Wars, cats and dogs are three pop culture topics discussed daily by millions of people on the internet helped the agency develop a concept that could touch and possibly connect with the millions of internet users specifically interested in Star Wars, cats or dogs.

By developing a TV spot that was emotionally engaging and that featured the new Volkswagen Passat and a little kid dressed as Darth Vader, the agency and its client increased the likelihood that internet users might like the final spot, and possibly react and talk about it on the internet. Deutsch and Volkswagen focused on human experiences many consumers are familiar with, specifically all members of a family—and allowed viewers to engage emotionally. Within weeks after its first appearance, "The Force" became a blockbuster online and after the first year was seen by 50 million viewers. This represents a mighty success that many consumers and advertising professionals will remember for years to come.

COMMUNICATING IDEAS

Not all ideas are destined to have a long trajectory. Some are short and sweet, and quickly executed, and others never get off the proverbial drawing board. While many factors are at work in the translation of an idea from imagination to reality, the way an idea is communicated and executed greatly affects the trajectory of influence and success of the idea.

There are many ways to communicate an idea. Often the idea, as you see it in your mind, has a certain medium or communication channel attached to it. Just as you learned to generate multiple ideas before evaluating and selecting one, you need to look at your idea through different mediums of communication.

There are two reasons that considering the communication medium of an idea is important: First, communicating through the most appropriate medium helps you share your idea with others. Second, seeing the communication medium as a flexible factor, provides another chance to see a new connection—a new communication option—that can enhance your idea and make your idea more impactful.

As an example, imagine that you have an important presentation to give at work. You need to share a new idea with your colleagues. The standard form of presenting at a business meeting involves software such as PowerPoint and coworkers sitting around a table in a conference room. You are working on the presentation, but you have a problem: putting the idea into words is not capturing the idea as you first envisioned it. You think back to when you had come up with the idea originally—it was full of color and life and images. When you came up with your idea, you most likely had not thought of it as a series of bullet points. Yet bullet point lists are one of the most common ways that ideas are communicated. Human beings take in 80 percent of their information visually and while printed words are visual, images can carry universal meaning and have greater information and emotional connection than words. Knowing this, you decide to switch from bulleted lists to images in your presentation. Your presentation is not only refreshingly clear to your audience, but it translates the idea quickly and with enthusiasm.

You Are a Cartoon/ Comic Author (Part 3)

Again, buy a local Sunday paper and pick a new cartoon/comic. White out the text in the word balloons and write your own copy.

By using visuals and breaking out of the mold of corporate presentations, you help your audience experience the idea at a closer level to your original experience.

An example is the presentation of former student Kristina Shigaeva when she dressed up as

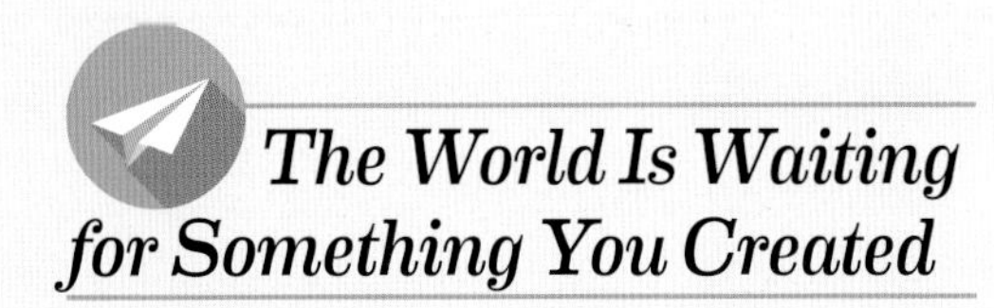

The World Is Waiting for Something You Created

Good ideas are our most precious asset. The world is waiting for something you created. What is it?

The "The World Is Waiting for Something You Created" exercise is credited to Jung v. Matt, London, http://www.jvm.com/en/home/index.html.

detective to present her case about the English sought-after artist Banksy.

For a research assignment to introduce the British graffiti artist Banksy, Kristina Shigaeva chose a novel approach to get her classmates' attention. Instead of presenting the basic facts and visual examples of Banksy's work via some PowerPoint slides, Kristina impersonated a British detective dressed in trench coat with hat and a dossier stamped "Top Secret" and "Classified" under her arm. Then, she introduced the villain and used several exhibits to show evidence of Banksy's work. Through the creative use of role-play Kristina presented her core concept and research findings in a fresh and engaging way.

This technique can play out on many levels in many different industries. What is important to note is that the ideas that usually have the most impact are the ones that are communicated clearly and in such a way that allows the audience to connect immediately.

While choosing the right communication medium for your idea can increase the idea's trajectory, choosing the incorrect medium or introducing too many communication elements, can also mean running the risk of obscuring the idea. I recommend the following when thinking about how you are going to communicate your idea:

- Keep it simple.
- Know your audience and help connect the idea to their needs and wants.
- Develop a consistent style for the communication, whether it is line drawings or 3-D effects, make sure the medium supports the main message of your idea.
- If possible, introduce an unexpected element that helps communicate the core idea in a memorable way.

Most important, though, know when to communicate an idea. Sometimes ideas are shared eagerly or too early and sometimes with the wrong people. This can have an immediate negative influence on the longevity of the idea. Know who you can trust with rough ideas that are in the development stage. Look for people who are good listeners, who don't pass immediate judgment and who can offer effective encouragement for the continued execution of the idea. These people can sometimes be hard to find, but when you discover them, be up-front in asking them to be a sounding board for you and your ideas. Maintaining a network of people that can help encourage you as you nurture an idea is a great way to help your ideas come to fruition.

COMMUNICATION MEDIUMS

While there are many communication tools and technologies, from pen and paper to text message, this book focuses on the core communication mediums that engage the senses and communicate information at various levels. You might want to consider the following core communication elements:

- Storytelling
- Sight or visual imagery

Sight + Seeing

Touch + Feeling

Taste + Texture

Sound and Hearing

Smell + Aroma

- Sound
- Environment (includes scent)
- Attitude

Some mediums are straightforward core communication tactics, such as visual imagery. Others are more obtuse and instinctive, such as attitude. Being conscious of the medium through which you choose to communicate your idea or using a combination of the factors above to enhance the presentation of your idea will not only help you create a memorable experience, but can also spawn new ideas that further separate your idea from the competition.

The following are core mediums for idea communication and their roles in effective information sharing.

STORYTELLING

Storytelling is one of the oldest forms of informative communication and the sharing of ideas. Traditional storytelling uses words, language, sounds and gestures to create a dramatic and memorable tale. While traditional storytelling exists today almost exclusively as a form of performance art, storytelling is alive and well in urban legends and even the gossip at the water cooler.

Well told stories make an idea memorable.

- Stories and storytelling exist in all cultures and languages.
- Storytelling is ingrained in our communication ("talking shop").
- Stories put knowledge into a framework that is true to our everyday lives.
- Stories are tools that help people see connections, context, and relationships in new ways.
- A story is a simulation: The viewers' minds and imaginations take on the role of the protagonist.

Stickiness Factors

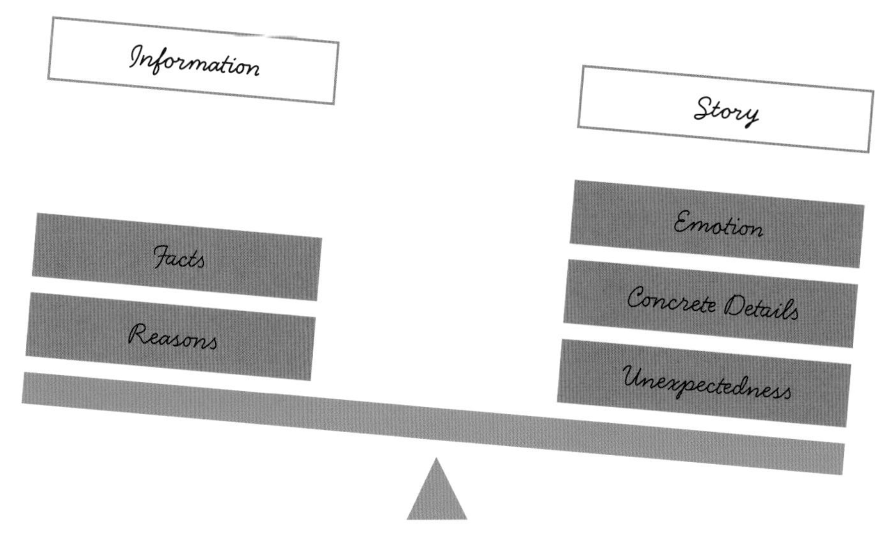

Adopted from a lecture note by Brenna McCormick, Boston, MA.

Storytelling as a means of memorable communication is the subject of Chip and Dan Heath's book *Made to Stick*. They argue that stories are a vehicle for creating communication that people remember through the "sticky" information that is woven together through emotion and examples. Storytelling creates an easy-to-remember lesson that is also easy to repeat thereby creating a viral communication effect and ultimately effective communication.

On a basic level, a story is made up of a plotline, characters and conflict (see illustration on page 83). When these elements are employed skillfully for advertising and marketing communication, they can have a positive impact on how an audience connects with a campaign. An excellent example of this is the Subway campaign featuring Jared, a man who lost weight by eating a diet that consisted of Subway sandwiches. Jared's story, a traditional underdog tale in which Jared triumphs over his obesity, ultimately repositioned Subway as a healthy alternative to fast food, a position that has had much longevity beyond Jared through weight loss shows such as *The Biggest Loser*.

According to the brothers Heath, the Jared Subway story contains all of the elements of a "sticky" idea:

- **SIMPLE:** Eat healthy Subway subs and lose weight.
- **UNEXPECTED:** Lose weight by eating fast food.
- **CONCRETE:** Visuals including oversized pants, a diet of sandwiches, loss of body mass.
- **CREDIBLE:** Endorsement from real person withstands comparison to reality.
- **EMOTIONAL:** We care about Jared as the Everyman who reaches his potential.
- **STORY:** Protagonist triumphs over odds. Inspires us to action.

Note that it is the last element of the sticky idea, the story, that inspires us to take action. Due to this element of action, stories make for great segues into more traditional presentations. Storytelling as a communication tool sways the audience through an emotionally charged narrative that educates toward an example that people can act on.

At its heart, a story is an idea.

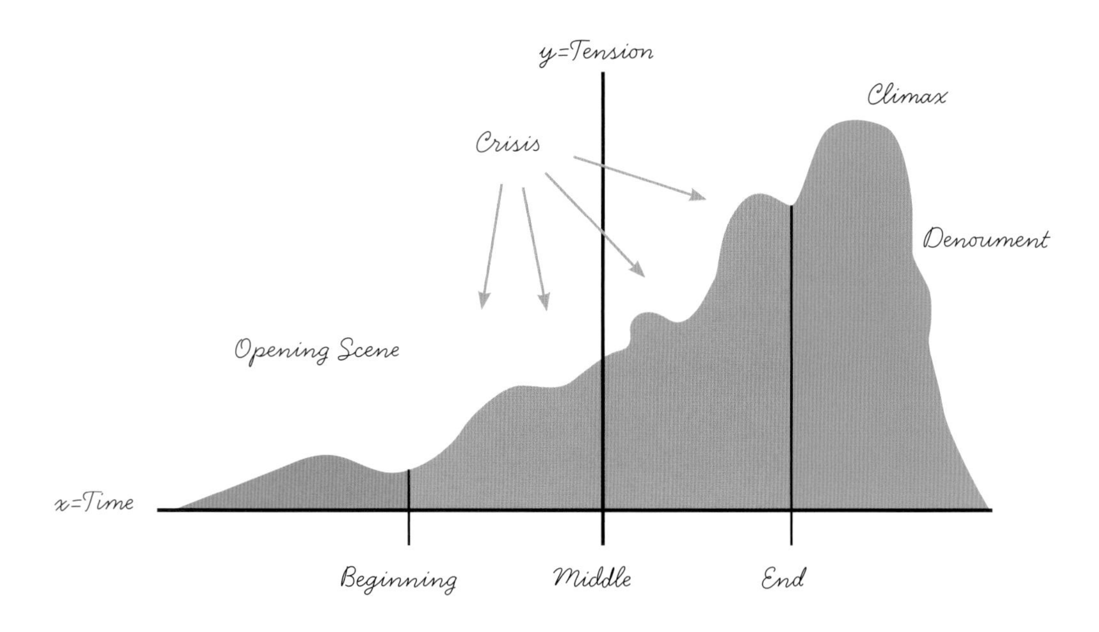

Classic Storytelling Structure.

How you package that idea is what makes a compelling story (or ad).

- **PLOT**
- **CHARACTERS:** protagonist & antagonist
- **THEME:** concept, moral (idea)
- **CONFLICT**
- **SETTING**
- **LANGUAGE, TONE, PACING**
- **HOOK, FORESHADOWING**

The elements of storytelling can be ingrained in any communication process to lengthen the trajectory and "stickiness" of an idea.

Inspiration Point:

Forms of stories exist that transcend time and culture:

- **MYTH:** usually a story of origin, nature, or gods and heroes
- **LEGEND:** passed down within a culture, usually involves historical basis and larger than life exploits
- **FAIRY TALE:** a story with magical deeds or moral lessons
- **FABLE:** teaches a moral lesson
- **URBAN LEGEND:** appears magically, spreads virally, elements of horror and humor
- **CONSPIRACY THEORY:** explains a historical or current event as result of secret ploy
- **PROVERB:** short saying that is simple and profound

Inspiration Point:

How an idea is spun into a story can enrich the experience for the listener, and add credibility to the story or elicit emotion. Some mediums to consider when telling your idea as a story:

- **SPOKEN**
- **SONG**
- **WRITTEN:** poetry, prose, novel
- **WORD & IMAGE:** comic, graphic novel, picture book
- **VISUAL/PICTORIAL:** movie, photos, flip book
- **PLAYS/THEATER**

Retail Environment Observation

With your sketchbook or a notebook handy, head to your local mall or a favorite shopping area. Walk around and observe the elements that make up the environment of the store spaces. Pay careful attention to how the space engages your senses: sight, sound, smell, touch and taste (if applicable). Make notes on what elements are used to define the store space and enhance the customer experience. Consider how they convey the brand of the store. Compare one of your favorite stores with another store that you do not like. What are some of the contrasts? What are the goals of each environment? What are the details of the environment communicating to you in both of these spaces?

Adapted from a class exercise provided by Brenna McCormick, Boston, MA

- **"TWISTERS":** using Twitter to tell stories in 140 characters or less

SIGHT OR VISUAL IMAGERY

The oldest form of communication, visual imagery can be traced back 32,000 years to the cave paintings of the Aurignacian culture. The power of visual imagery is that it is universal and not restricted to languages.

Similar to the early cave paintings, visuals can translate emotions as well as instructions. Visual imagery in the form of informational graphics allows you to travel to a different country and still successfully find a restroom. In the form of photojournalism, the image helps capture and express the emotion of a specific moment.

The act of seeing—using our sight to process information—works differently than when our brain processes words; we see visuals by being open and receiving information rather than processing and filtering. Processing or reading images involves impressions, intuition and feeling in combination with information. This is what allows visuals to connect with us emotionally, on a deeper level than words, and to defy the boundaries of language.

Keep in mind though that seeing is not always perceiving:

> *In 1500, Leonardo da Vinci said, "[The average human] looks without seeing, listens without hearing, touches without feeling, eats without tasting, moves without physical awareness, inhales without awareness of odor or fragrance, and talks without thinking.[1]" Da Vinci trained himself to see ideas and inspiration in nature at an almost superhuman level that has only recently been duplicated by modern photography technology.*

Several of my former students have developed some practical exercises that have helped increase their awareness. Lauren Biese started an Instagram account and uses daily photographs to explore different perspectives when looking at objects. During her internship, one of her photos was picked up by the local media because of its unusual perspective. "I just portrayed the scene from a skyward angle rather than straight on so viewers were looking at the scene from a different POV than a regular photo," said Biese.

Matthew Fiorentino has continued his creative journey (see page 160) and incorporated exercises from Michael Michalko's *Thinkertoys* into his daily routine to improve his creative thinking skills. "Perhaps one of the easiest ways to experience this shift in perspective is through color concentration, an exercise you can find in Michalko's book. Take a moment, look around the room and search only for the color blue. Notice the patterns that emerge, the blue objects you hadn't registered before, even the absence of blue. Whatever your experience, you are now looking at your world differently and picking up signals and potential connections you hadn't picked up before. Finding, interpreting and producing something new from a connection like this is what sits at the core of creativity," says Fiorentino.

SOUND

Like visual imagery, sound is a powerful universal communication tool. Music can influence emotion and set a tone, but in order to clearly communicate information it is usually combined with storytelling in the form of lyrics.

Sound is a powerful emotional driver, as it bypasses the rational mind and connects on a deeper and more emotional level than words or images do. Before story there was sound which evolved into music. Music exists in all cultures and while it has unique cultural characteristics, it can be interpreted and understood as a universal language through the use of sound to influence emotion.

Leverage music to influence your creative processes:

- Using music can create a sense of safety for creativity.
- Music can set the tone for an emotion you need to tap into.
- Music can also be leveraged to change emotions.

ENVIRONMENT

We have spoken in previous chapters about Place as one of the 4Ps of creativity; this is because the environment that surrounds us sends subtle messages that indicate behavior or information. Leveraging the environment as a way to communicate an idea can be a powerful way to share the idea with your audience, as it allows for a full sensory experience. Within an environment you can manipulate sight, sound, scent, touch, taste, lighting and even traffic flow. Environments communicate ideas in holistic and sensory ways that often make them memorable. Examples of using the environment to communicate ideas can most commonly be found in retail stores.

Apple Stores clearly convey the core idea of brand through an environment. The Apple Stores are created with a unique consistency between product design and architecture of store space. The goal of the environment is to cultivate the feeling of attending an event rather than visiting a retail store. For ease of task, the store space is divided into three areas: play, purchase and learn. Two of these areas are known to customers as The Studio and Genius Bar. At the core of the Apple Stores is the Next Generation Learning approach to selling, which allows customers to experience and take advantage of the tools available in the products. Through the three spaces, Apple creates a unique destination environment that Mac users everywhere are as enthusiastic about as they are the company's products.

ATTITUDE

Within the marketing, communication and advertising industry every presentation of ideas and

Visualization of Concepts, Part 1: Beauty

The world is becoming increasingly visual. In order to communicate effectively we need to come up with innovative, original and creative ways to show familiar concepts in unusual ways and unfamiliar concepts in familiar ways. Visualize Beauty with 9-12 images/key visuals.

The presentation can be produced in an abstract, concrete, symbolic or descriptive way, or can also make use of analogies. The key visuals can be in relationship with each other, e.g. tell an overall story or script or can be independent from each other.

This assignment should encourage you to be playful, take risks and experiment (try out new things you might not even think of).

The key visuals should have an appropriate size of 8 ½" × 11" to present to an audience of 6-10 people. You can use any visual design tools or elements available to you (e.g. photography, painting, drawing, collage, and objects).

concepts turns into a pitch where clients, peers or people at higher ranks buy into what we are presenting or trying to sell. Every time you present and communicate ideas, your audience experiences not only your ideas and concepts but also your personal creative attitude.

Attitude relates to your own feelings, self-understanding and behavior, and how you engage with the world and the people around you. Your attitude is connected to your personality and it influences how others perceive you. Creative attitude is often associated with the complex personality characteristics of so-called creative people. These characteristics include being curious and interested in exploring new things, being imaginative and realistic, humble and proud, passionate and objective, and playful and disciplined. Being confident in your work but also being open to constructive feedback and expressing courage when presenting ideas and concepts can help shape a positive attitude. Seeing problems as opportunities, and confronting challenges as they arise, as well as practicing and nurturing your creative skills are additional elements that can influence attitude in a positive way.

For many of my former students, creative attitude has grown from the understanding that creativity can be a part of life. Creative attitude becomes a way of looking at life, a belief that life becomes richer when creativity plays a part in it.

CHAPTER EIGHT

CREATIVITY AND PLACE

When I worked as an art director under the guidance of the famous agency creative George Lois in the late 1980s, our offices did not have any doors. Employees were encouraged to hang up any work-related items such as idea scribbles, images, drawings and layouts on our office walls. When walking through the agency and passing each of the offices, we could easily see the projects everyone was involved in. This also allowed Lois to see and review each person's work when he toured the agency early in the morning every day. Even then, Lois was taking steps in the right direction in terms of the sharing of knowledge. However, the organizational structure of his agency, as well as many others during the 1980s, 1990s and early 2000s, did not yet support or facilitate true collaboration. Back then the employees still were divided into various disciplines and departments of art and copy, media, account services and production, and cross-collaboration was not often practiced. But times have changed substantially. Today company heads put a lot more thought into the physical, structural and cultural work environment.

According to American creativity researcher Teresa Amabile, individual creativity exists as a function of three components: expertise and special

The open and collaborative office design of the agency Anomaly, New York.

knowledge in a specific domain, creative-thinking skills, and both intrinsic and extrinsic motivation. Additionally individual creativity and creativity of organizations are also influenced within the context of the environment. From the interviews that I conducted with creative executives, it became clear that many agencies have started to emphasize the physical environment by deconstructing the traditional workplace, of the Mad Men generation (a time frame spanning the 1960s and lasting through the 1990s). Numerous agencies I visited were either in the process of breaking down the walls or had recently completed a deconstruction process. Traditional cubicles and offices hardly exist anymore. The end result is seen in the way that people interact more openly with each other.

According to Marshall Ross, chief creative officer at Cramer Krasselt, one of the things his agency has done is to knock down walls and doors in the thinking areas. The same kind of emphasis on openness was reflected in the interview with Lynn Teo, former chief experience officer at AKQA, who said, "Literally, as in the physical space is extremely open. There are no little cube offices." Doug Spong of Carmichael Lynch Spong captured and articulated the reasons why a physically open environment leads to more openness between employees: "We have a very open collaborative environment. We intentionally designed this space to take down traditional drywall with doors that lock people out and shut light out from the central halls. We have close to 80,000 square feet of space and only a few conference rooms. We created an open space because we recognize that the future for us as an agency is about getting disciplines, departments, talents, giving skills and gifts to work better together with a high degree of frequency and more sharing." Both the physical and social environments have a strong impact on creativity and the cultivation of a creative culture.

The business owners and managers have given special attention to the interior design of the physical environment and workspace in each of the agencies I had a chance to visit. When Tom Moudry of Martin Williams in Minneapolis walked me through the agency, I noticed that the rooms looked more like the living rooms or dining rooms in a private home rather than rooms in a conventional office. Pieces of art and toys could be found in every corner of the agency. I still remember the large stuffed zebra head that hung on the wall of one the living rooms furnished with carpets, couches and cocktail tables where our interview took place.

All of the workspaces I visited encouraged employees to meet and share ideas. Martin Williams built numerous rooms with glass that provide an open view over the city landscape and beyond. "It's collaborative, open, and I think we've made great strides in that," says Tom Moudry proudly. "We have a lot of common areas and our philosophy was to make the private areas smaller and more transparent, and the communal areas more open." This allows employees to step into a thinking chamber that provides a quiet zone sometimes necessary for both concentration and relaxation when working individually or in small teams. The communal areas encourage employees to bump into each other and start conversations.

Collaboration was the most frequently used word that came up during the interviews with creative executives. All of the interviewees mentioned that collaboration among their employees and between departments and offices is the most important concept embraced by highly creative agencies. Marshall Ross describes the agency practice at Cramer Krasselt: "We keep the work very exposed. Work-in-progress is always out in the open for people to see because we want that constant level of critique. We want people constantly wondering if this is good enough." When describing the atmosphere at Riester, Tom Ortega emphasizes a "very open climate, very open atmosphere." He also says that employees tend to be fairly collaborative. Woody Kay, creative director at Arnold Worldwide says he has "always felt, because advertising is such a collaborative medium, that we really need to find a way to get people to collaborate." This desire has been addressed by Arnold's decision to build a completely new office space in downtown Boston. The plans will take advantage of an open physical environment that facilitates better collaboration and cross-pollination among the several hundred employees across various disciplines.

You Are a Cartoon/ Comic Author (Part 4)

Now it is time to create your own cartoon/comic. Spend some time and develop as many ideas, concepts and stories for a cartoon/comic as you can. Once you have developed a good amount of ideas (approx. 50) pick your best one and draw/write your own cartoon/comic.

According to George Lois, creativity is mainly related to the skills of an individual and a big idea could never be developed in a team setting. As we know from earlier chapters, the individual problem solving and creative thinking processes and skills are important contributors to the overall creative end product. However, collaboration can strengthen the overall output of creative ideas.

Teresa Amabile argues that creativity can come from anyone and that ideas from all ranks can be tapped. With the organizational survey instrument KEYS mentioned in the bonus chapter "Creativity and the Evolution of the 4Ps" (available for download at www.breakthroughthinkingguide.com),

Amabile developed a tool that assesses the work environment of any company and gives insight into how well an organization is equipped for encouraging and producing innovation. The instrument measures several key areas that can enhance or stifle creativity. These areas include organizational encouragement, supervisory encouragement, work group supports, sufficient resources, freedom and challenging work.

Organizational encouragement is an indicator of how creativity is supported and encouraged by the culture of an organization. This includes the fair judgment of ideas as well as reward system for developing new ideas. Additionally a shared vision among the individuals in the organization is a contributing factor. Encouragement within an organization illustrates that individuals have the ability to express their ideas freely, even if these ideas are off the wall or ostensibly unrealistic.

Supervisory encouragement looks at the way in which goals are set and how team members are being supported and valued. Some examples of this include delegating responsibilities, giving immediate and timely feedback, boosting confidence, mutual respect between employees and supervisors, and being part of the decision-making process.

Work group support takes into consideration how diverse skills are represented within a group of employees. It also looks at how open a group is to new ideas and how team members support each other as well as how well the group communicates.

Sufficient resources measures whether or not a group has access to resources such as funds, materials, facilities and information.

Freedom addresses an employee's ability to control aspects of the work produced. Some examples of this include whether they have the power to decide what they work on and how they can complete the given task. Employees should have the ability to initiate projects and the allocation of time and assistance for individual efforts.

Challenge looks at how stimulating and important the work is.

Amabile's instrument also assesses two components that can be dangerous to creativity: organizational impediments and workload pressure. Organizational impediments include internal politics, destructive internal competition, risk avoidance and harsh criticism of new ideas. Workload pressure looks at how realistic or unrealistic deadlines are and the existence of any distractions from the production of creative work.

All of the agencies that I visited appeared to give their employees encouragement and support, which was often expressed by a very individual corporate culture. Rob Schwartz of TBWA\Chiat\Day introduced the concept of a pirate culture and it has been integrated throughout the agency. Schwartz had done some research and found that "pirates have the reputation of chaos and flamboyance, and their actions always seem very haphazard, like 'Oh, there's a ship, who's not drunk, let's go, let's take it!' But when you dig in a little deeper to these guys, and I'm talking about the seventeenth century, you find that most Caribbean pirates were insanely organized. They knew that the final output was going to be this sense of chaos, but the preparation to get to the illusion of chaos was methodical." At TBWA\Chiat\Day in Los Angeles the pirate theme becomes obvious when walking through the huge office space located in a former helicopter hangar used by Howard Hughes. This includes visual icons and images of skulls and bones, which appear throughout the physical space. A basketball court also has been built into the office. Such elements create a spirit of risk taking, rebellion and being different, which the agency encourages. According to the TBWA\Chiat\Day website, "Pirates don't live by rules and conventions, they break them. They seize

The office space atTBWA\Chiat\Day is located in a former helicopter hangar used by Howard Hughes.

upon every opportunity, creating their own when none can be found."

As TBWA\Chiat\Day has demonstrated during numerous award shows and industry festivals over many decades, the piracy theme, organization and effectiveness can coexist well. "What I observed was that when we are organized from a management sense, an org chart sense, and in our pitching process and in our production process, we are then liberated to focus on the creativity. Because the biggest enemy to creativity is chaos—organizational chaos" says Rob Schwartz.

Organization and structure is also important to David Droga. "There's a certain structure here, but the structure allows for the chaos of everyday conversations and thoughts and tangents and being lateral and being brought back down to ground again because the structure makes us not lose ourselves," says Droga. Yet any organizational support can only do so much if your company does not employ the right people. Droga points out that he employs the best strategists and the best creatives. The concepts of best-in-class and world-class excellence go together and can be felt in the office. It is represented by the open office layout, where the employees are served a company dinner if they would like to stay a bit longer. There was "a feeling of esprit" that they knew that they were the best. "It was one part religion and one part ethos mixed with athleticism and competitiveness," Droga states. "I think

Visualization of Concepts, Part 2: Journey

The world is becoming increasingly visual. In order to communicate effectively we need to come up with innovative, original and creative ways to show familiar concepts in unusual ways and unfamiliar concepts in familiar ways. Visualize the idea of journey with 9-12 images/key visuals.

The presentation can be produced in an abstract, concrete, symbolic, or descriptive way, or can also make use of analogies. The key visuals can be in relationship with each other (e.g. tell an overall story or script) or can be independent from each other.

This assignment should encourage you to be playful, take risks and experiment (try out new things you might not even think of).

The key visuals should have an appropriate size of 8 ½" x 11" to present to an audience of 6-10 people. You can use any visual design tools and/or elements available to you (e.g. photography, painting, crawing, collage, and objects).

it's a very collaborative, forward-thinking place. I like to think that there's a very generous culture in this agency—generous in how we share—and it's not 'kumbaya-ish' or we're all in it together. Creative people are as spectacularly selfish as they are gener ous, but I feel like a lot of people are very confident in their abilities, so they're generous with their thinking, generous with their time. And they are competitive too. I think I'm also a big proponent of friendly competitiveness."

The culture of each agency acknowledged the fact that one must know the rules of the game. This means that they need to respect the various processes and regulations of the agency. However, the fact that rules must be broken in order to create original and innovative work is also accepted within each culture. In recent years, the roles of the so-called creative have changed as well. Several agencies are still organized according to the different disciplines such as production, account management, media, strategy and creative. However, all of the agencies that I visited are making an effort to integrate and mix the different skills that the various departments bring to the table, combining them during all phases of the work process.

Tom Moudry of Martin Williams pointed out that every employee, including the receptionist, is encouraged to think creatively and encouraged to participate in every agency assignment. This means that anyone can contribute to the ideas and they do not necessarily have to think within their discipline. The same idea is echoed by Lynn Teo, who says that "an intern could be with us during a brainstorming session, and it could be that that person's idea is the one that has the most legs. So I do think that the organizational structure has to be flat." Many agencies are trying to create organizational structures in which the different departments interact more frequently with the freedom to share their ideas, no matter what their background or their position. Such structures can not only lead to more collective creativity and better products within the agency, but also can strengthen the creative performance of each individual.

Increasingly agencies are encouraging all departments and all employees to be creative. Roger Hurni, chief creative officer and founder of Off Madison Ave in Phoenix, focuses on creating an environment that is very collaborative and "that physically doesn't have walls." His second focus lies in "mixing everybody up amongst everybody else," ensuring that as many different skills are working together as possible. Hurni achieves this mix by maintaining a very flat organizational structure at his agency. "There's not a lot of hierarchy here as far as direct reports, and there's no chain of command if you want to get an idea here's how it gets approved. We don't just have an open door policy, we have a no door policy here, which goes back to the environment," Hurni says.

Mullen, a Boston-based agency, used to be located in a mansion in the outskirts of the city. "The old building had long, narrow hallways and little offices, you know, off to the side, and wings that shot out. The result was tremendous isolation, so it was really hard. Digital was down in the corner someplace, separate from creative, separate from user experience, separate from public relations, separate from social influence, and we all might have met each other in a conference room or seen each other at lunch in the cafeteria, but everybody worked in their little, separate office that had a door and a window, and it was closed off. And if people knew each other and bumped into each other, it was good, but we didn't have an environment or a physical place that helped achieve that at all," says Edward Boches.

Mullen's decision to move the office into downtown Boston can be seen as a major success factor in attracting talented employees. According to Edward Boches, the move allowed Mullen to leave a traditional office setting and design their new office space before moving in. The interior design and office layout of the new space allows employees to collaborate and share ideas. A greater and better integration of different skills into every new business pitch has enabled Mullen to become one of the most creative organizations and to win many new clients. Boches explains, "I should be really careful and make a point that we define creativity as the things that come out of the creative department, but I think there's as much creative thinking in account planning, in media, in the connected strategies we come up with, even in the ways in which we service business via the account group, as there is in creative. So we challenge everybody in a number of ways, making sure they're learning the technologies and thinking about *how* to be creative in those new technological spaces, whether it's location based or mobile or new things that are happening on the web or the iPad."

Even though some of the traditional departments still exist at Mullen, the traditional creative teams no longer exclusively develop creative ideas. The person responsible for business development provided several insights and developed ideas for apps and other components typically not included in traditional campaigns. "One of my most creative guys in this company is our new business development guy, who runs an iPhone app business on the side. We're doing iPhone apps nonstop for a lot of clients. He thinks up every one of them himself. He's an ex-account guy who's now on our new business group who thinks up iPhone apps, and he's incredibly creative about them. We've done iPhone apps for Lumber Liquidators, FoxWoods, Century 21, Stanley, Timberland and lots of other clients. He's done them all," Boches adds.

Several agencies have further developed their concept space and collaboration. In addition to describing the Goodby Silverstein & Partners climate and the physical space as "open and collaborative," Rich Silverstein mentions their "kitchen," a room designed to provide the physical attributes

"Every time the cukoo clock chimes we rotate seats." —Mother New York

similar to an open and warmly designed kitchen in a home, where everyone gathers and shares ideas and truths one normally does not talk about in a formal dining room, living room or office. The kitchen was also mentioned by Andrew Deitchman of Mother New York, an agency that has taken the concept of open space to another level by placing their kitchen at the entrance of the agency. The receptionist is situated in the middle of the kitchen: a special place where employees come together to enjoy coffee in the morning or an after-work drink before leaving for the day. The kitchen creates a centerpiece within the agency that acts as epicenter where employees, visitors and clients can mingle, run into each other and exchange ideas. Deitchman says, "The receptionists welcome you and it's like 'oh, come sit down in the kitchen and we'll bring you some coffee.' It creates an energy source in the office in an ongoing basis, because everybody is constantly going up and down into the kitchen."

Compared to many corporate office environments Mother's physical space is very raw and imperfect. According to Deitchman, this imperfection creates a casualness that allows everyone to stick work, or anything else they like, up on the wall. At Mother, everything is about change and everything is in motion. Client projects and creative work are always pinned up on the walls to represent work-in-progress and what's next, allowing employees to stay informed and get engaged in projects that they might not be working on actively. Seeing current work from various client projects gives everyone an overall sense of where the agency stands at any given moment. Even the office furniture is secondhand and swapped out constantly. "People are like 'Oh, that's a new couch, that's cool.' It's about a sense of imperfectly perfect and that the way things are today may not be the way they are tomorrow in our space. Everything from what's in our fridge to the couches to how people sit," notes Deitchman.

Every three months the agency changes up the seating arrangements so that no one can get too comfortable, allowing staff to get exposed to new tablemates every three months. "Nobody has an office, and one month you're sitting next to somebody who's a producer, somebody who's in finance, a creative director or a designer. And the next month you're sitting next to someone who works in brand experience and so on. So you're constantly exposed to new people with different personalities," says Deitchman.

This constant change and the sense that there is no permanence is paired with permanence in the environment, which is incredibly friendly and warm. Entering the agency, one immediately feels at home, and visitors and employees frequently say they'd love this to be their apartment or their house. This mix of physical and emotional environment creates an office in which employees do not want to leave; they just hang out. "And part of that is just having beer taps for people to help themselves and programming the space in interesting ways. It's not just about throwing parties. It's about having an environment where people want to bring their friends and hang out and spend time there. I don't want to say it's too calculated because it's not, it's just very naturally who we are, but at the same time, I'm really proud of it because it informs and drives our culture in a very significant way," adds Deitchman.

The creative leaders represented in the book all tap into the resources and creative problem-solving skills of all their employees. As leaders they are in tune with the talent employed at their companies and utilize it in the best way possible. Many creative leaders interviewed for this book mentioned that they are constantly in touch with their employees. They make themselves available when employees need feedback or would like to discuss something. All employ either a "no door" or an "open door" philosophy, which means that they are always accessible and available to others. Margaret Johnson of Goodby Silverstein & Partners says, "You can come see us anytime. We have a lot of great creative directors and associate creative directors, and I think that support system really helps the younger creatives who are rising up. The same goes for the account side. There's kind of a structure in the agency to support everyone at every level so it works out nicely." Several other agencies have put in place a process that enables, requires or encourages employees of all ranks and discipline to participate and contribute to the projects the agency is working on.

Whether it is a company, an advertising agency or a nonprofit, every organization experiences day-to-day routines, where work is being completed with established teams and in familiar group settings. In order to optimize and standardize business, agencies often employ specialists over a long time in a specific skill category. For many years, traditional agencies have established experienced and highly specialized teams typically in the areas of creative, management, media and production. These teams focus on specific categories such as automotive (e.g. Mitsubishi), OTC drugs (e.g. Nuprin) and fast food (e.g. McDonald's). Though there are good reasons for specialization, creative agencies today are trying to mix up teams and get fresh and diverse skill sets for every client as early in the process as possible. Chris Foster sums up the people aspect of managing workgroups: "Creativity does not happen in a vacuum. Creativity, as it relates to my per-

Openness can be seen in several aspects at Big Spaceship.

spectives, relates to the people. That is the thing that makes creativity happen: People of different cultures, different backgrounds and different perspectives all rubbing together. They all come at a problem from different angles, and from that, you get that sort of dramatic tension where creativity is sponsored." Lynn Teo, customer experience expert and former chief experience officer at AKQA and McCann Erickson in New York, points out that managers have to make sure that the organization structure empowers creative work. Establishing flat structures and reducing hierarchies in traditionally large agencies has been one of the many challenges in managing and fostering a creative climate. Woody Kay, executive creative director at Arnold Worldwide in Boston, says that they are "trying to get a much flatter structure so that everybody who touches the product is empowered to talk to the client. Ultimately, whether you're pyramid or flat, the objective is to keep the work pure."

Doug Spong believes that "creativity is not limited to the twelfth floor, to our creative department. We are all expected to and encouraged to be creative in everything we do." David Droga of Droga5 claims that "creativity comes from the agency and the culture. And the culture is now bigger than any department." Departments are becoming much more integrated and collaborative with each other, a fact which results in more agility and which translates into quicker processes and better ideas. A small number of companies has even gone further and abolished the word *creative* from their business cards, as well as other departmental labels. Michael Lebowitz of Big Spaceship concludes that everyone in his organization is creative and must be proficient in creative thinking and problem solving. "We're the only agency that I know of in the world that has no creative directors. Nobody has *creative* in their title, I don't allow it. No one directs creativity in a way that [means] everyone is responsible for

creativity. We don't call people creatives, which I think is one of the most awful things about the industry, [meaning] that somehow there is just one group of people who are 'the creatives.' So everyone here is creative, that's just a baseline. Everybody participates in creativity. [Everyone] is responsible for and has the mandate of bringing creativity to the table."

But creativity and collaboration can become more challenging as organizations grow. Several agencies have developed electronic tools that encourage collaboration by providing opportunities for employees to post and comment on their coworkers' ideas. Tim Leake, director of growth & innovation at RPA and former creative director and director of creative innovation of Saatchi New York, describes what can happen when agencies miss out on developing tools for sharing knowledge and ideas. "It is sort of a shame that we don't somehow get like-minded people to get together, because we can get great things to happen. So like-minded people would sometimes find each other, but we couldn't really collaborate because we didn't work in the same pieces of business. We all got frustrated and left."

Many agencies do their best to provide as much organizational support for their employees as possible so that they can be the best that they can be. Blake Ebel, founder of Fear Not Agency in Denver and former chief creative officer at Euro RSCG Chicago, believes that "it's important [to get] people what they need to succeed, whether that's the right equipment or the right training." Similarly Roger Hurni said that the agency supports its employees "in any kinds of seminars they want to go to." They send people as far away as Paris and as close as down the street. "It just depends on what it is and what they need to do in the organization," he says. This kind of support allows the employees of an agency to get inspired by outside stimuli and be able to come up with more interesting and innovative ideas that they may not have come up with otherwise.

Every idea is welcome at Euro RSCG.

A growing trend for agencies is to invest a lot time and money into outside support and inspiration because it reflects an ostensible investment in their future. Robert Sherlock says that his agency invests "an incredible amount of money and time because we believe it's exactly right. It is developing and nurturing and creating basically better employees for themselves and for the company."

Agencies like Goodby Silverstein & Partners and Fallon go further and bring creative talents from the outside into the agency without connecting the talent to any specific project. Fallon regularly hosts exhibitions and performances by local artists to connect with creative activities that lie outside the projects that the agency is working on. Margaret Johnson considers the exchange with creative people outside the agency a necessity. "We do a lot of things with music. We bring bands in; or we do a lot of things in the arts, like we created our own documentaries or bring in lots of directors and talent to share all the creative things that they're working on. So I feel like the environment here feels really creative and that is an interesting rub, because I think you need the things outside of work to fuel the things inside of you."

In some cases the outside work can inspire projects the agency is working on down the road. "We have a lot of bands that come and perform for the agency and a lot of times that'll spark something," says Johnson. "You hear a piece of music and then maybe two months down the road you're finishing up on a commercial that's going on the air or something really cool digitally that you're going to do as a stunt or online, and you remember that piece of music, and it may shape the idea in a different way than you had originally thought. You bring that with you. You, kind of, are able to infuse that piece of music into an idea that you didn't have to begin with."

David Droga believes in the combination of art and technology and also in supporting his employees' outside lives. "When people need extra training, whether it is something that is fundamental to helping them here (at work), we encourage them to pick a course and we will support that. But there are times when the course will have nothing to do with what this agency does, but it contributes to their personal growth. If it's not outrageous and we can do it, then we will definitely help. We're constantly offering seminars and courses. One can be as ridiculous as learning how to do taxes, which everybody needs. Or someone might want to do a whole class on knitting. They're equally complicated, taxes and knitting; there are some parallels between the two. Also, we're linked to the new museum; we are deep believers in the expression of all types," says Droga.

R/GA also embraces the interests that their employees have outside of work. Bob Greenberg, the CEO of the agency, collects art from the "out of bounds" people who might be considered at the outskirt of societal norms. Looking into different disciplines and learning from them can ignite new inspiration and allow for people to have insightful and unique ideas that they could have had otherwise. In many of the interviews that I conducted, it seemed clear that the creative executives encouraged their employees to have interests outside of work and to get inspiration from these sources. Marshall Ross, the chief creative officer of Cramer Krasselt, says that "the people who are good, or who are successful within creative organizations, are people who are learning constantly from lots of different resources. They learn from their friends; they learn from their peers." This was also reflected when I asked our interviewees how they like to stay inspired and creative. Many of them pointed to the fact that they seek inspiration from outside of their industry and by embracing their surroundings. Rob Schwartz says, "I see inspiring things, and sometimes I go 'Ooo, I can use that for this project.'" For Rich Silverstein, it is the juggling of sport, business, family, pleasure and arts that provides energy and insight during his creative process. "It's a love of what's going on in the world, rather than what's going on in advertising. I mean, what's in my room reflects things that I'm interested in. Like kitty cat art, New York City, books, information, sport, design, craft, heritage, all those things," says Silverstein.

Throughout the interviews, another concept emerged that I call collective intelligence. As we have seen, collaboration plays a great role in a modern organization, requiring the combination of many different areas of expertise. However, collaboration is no longer limited to the conversations during meeting times: when everyone who is involved with an agency project is in the same room. Agencies are turning into gallery spaces and museums, where every project is openly displayed and presented for everyone to see. Every employee is encouraged to look at and be aware of all the work that the agency is producing. All are encouraged to participate in the process, regardless of their rank, position or department, in order to create and produce the best work possible.

Marshall Ross, chief creative officer at Cramer Krasselt, said that his agency utilizes something called the "show and tell blackboard" upon which people can post any ideas that they want to share with others. "What we do is not a solitary thing," says Doug Spong. "This is not an individual sport.

It's a team sport. And what our employees love to do is to be around other highly creative people that they can feed off that energy, that passion, [people] they can actually learn from."

In order to produce the best work possible, agencies are beginning to understand that teamwork is crucial and truly the key to breakthrough thinking. Ideas are not exclusively tied to the creative department and where they originate no longer matters. They can come from anywhere. Tim Leake adds, "You have an environment where it's okay that that idea got said by an account person and now the creatives are going to go do something with it." At Euro RSCG, "anyone's idea is welcome to the wall... whether you're a planner, producer, creative—it doesn't matter to me," says Blake Ebel.

These public displays of ideas, as well as the participation and creative involvement of different individuals, are a perfect example of what Teresa Amabile describes in her various Harvard Business School Press articles and the KEYS elements assessment. The process of combining and including the collective intelligence of every employee will lead to a learning organization. This kind of environment can help an agency push boundaries and reach new insights. The documentary *The Pixar Story* by Leslie Iwerks allows viewers to see the inner workings of Pixar Studios, a highly creative organization. It is a place where employees embrace learning from others as well as from each other. Ed Catmull describes several insights in his Harvard Business School Press article "How Pixar Fosters Collective Creativity." He says that is "of great importance and something that sets us apart from other studios. It is the way people at all levels support one another. Everyone is fully invested in helping everyone else turn out the best work. They really do feel that it's all for one and one for all. Nothing exemplifies this more than our creative brain trust and our daily review process."

Brain trust at Pixar is when people get together when they need assistance and present their ideas to others. "There's no ego," says Catmull. "Nobody pulls any punches to be polite. This works because all the participants have come to trust and respect one another ... The problem-solving powers of this group are immense and inspirational to watch."

Another element of the culture at Pixar is what Catmull calls "the dailies," which is a process for giving and getting constant feedback in a positive way. He says that this process has a few benefits: "First one, people get over the embarrassment of showing work still in progress; they become more creative. People learn from and inspire each other ... and there are no surprises at the end."

Catmull speaks about a peer culture that is open to criticism, where everyone helps each other in order to become better at what they are doing. Every employee is encouraged to actively participate in making the organization better in every possible aspect. This means that communication among employees is open and can happen independently of rank, title and discipline. Digital technology certainly has helped encourage this and allows people not to be tied to just one kind of communication channel. Managers and leaders that used to be inaccessible from the outside are nowadays available via LinkedIn, Twitter, Yammer or through internal communication tools and platforms—or simply through an open-door policy.

Within the open spaces of the many agencies I visited, a few offices still do have doors. However, the creative minds behind those doors encourage the open-door policy in their physical environments.

The "learning environment" or "learning organization" is another key aspect confirmed throughout the interviews as well as a concept that is mentioned in Catmull's article. He says that at Pixar they adhere to a few principles on a daily basis.

Hello!

Imagine this situation: You just finished a job interview at a company. Now you're on your way home thinking, *Shit, I probably blew it. That wasn't very good.*

But you have the mobile phone number for the CEO or Chief Creative Officer and you think, *I'll send him a text message to convince him that I'm the right person for the job.* Your message is limited to 160 characters, including spaces.

What do you write?

Have fun with this assignment. If you do a good job, you will be invited back.

The "Hello" exercise is adapted from a copytest by Jung v. Matt, London, http://www.jvm.com/en/home/index.html.

First of all, everyone must have the freedom to communicate with anyone. "This means recognizing that the decision-making hierarchy and communication structure in an organization are two different things." He mentions that people from different departments need to feel the freedom to communicate with each other and collaborate, and that hierarchy is not an issue when it comes to communication. Secondly, it must be safe for everyone to offer ideas. This means that no matter what someone's position or discipline, anyone has the power to give his or her opinion or offer an idea. Finally, Catmull says, "We must stay close to innovations happening in the academic community."

This refers to the idea of breaking down the walls between different disciplines and departments, as well to being in touch with the latest technical developments and research findings. Catmull also emphasizes the idea of "unplanned collisions" which I mentioned in earlier examples. "Most buildings are designed for some functional purpose," he says, "but ours is structured to maximize inadvertent encounters... It's hard to describe just how valuable the resulting chance encounters are."

The Pixar documentary also provides a valuable lesson expressed by Steve Jobs: "The last trick does not work anymore," he said. This means that in order to duplicate a successful product, for example a computer or movie, we should not just apply a formula that might have been responsible for our success in the first place, but take on every challenge and product innovation with a fresh perspective and consider new situation specific solutions. Jobs speaks of the "second product failure syndrome" that often happens after launching the first successful product. According to Jobs, developing a second product does not automatically lead to a successful launch based on the fact that the first product was successful. In creative industries this is even truer, since the "production of creative products and/or campaigns" is the whole raison d'etre[1] of these industries. Every new client and each new project requires the creator or the agency to hit the reset button and to come up with something innovative, new and original. This is a concept that is quite different from traditional manufacturing, where ideas and products are developed but then produced for a relatively long time. Rich Silverstein is very much

Everyone is responsible for creativity at Big Spaceship.

aware of this situation. "The agency has to remain fresh by constantly being relevant and reinventing ourselves every five years," he says. "You cannot rest on your laurels. I'm in the hall of fame in the Art Directors Club[2] and also in the One Club.[3] Well that's pretty impressive, you might think, but it means nothing. Because a young person can come in and it's 'what have you done for me today?' You have to come up with an idea each day. So we have to reinvent the company. We can't rest on what we did twenty years ago or even five years ago. Or even last month."

Being innovative requires a person or an organization to challenge the status quo and to be open to new possibilities. This openness can be experienced and observed in all of the agencies featured in this book. Yet nobody illustrates this better than Big Spaceship and Mother New York. Michael Lebowitz of Big Spaceship struck me as unusually open to everything new, whether it was a new intern, a request for an interview or a new project. Openness can be seen in several aspects at Big Spaceship. First, there is Lebowitz's organizational philosophy that the "company is a canvas." This is an excellent metaphor for a learning organization, where collaboration and learning take place and where new thinking and ideas are a must (this will be discussed in more detail in the next chapter). The physical space and the way the different disciplines are organized demonstrate how important the concept being open is taken at Big Spaceship, where technology turns into tools, palettes and possibilities.

According to Lebowitz, "The output of the company is not design, and it's not technology, and it's not project management and production or account service, and it's not strategy. It's the amalgamation of all of those things, so why would we organize ourselves as though the output is one thing at any given time, rather than all those things at any given time? I sort of fell in love with the cross-disciplinary approach, and I'll never go back."

Lebowitz has identified the power of the physical space and designed a workspace environment that not only fosters collaboration, but also positively influences how his employees feel about the company and each other. Since many different talents collaborate and influence each other's individual creativity, as well as the overall creative product Big Spaceship delivers, openness is also illustrated by the physical space where everyone works. Lebowitz explains the rationale behind why his office resembles an open factory space. "We seat people together in cross-disciplinary teams, and our space has gotten a little small for us."

One day Lebowitz had an aha moment and reorganized the team and put people in the aisles between the tables. That way, they concentrate outward, toward their computers and, as soon as there's a problem to solve or a moment of inspiration, all they have to do is turn their chairs inward and they're conferring with each other. "Reduce the friction involved in collaboration to as little as possible. Because the half-life of inspiration is really short. By the time you have set up a conference room meeting or tracked somebody down, your enthusiasm for it may have dissipated and you won't get others as excited as you are about it or a little problem has already snowballed into a much larger one while you were waiting to find a place to get everybody together. The openness of the plan is very intentionally oriented toward rapid communication. What we're doing more and more of is trying to identify the different types of behaviors outside of that, so we can create physical space that accommodates those behaviors. So I've noticed there are more people who are taking laptops and going to sit on couches to, sort of, type quietly. Okay, so we need more lounging and relaxing space, so how do we build up the space so we have more of that, and it's not that I want people doing that all the time, but I want the opportunity for it, so they can fold themselves in and out of the communal space as they need to," says Lebowitz.

He describes that many traditional agencies still employ a more top-down approach and processes that require employees to fit in. He argues that following a certain production process might favor people with certain talents and not consider someone with possibly different or inadequate talents. But Lebowitz sees an opportunity to change and improve any process in order to maximize the different talents of many people. "If you take my approach, where the teams are responsible for figuring out how to do it, and it's grassroots, and it bubbles up, then it can, at its best, extract maximum talent out of everybody, as long as they are committed to the collaboration and the caring part of it. Because collaboration is the interface of talent and knowledge and vocation. And taking care of each other is the personal, 'I actually care that you do well, not just that I do well,' and that actually creates transparency. No one can hide

Know Your Audience

Invent a product that every retiree (a person of age 70 and above) in America would buy.

in a system where people are taking care of each other. It's really clear when somebody isn't. That builds trust and surfaces problems quickly," says Lebowitz.

Andrew Deitchman of Mother New York expressed a similar approach. "We have creative directors for every discipline; we don't have account management in the traditional sense from an agency perspective." Mother dismissed the idea that an agency requires someone who essentially is just a liaison between client and agency. When Mother was founded in London in the 1990s, a greater emphasis was put on the realization that creative people need to take responsibility for understanding the client's business, and clients need to sit around the table along with the agency. "If a client wants to talk about copy, they should talk to a copywriter, if they want to talk about strategy, they should talk to a strategist and not to an account person, who is then going to interpret that and kind of play the game," says Deitchman.

Mother tries hard to eliminate as many walls as possible and to get as many people as possible to have direct conversations to keep the organization flat. This helps prevent people from saying, "Well, that's not my job" or "I'm not a designer" or "I don't have an opinion on that." Deitchman insists that everyone should have an educated opinion and says, "[Surely] you can say [whether it] look[s] good or not [or if] you like it or not? So all of this sort of breaks that down. At the same time, every discipline is required to solve the client's problem in creative ways."

Mother embraces the different disciplines of arts and technologies, where employees are celebrated as equals to a degree I have rarely seen in any agency or corporate environment. Diversity plays a huge role here, and there is a clear focus on bringing people from different disciplines together who respect each other. Treating one another as peers is just as important as getting people within disciplines to do so. Deitchman believes in "being generous with your ideas—it will always come back." The culture at Mother is obviously very open—and the fact that the organization does not shy away from exploring different disciplines and collaborating is truly reflected in the exceptional work produced there.

CHAPTER NINE

CREATIVITY AND PHILOSOPHY

During the interviews with various creative executives, the dimension of *philosophy* emerged in addition to the 4Ps: place, person, process and product. A clear overarching agency philosophy can influence the climate of an organization and, when paired with a focus on the creative product, can define a creative organization internally and externally, helping it to stand out among the competition, and provide an organization with its intrinsic motivation.

Across the board, I noticed that each one of the agencies that I visited had something special and unique beating in the hearts of those interviewed and their employees. An invisible force represented a mix of belonging, optimism and a can-do attitude. Among the employees and throughout the agencies, I detected an attitude of "There is nothing that can't be solved!" It was a pledge that seemed cult-like or emblematic of elite military groups such as the Navy SEALs. Everyone I encountered seemed excited and motivated to be part of his or her respective agency. Motivation is something all individuals possess and is usually expressed as a driving force influenced by intrinsic and extrinsic factors. Based on my interviews, I believe that an organization as a whole

The pirate culture at TBWA\Chiat\Day is apparent in many different ways.

can have intrinsic motivation as well, and that it is manifested as the agency philosophy.

All of the creative executives describe their respective company culture as one that places a strong emphasis on creativity. This emphasis often is reflected physically in the spaces in which employees work fully engaged and collaboratively in open environments. Beyond this, many of the executives mentioned an aspect that I would call an overarching philosophy or ideology. The agency philosophy influences the culture and represents the organizations' intrinsic motivation to be the best within their domain of expertise. Often the company's founders or leaders' commitment to creative excellence represents that intrinsic aspect of motivation that is seen on an individual and personal level.

Rich Silverstein and Margaret Johnson, executive creative directors and partners at Goodby Silverstein & Partners, say that "creativity is everything" and that it represents the core of their agency. As Silverstein says, "Creativity to our agency is [like] air or water. You die without creativity. It is why we're here. It is what we should be doing." Through creativity, Goodby Silverstein & Partners has developed a strong new philosophy to "make stuff people care about." The goal is to elevate their work to a place beyond advertising and to take on a bigger role in people's lives. Johnson said that all of the work that they produce at Goodby Silverstein & Partners is constantly put through a filter of questions such as "Who cares about this?" "Why is this a creative idea?" and "Is this going to make a difference?" If the answer to any of these questions is no, the team goes in a different direction. In this way, an overarching philosophy helps ensure that everyone in the organization is moving in the same direction. Says Johnson, "it helps when everybody has a north star, and we are all working towards the same thing."

TBWA\Chiat\Day uses the philosophy of "Disruption" and "Media Arts." According to TBWA\Chiat\Day, disruption represents "the art of challenging conventional wisdom and overturning assumptions that get in the way of imagining new possibilities and visionary ideas," and is a concept that can be applied to many aspects of business. Combined with TBWA\Chiat\Day's culture of piracy, the leaders are taking creativity one step further and are constantly pushing themselves to deliver more than what is expected of them.

David Droga of Droga5 produces great creative results by bringing together the best minds in planning and strategy, and mixing them with the best creative skills in storytelling, production art direction, copywriting and digital software development. Droga says that his overarching philosophy is "to build the most influential creative business in the world." He acknowledges that his philosophy is ambitious and "ridiculously a stretch," especially when he wants to achieve this within an entire industry.

Droga is aware that in order to succeed, he has to overcome several challenges. "We have to be successful for our clients," he says. "We have to contribute to society in a positive way; we have to rub up against other industries; we have to influence pop culture; we have to bring in the best new talent; we have to elevate our industry. I want to do great things with that, and as I said, that's our goal, we have to build the brands of the twenty-first century, but at the same time, it's creativity with purpose."

For Droga, creativity is the fuel and the foundation of his agency. "It's not biased toward the creative department. We are a creative company so we have great thinkers across many functions. While we're a celebrated creative agency, our special secret source in the agency is our strategic thinking." Droga considers himself lucky to be living in an era where "we can do great things with our imagination" and where communication is the newest and most powerful instrument needed in order to make a positive impact on the world. As he explains, "Creativity is no longer a sort of cute-little-nice-thing to have. It plays a massive role in society, and I'm glad that we're part of it. I'm also glad that we're in a time now where advertising isn't this one little pigeonholed thing where it's just about selling soap powder on TV and print ads. There's nothing wrong with those things, but we can do so much more than that. We can help raise awareness of prices or raise money or contribute to pop culture or build industry—save industry. We're not going to cure cancer but maybe we can help the doctor who is. And I feel like we want to touch and influence and make better every day. Everybody, communication and messaging and education, play a part in all fabrics of life, and that's not to say that all advertising is good advertising. I get it, I know. I understand that 90 percent of advertising is garbage, and it's pollution. That's why I like to operate in the 10 percent that's actually trying to do something better."

Michael Lebowitz of Big Spaceship explains that his philosophy is "take care of each other"

Visualize Your Personal Future

Create a mental image of where and how you see yourself personally within the next year. Use magazines, newspapers, art supplies, items found in nature and paper, and create a collage that represents your idea visually. (This exercise can be repeated regularly).

combined with the concept that the "company is the canvas." In other words, every employee is a creator and artist. Lebowitz provides an interesting concept to managing for creativity and developing one of the best creative climates within the marketing communication and advertising industry I have come across. The teams at Big Spaceship are responsible for figuring out how to accomplish the work that needs to be done and to deliver the creative products and solutions for which their clients are looking.

The two concepts provide a philosophical framework that enables and, at the same time, challenges employees to be creative and to live a creative life that goes beyond the domain knowledge of the specific discipline in which they work. Lebowitz says that his philosophy has developed over time. He also acknowledges that each individual employee plays an important role in his organization. He is keenly aware of the duality between the individual and the group. "It's how people interface with each other," he says. "So the individual is obviously part of a wildly important component, but it is a component; and openness to others' points of view, and then willingness and an interface for collaboration with people who do other things and have other crafts. Those are the primary things ... for me the thing that makes ... great things in innovation come from great things bumping up against each other. Because the actual creativity in my mind, how I think about it is what emerges out of the connections between people rather than what emerges out of a person."

Andrew Deitchman, the CEO of Mother New York, says that his overarching agency philosophy is "unlocking creative potential." Like the other agencies that I interviewed, Mother New York holds creativity at the core. But Deitchman uses creativity for something beyond advertising and communication. Mother's purpose lies in unleashing creativity where it does not yet exist, be it among clients, consumers, products or everything surrounding them. "Did we unlock something?" he asks after each creative production. "Did we unlock creative potential in this brand, in this individual, in a company, in ourselves, in some way?" Mother is constantly weighing whether or not they achieved that goal, and, if not, how they can redo or make adjustments.

Deitchman also sees Mother as part of redefining the changes currently going on in the advertising industry. Instead of calling Mother an advertising agency, Deitchman uses the term "a modern creating company." As a long-term goal, Mother wants to be better known and more relevant to creators on a very broad scale. Deitchman draws a comparison to Goldman Sachs in the financial services industry and to any parents' positive reaction when they hear that their child got a job there after graduating with a finance degree. Ten years from now Deitchman would like Mother to become the Goldman Sachs of the creative realm.

"Whether a kid is coming out of journalism school or film school or design school or architecture school or something involving technology and so on, and he tells his mom and dad his first job is at Mother ... 'Oh, my God, I'm so happy for you!' They know what that is. They are excited for him because our brand becomes this celebrated company that has very wide, very open arms to a very broad group of creators. Because we've always embraced the fact that the definition of us as a company is incredibly broad. It's more about attracting the most creative people and the output could be anything," says Deitchman.

He sees Mother continuing to expand because marketing and entertainment are becoming the same thing, because public private partnerships are happening, and schools and playgrounds are going to be funded by brands, and because of how Mother integrates technology at a festival to provide people with the best possible experience. "It needs to be something interesting and creative, and it's going to bring together a very diverse set of minds. People who are tech people, people who are architects, people who are writers and storytellers. The company will be made up of many different types of creators, who are going to need to come together in interesting ways in order to be successful and because of this, there's a potential for much invention to happen. I think clients will be coming to companies like us for outsourced innovation, in a much broader way, not just for ad campaigns, particularly as they are bringing more and more of that in-house. And so we have to think of ourselves as this very broad sort of creative magnet and creating company, not a company that's going to create messages for clients or create bespoke content based on paid media," notes Deitchman.

Mullen's philosophy, "Advertising Unbound," represents a culture that is "entirely about limitless possibilities and a relentless belief in a future that is bigger than the past. It is how we started our company. It's how we built it. It is how we continue to evolve and innovate."[1] Edward Boches reflects on how and why this philosophy was developed. "We used to have a line, which was 'Relentless creativity that built brands and businesses.' And we got rid of all that and we came up with one word: *unbound*. And we have that embedded throughout the company in whole bunch of ways. We have a piece of artwork upstairs in the café. The word is on our business cards, and the word is in every video that we do, and the word is spoken throughout the company. All it essentially means is that you have to be open-minded to anything as a potential solution. You can't be bound by tradition, you can't be bound by advertising, and you can't be bound by the idea of thinking we're in the business of making a message. You have to believe that the solution to a marketing problem or a creative problem or a client's objectives could be anything. It might be a new product that we invent for them. It might be a digital experience or a platform. It might be an iPhone app. And I think we probably came up with that word approach because historically we were a traditional ad agency that made print ads, radio spots, TV spots, etc., and that was in our muscle memory as the product that solved every problem, and sometimes institutional muscle memory is hard to change. You can't change it in increments; you've got to leap way over here and say, 'This is the new target.' And when we put that word into effect and tried to change everything by aspiring to that as something we wanted to reach but also something we wanted to change," says Boches.

The Mullen example represents the way in which an organization's philosophy can permeate everything, and everyone who works there becomes the glue that holds it together. It is clear that *unbound* is a concept that is ingrained in everything that is done at Mullen and is the driving force behind the creative work that is being produced.

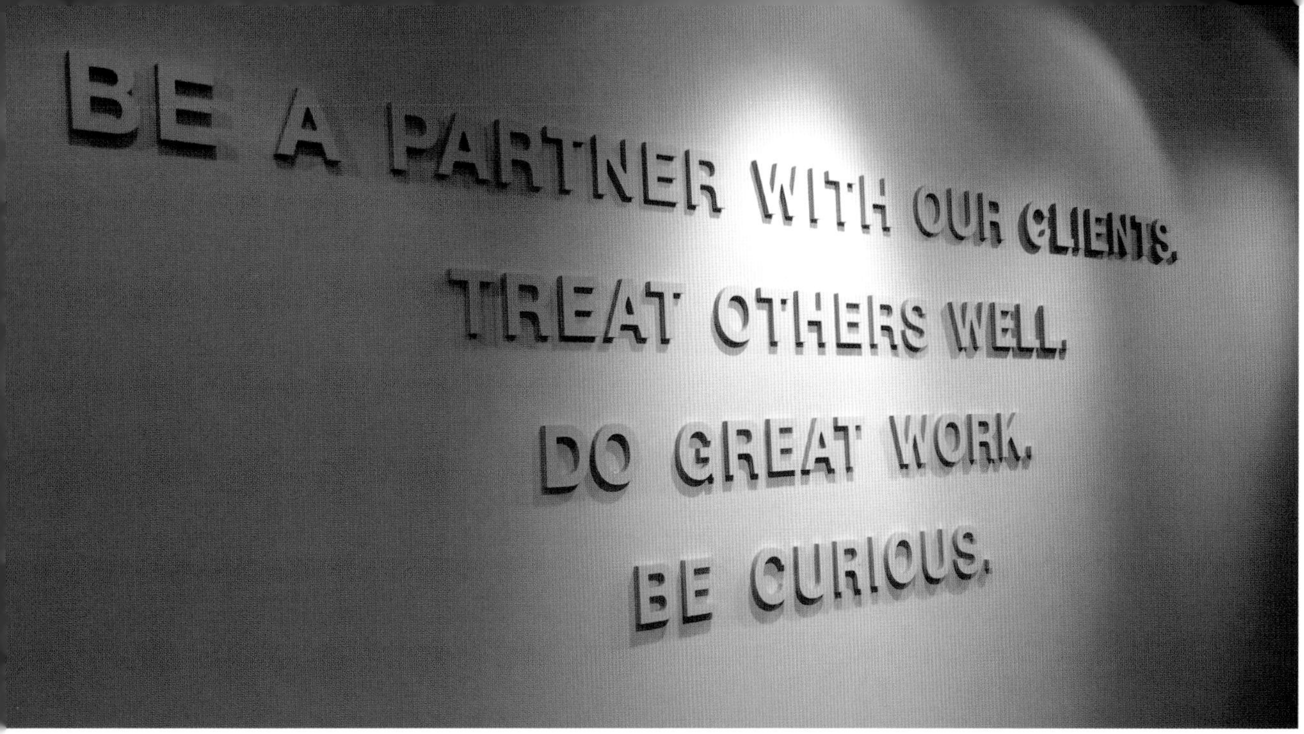

Martin Williams's agency philosophy centers on people, relationships and the right climate.

For Off Madison Ave, creativity is truly at the heart and soul of everything they do. According to Roger Hurni, creativity is a hodgepodge of personal and work experience and personal opinions. It is all about allowing employees to dig out what the best ideas and solutions are for their clients' problems. "It's messy and it's unstructured and it can be sort of difficult to navigate to a point where we have something we want to put in front of a client, but at the same time, it sort of works for us," says Hurni. That is why Hurni has added an overarching philosophy that holds the messiness together. "Our mantra is *outthink, outperform*. And so we try very hard to hire and inspire people to be better than they are and to be a part of something larger than themselves. If they can do that they'll find their own sort of gratification and their own careers take off and it sort of feeds into itself in terms of being very motivating and very creative in its approach." According to Hurni, the focus on creativity paired with his philosophy has allowed Off Madison and its employees "to not just go with the flow, but to zig when everybody zags."

Marshall Ross of Cramer Krasselt has a simple overarching agency philosophy. "It's a popularity contest. And the brand with the most friends wins. Done. So we try to build brands, and we try to make work and deliver ideas for brands that are inherently likeable and that are built for helping brands not just to transact business, but literally build a friendship base, because brands and, most of all, friends have friends." In order to achieve this goal of getting the most friends for his clients, Ross utilizes creativity as much as possible. "It's our product. And I think what's important for an agency is to recognize that the definition of creativity needs to be very open. If we don't bring creativity, we don't bring surprise or novelty to readjust the positions."

According to Ross, his overarching agency philosophy and focus on creativity will allow him and Cramer Krasselt to not only adjust to the changes happening in the advertising and marketing industry but also to be a better leader. Ross says, "This is the most interesting time to be in business. So you just have to be in front of those changes ... you'll have to deconstruct those walls all over again and with a much quicker life cycle than anyone would have thought. You have to sort of embrace the fact that, almost like the fashion industry, you are on a never-ending journey of change, and the journey is going to go up and down and sideways and, you've got to be the right where the change happens. Or you've got trouble."

Martin Williams's overarching agency philosophy centers on people, relationships and the right climate. The agency philosophy hangs on the wall in the office in big letters and serves as a constant reminder of what is truly important to the organization. "Our philosophy is what's on that wall," Tom Moudry says. "We do have an overarching agency philosophy and we try to be collaborative and partners with our clients. I think if you're not it's very difficult to get good work done. We treat others well, we do great work and the last thing on our lobby wall is 'Don't be grabby.' And we say that humorously, but I mean it. There's a lot around here, and we'd rather have somebody steal a laptop rather than suck the energy out of this place. And one negative person can do that in a culture. I will help you steal a laptop over the weekend but don't steal our momentum or our enthusiasm. And people can do that—one person can have an extraordinary and devastating effect on the culture."

Susan Credle mentions the consumer perspective when she explains the agency philosophy of Leo Burnett. HumanKind is the guiding principle that makes everyone in the agency consider how consumers will feel when they are exposed to the creative product of the agency. HumanKind allows the agency to look beyond any facts and features a brand might have and focus on the benefits that people experience. Credle says, "Brands exist to make people's lives better in some way. It might make you hipper or cooler, or tougher, or stronger." HumanKind helps Leo Burnett in their quest to find the true purpose of a brand. Credle adds, "I think HumanKind is so important because it leads to better creative work. But I actually think it serves as a guide for the company."

If every brand is challenged to serve HumanKind, the world will ultimately become a better place. The overarching philosophy is closely connected to the ten principles that help Leo Burnett evaluate every idea they develop for their clients. The top three evaluation criteria are the most difficult to achieve, but they clearly include the concept of HumanKind and focus on the impact that an idea has on people: Does the idea change the way people feel? Does it change the way people act? Does it change the world? And HumanKind goes beyond communication and experiences. It allows clients and the agency to have a long-term perspective and to widen the services they offer. Credle says, "So HumanKinds are a brand's purpose. This isn't just good for a creative product but is actually good for future forward thinking and where you could possibly go as a business. And if you own that, it's really exciting. And especially today, when people want to talk with friends and communicate, you have to stand for something." Credle adds that it is not just about advertising anymore. It is all about doing good and having a cause. "I think that we have the moral responsibility in this business to not only do work that's good for the brand, but to do work that's good for the world," she says.

When I visited Fallon in Minneapolis, I immediately noticed a sign, reading, "We are Fallon." Chris Foster chairman, regional CEO, Saatchi & Saatchi Asia-Pacific and Greater China and former CEO of Fallon in Minneapolis explains: "[We are Fallon] is a our mantra. You see it, you feel it, there is a sense of pride, as sense of family, a sense of cohesion that goes beyond the task at hand. This isn't a job to most people: It is a calling; it's a pursuit. People really believe in the work we do here,

"The death of marketing as we know it." —Anomaly New York

and believe in its importance, and believe in the fact that we can change the world, basically. And that's really, really important."

Foster describes the agency philosophy as "our focus to do brave work that makes a difference." He says that Fallon's key focus lies on the creative product that the agency produces. Fallon achieves creative results through having a global view of creativity. Foster adds, "Even though we're based in Minneapolis, we make sure that we have a world view. That's born out in the fact that we have clients from around the world—we're doing projects in western Europe, we did some work with Thailand, we work with a bank in Abu Dhabi, and we have a multinational staff of people. So more and more, the world is a global place, and there's no reason we shouldn't be working on these types of clients and bringing that perspective to our American clients. Our goal is to do brave work that makes a difference, and we do that through a worldview of creativity."

Foster sees creativity as something that creates an unfair advantage. "If you have some kind of solution, some creative way of solving a problem that is or can be an economic multiplier, then creativity is a purpose-based thing. We're not here to make art films. We're not here to make the world a more beautiful place. We're here to solve business problems. So there's a very practical view of creativity that comes with the Fallon proposition, which has got to be attached to a business problem or has to get you to a better place as a result of that creativity thinking. So I think that's the nature of creativity for this place."

For Johnny Vulkan, cofounder of Anomaly New York, creativity represents the core of everything Anomaly stands for. He describes his philosophy: "Creativity makes the difference in something having an impact," and creativity without purpose is just indulgence. Vulkan is not interested in doing something new or crazy for the sake of it or in creating something to impress the industry. He says that "creativity is the holy grail" and that it provides the foundation for conducting a successful business. Creativity allows Vulkan to make positive change and to achieve positive business results for his clients. He points out that his job is commerce, not art, and that creativity must be applied to business problems. Referencing German designer Dieter Rams and English designer Jonathan Ive, Vulkan says the goal is not just to build a beautiful thing, but starting each project with a functional benefit that ends up being beautiful. Every project that Anomaly takes on has to work successfully, and aesthetics are an added benefit. This approach is a reminder of the Bauhaus movement and the belief that "form follows function" or "form follows business success" that is often achieved through originality and novelty.

WHY LEADERSHIP MATTERS

The philosophy of an agency is largely a reflection of the leadership of the organization. It takes a great leader to be able to home in on the creative potential of his or her employees and to use this power in the best way possible. A highly creative person must develop at least one or more specific domain skills and work hard at developing them. Individuals can achieve creative excellence with constant practice, tenacity and commitment—and by applying some of the concepts introduced in previous chapters. Mastering personal creative abilities is easier and more manageable than developing the creativity in organizations. Becoming a great leader who can lead companies toward creative excellence poses a greater challenge due to the complexity of creativity and the difficulty of managing the numerous factors that can influence the creative outcome.

Highly creative individuals do not necessarily make great leaders in a creative organization. The creativity 4Ps of person, process, place and product—framework provides a foundation for better understanding how creativity works. It may not be perfect and by no means is it all-inclusive. However, it provides a holistic model to look at four distinct dimensions that can greatly influence the creative outcome of any organization.

In order to discover what it takes to be a great leader, we need to understand how creativity happens at the individual level and how employees can be empowered in order to expand on it. The creative abilities of an individual depend on their ability and willingness to think divergently and convergently, as well as the way in which the individual uses creative problem-solving processes. Implementing a creative problem-solving process not only strengthens an individual's thinking ability, but also provides a framework for an entire organization that will increase the chances of higher creative output. As we have seen in the previous chapter, the physical place and the cultural environment are influential factors when it comes to the creative output of employees and the organization. Being aware of the many factors associated with the place component can provide leaders with managerial tools that can influence and improve any creative organization.

Creativity is complex, and many different factors can influence the outcome of creative people and creative organizations. Since it can be challenging for an organization to achieve creativity, it is important to understand how one can manage and provide leadership for better creative climates. According to Teresa Amabile, creativity cannot be managed, but we can "manage for creativity." Amabile's KEYS instrument provides a framework that any leader interested in creativity and innovation can learn and understand. Many executives interviewed for this book confirmed that creativity is the biggest asset they can provide their clients. Advertising executives are beginning to understand that their business is no longer advertising alone, but rather a business of ideas and problem solving.

Based on the interviews in this book, the focus in advertising is moving away from delivering creative pieces and moving toward making meaningful contributions that connect people and brands. Margaret Johnson of Goodby Silverstein & Partners says, "We only want to do the most innovative things. We want to effect culture. We want to be a part of pop culture." According to Johnson, Goodby Silverstein & Partners has such an impressive reputation within the industry that it attracts only the most creative and talented people. Johnson adds, "Everyone is really driven and interested in doing the very best work." According to Johnson, people want to work hard because they want to represent the company well, and they want to put the most innovative work out there for people to see.

Motivation, both intrinsic and extrinsic, is a key component that influences creativity at the individual level. Any member within an organization, whether they are an employee, a manager or an executive, is influenced by both kinds of motivation. Knowing what motivates creative people and what promotes creative excellence can help a manager adjust the various factors that drive motivation, and ultimately the creative end result.

A creative leader should not only be aware of how these two areas affect his personal engagement, but he should also understand how motivation can influence the creative work of his employees. Susan Credle, chief creative officer at Leo Burnett in Chicago, describes her experience with employee motivation: "When agency people are producing the work they are proud of, they stop talking about money and vacation really fast. So the motivation is the work." Lynn Teo believes that creatives are motivated by expression. "I think it's that need to leave a mark on something. I think passion is probably the thing that drives motivation," says Teo.

Alternatively, Doug Spong believes that the motivation for creatives is not about money. "For all people it's as much their avocation as it is their vocation. I don't believe we have anybody who feels like they simply show up to collect a paycheck. Our people here love the art and the craft of what they do." Blake Ebel approaches motivation from the perspective of support and encouragement. He says, "I want them to be selfish in the sense that I want them to be constantly worried about what great work they've made this year." Ebel encourages his employees to create the kind of work that wins awards and makes them money.

Michael Lebowitz looks for people who want to be doing the kind of work Big Spaceship specializes in or who want to explore and are not necessarily looking for stability and equilibrium as the defining factor for their job. "It's not that they don't have the same external motivators as fame and fortune, and all that stuff. But if you asked any given person what their favorite thing is about working here, they would say the team and the culture, ninety-nine times out of one hundred, guaranteed. That's what real motivation looks like, living up to the team and the culture. They want to pay homage to the people around them; they don't want to let each other down; that's motivating. Motivation is a personal thing, and it varies from individual to individual, so there's no one-size-fits-all answer."

WHERE UNPLANNED COLLISIONS HAPPEN AND ENERGY FLOWS

As I mentioned in the previous chapter, it is important to design the physical place in order to increase accidental collisions and sharing of ideas. All of the creative executives interviewed for this book understand the power of the physical environment and the impact that it is has on the creative work that is produced by the agency. Many traditional agencies have started the process of tearing down the walls in order to create an open and collaborative climate. Blake Ebel, former chief creative officer at Euro/RSCG in Chicago, explains, "We've created a real open environment. The actual space itself is very open so there is a lot of energy. You can hear a lot of people running and walking up and down the halls, and I think that's a good thing."

Chris Foster, former CEO of Fallon in Minneapolis, says, "Creativity, I think, is just a sense of energy and movement, so even in the way we have designed our space here, you kind of look. We have a round room; we have a central staircase;

Visualization of Concepts, Part 3: Connection

The world is becoming increasingly visual. In order to communicate effectively we need to come up with innovative, original and creative ways to show familiar concepts in unusual ways and unfamiliar concepts in familiar ways. Visualize *Connection* with 9-12 images/key visuals.

The presentation can be produced in an abstract, concrete, symbolic, descriptive way and/or can also make use of analogies. The key visuals can be in relationship with each other, e.g. tell an overall story or script or can be independent from each other.

This assignment should encourage you to be playful, take risks and experiment (try out new things you might not even think of).

The key visuals should have an appropriate size to address an audience of 6-10 people. You can use any visual design tools and/or elements available to you, e.g. Photography, Painting, Drawing, Collage, and Objects.

people have to bump into each other; people have to run up and down; people have to have spontaneous meetings. You have to gear yourself up for spontaneous interactions so that magic can happen. Space doesn't make an agency, but it certainly helps with energy flow."

Both executives believe that effective leaders should take charge of the physical space in order to optimize it for maximum creative potential.

The physical and cultural environments also play an important role in supporting the philosophy of the agency. As we have seen in some of the samples, the employees of highly creative agencies seem to be generally happy people and more effective workers if they really understand and embrace the philosophy of the agency. This is the reason many leaders display their agency philosophies in the office, thereby making that philosophy a part of the environment.

As described in chapter eight, several other agencies that I visited redesigned and modified their offices in order to encourage unexpected collisions. As Edward Boches of Mullen says, "I want there to be unexpected collisions, and a lot of them. Even those who have closed offices—they're all glass, sometimes two people to an office—and you can't come out of your office without bumping into other people. It makes you realize that everything you do is connected to what everybody else is doing."

These collisions and run-ins allow for the exchange of ideas at spontaneous and unexpected moments and can result in the production of even better, more innovative ideas. There are definitely benefits to having planned meetings, but these do not allow for as much spontaneity as random run-ins do. Many agencies are trying to create environments that not only encourage open discussion and collaboration, but also encourage the sharing of ideas at unexpected times. David Droga says, "There's a very structured thing here where, as I said, the strategic planners are engaged very early. We make sure that people are having lots of conversations. So the idea is not just in a complete vacuum. It's not just thrown in a sandpit and like 'Hey, let's see what comes out!' There are lots of conversations and thoughts. We're a corridor conversations type of place. There are more interesting things reeling ahead in the most unlikely of places." Droga says he loves the contagious nature of creativity "when it's free-fall and freestyle sort of talking and conversations. Just casual, I think the best stuff comes from casual [interactions]. It's not forced. You can't force creativity. You can't force collaboration. I just feel like [it is important to] create a safe environment."

OPEN SPACE IS NOT ENOUGH

Tim Leake, former creative director at Saatchi pointed out, "It's sort of a shame that we don't somehow get like-minded people together, because we can get great things to happen by doing so. At Saatchi we sort of have an open space, but open space with desks and lots of meeting areas, which works okay. It's not enough to be this 'let's collaborate in the hallways' kind of mentality, and not quite closed enough to feel like I've got privacy." An open space in itself does not make a creative climate.

Michael Lebowitz of Big Spaceship has spent a lot of time thinking about the way in which his employees are seated and how he can influence and improve the way in which knowledge is shared and projects are managed. For years, the interactive industry has been faced by the challenge of creating multidisciplinary teams and integrating specialty knowledge—ranging from visual design, navigation design, user experience design, information architecture, concept development, strategic planning and consumer insight to programming, systems engineering, coding and project management. After rearranging the way his employees are seated several times, Lebowitz finally developed a model, where people of different skills are seated next to each other and can communicate in order to share the knowledge necessary to create the best possible solution for a client. The physical attributes of an agency then influence the way people interact and collaborate with each other.

Lebowitz thinks that the reason people work at Big Spaceship is more about getting to work with each other than it is about getting to work with the things that come in from outside. He has worked hard at providing the right environment that makes the agency inherently motivating and inherently exciting. He also points out that letting people be themselves and allowing them to have a sense of autonomy plays a big role in how the work gets done. "I don't tell people how to get their work done. I just say there are these values that we have, these five principles, and if those five principles are in equilibrium, I'm happy, and the business will be successful, and the rest is completely up to you. And that has stood us in good stead for a long time," Lebowitz says.

CONSTANT LEVEL OF CRITIQUE

"One of the things we've done in many of the thinking areas is knock down walls and doors... and I think some of your best thinking, best interactions happen in hallways outside of offices and over thinking tables," says Marshall Ross, chief creative officer at Cramer Krasselt in Chicago. In addition to maintaining an open environment, it is also important to collect as many ideas as possible within an organization and to allow every employee to participate, no matter what their discipline or rank. Ross adds that "One of the things we do here is we keep the environment very open; we keep the work very exposed. Work in progress is always out in the open for people to see because we kind of want that constant level of critique. We want people constantly wondering if this is good enough."

The open space environments and increased sharing culture also allows for filtration of good and bad ideas. Margaret Johnson of Goodby Silverstein & Partners speaks to the concept of "fail faster." In an industry where ideas, creativity and innovation are the raison d'étre, the generation of many ideas is not the only thing that counts. It is also important to establish a process that filters out good ideas from the ones that may not be as good. Mark Hunter, chief creative officer at Deutsch LA, says, "I kind of believe that ideas should get out in the open and they should get some air and some sunlight on them. If they're going to grow, they're going to grow, and if they're going to die, they're going to die—the sooner you find that out, the better."

Several leaders interviewed for this book encourage rapid prototyping and testing so that bad ideas can be identified earlier in the process. Displaying ideas on the walls throughout the agency instead of showcasing awards is a practice at Mother New York. Andrew Deitchman says, "If you come into our space, you'll see our works in progress surrounding us. That anybody who kind of walks up is like, 'That's really cool' or 'Oh, I'm not sure about that.' Everybody is surrounded by unfinished work. [However], a lot of other agencies that you visit display, a cabinet of awards, and there's a loop playing of finished spots. For us, it's graphs of paper constantly up against the wall."

This helps Mother create an environment where ideas are expressed and shared early in the life of a project. It's also part of Mother's culture to change an idea and improve any project up until the last minute. "I think there are some organizations that are great with, 'Oh, that's a terrific idea' there are some organizations that are so focused on the end product in a pure sense. For us, nothing is done until it is done. So a big part of it is an appreciation for the craft. We ask: Was the writing perfect? Can we tweak this? Could it be better?" says Deitchman.

POSTMORTEM OR DIE

The postmortem is another excellent tool that any creative leader can use to better manage the organization and its creative climate. In order to stay profitable and successful, most companies have to focus on a specific number of services. This often leads to specialization and the repetition of the same process based on its initial success. Even in fascinating and exciting industries like marketing, advertising, film, media and entertainment, where creativity is highly important, standardized production processes and procedures can lead to less creative experiences for employees. Individuals working in creative industries are typically curious. Therefore it is important to encourage as much creativity and freedom as possible. Typically they have an internal desire to learn more and are inquisitive about their surroundings and the world, just like Curious George developed by Hans Augusto Rey and Margret Rey.[2]

However, as a learning organization, it is important to manifest and embrace this concept on a larger scale and to continue to be curious even when things are not working well. Being conscious about what projects have and have not worked in the past is the first step toward creating an environment for continuous learning. Everyone at Pixar is asked to get more out of postmortems. This requires several people or teams to take a closer look at every project and analyze the elements that worked successfully and which ones did not.

During these postmortems, it is important not only to acknowledge the successful elements of a project, but also to recognize any mishaps and mistakes that were made. If the negatives are ignored, these sessions will not be nearly as productive and helpful for the future. One suggestion made by Catmull in his article, "Pixar Fosters Collective Creativity," is to vary the way in which these postmortems are conducted. He advises participants in the postmortem to think of five things that they would do again and five things that they would do differently in order to have a balance between the positive and the negative aspects of a project.

Twyla Tharp, world-famous choreographer of Movin' On, provides a similar framework, which she calls "concept of failure." In her book *The Creative Habit,* she says that it is important to be willing to fail and not to deny failure. In the end, failure can provide us with great opportunities for instigating change and progress in an organization, as long as both are welcome. This is a concept that is important in other contexts as well, including classroom projects. Rather than allowing an often-misguided need for "perfection" to drive us, we should reflect on our work and analyze what makes it successful. We should consider what could be added, changed or removed in order to make it better. By embracing failure and approaching a problem with a more realistic outlook, we can come up with bolder ideas that we would not have come up with otherwise.

Margaret Johnson embraces the concept of failure when she develops creative work at Goodby Silverstein & Partners. In order to create original and innovative concepts, many agencies are taking risks and pushing themselves, their employees and clients. Johnson fosters a climate in which failure is accepted and discussed openly. Doing so minimizes the risks that exist for agencies that are constantly trying to push the limits of what has been done before. "One thing that we have been saying lately is 'Let's try to fail fast.' Let's come up with a lot of ideas, do it quickly, and realize early on that it is not going to work so we can switch gears. You don't want to spend a ton of time on something and find out six months later that it was a bad idea," Johnson says.

Postmortems require that one accepts failure and then analyzes what went wrong or what could have been done differently. Postmortems are an important aspect of learning environments. Postmortems provide an opportunity to take a step back and assess what worked successfully and what needs improvement. Idea development, prototyping and the launching of new products are usually the most exciting activities in creative companies. However, being innovative all the time can be difficult economically, since the rewards for outstanding ideas are usually financial. Bettina von Stamm illustrates this in the Creative and Implementation Cycle in her book *Managing Innovation, Design & Creativity.* If managers used postmortems more frequently, employees would experience the sweet spot that exists between rules, procedures, routine-and-known solutions, constructive reviews, challenge, developing new solutions, commitment and experimentation. This is the bridge (or the mental space) between daily job activities and the exciting projects someone might get involved with based on the cognitive surplus. Identifying areas and projects for cognitive surplus within the organization can foster success, commitment and opportunity for small changes on an ongoing basis.

THE FREEDOM TO TAKE ON CHALLENGES

Freedom and challenges are two topics that emerged during my interviews and can be analyzed from a managerial perspective. Across the board, everyone interviewed encourages their employees to have as much freedom as possible and to pursue different kinds of ideas without many parameters. Many leaders say they give their employees the freedom to solve the problem at hand however they see fit, but they make themselves available for support, if needed along the way.

Rob Schwartz of TBWA\Worldwide and formerly of TBWA\Chiat\Day gives employees the freedom to do anything necessary to get the job done. He tells them, "Don't be afraid to be a genius." AKQA gives its employees tremendous freedom in terms of how they approach a problem. Lynn Teo says, "There's no right or wrong way in how they like to work." Doug Spong of Carmichael Lynch Spong in Minneapolis speaks of freedom in the workplace slightly

Map Visualization: The Way from Home to Work

A city or street map represents the earth in a two-dimensional way. Based on the idea of a street map, present your daily path: the way from home to work (or school) in 9-12 images/key visuals. Consider the use of elements that are related to maps such as symbols, directional information and topographical information.

The map, in form of a visual guide, represents the basics for developing personal problem solving strategies. You can develop innovative solutions or visualizations that go far beyond the traditional concept of a map by

- watching precisely your point of departure and final destination
- analyzing events or encounters that happen during your travel journey
- examining what can be represented by maps
- being conscious or aware of your personal travel experiences

You can use any visual design tools or elements available to (e.g. photography, painting, drawing, collage, objects). This assignment should encourage you to be playful, take risks and experiment (try out new things you've never tried before).

The key visuals should have an appropriate size to present to an audience of 6-10 people. .

NOTE: The special aspect of this assignment lies in the connection of two points of travel and its visualization separated by elements of time. The simple information "going from a to b" should be moved into the background: The *how* is what's important and not the *what*.

Adapted from Wilde, Judith, and Richard Wilde. *Visual Literacy: a Conceptual Approach to Graphic Problem Solving. New York: Watson-Guptill, 1991.*

differently and says, "I think we know that if we're not a little uncomfortable in terms of the ideas sometimes we're not testing the boundaries of that. So we do encourage people to test the perimeters and see where those boundaries may be for a client's brand or for ourselves for that matter."

However, freedom also comes with responsibility and accountability. Blake Ebel says that in his agency, creatives have a tremendous amount of freedom to own projects, to make them their own and then to make them great. "Putting that responsibility on them then holds them accountable for [the project]," he says.

David Droga expresses the duality of freedom and challenge by saying that he gives his employees freedom "as much as possible without becoming a free for all. Freedom with context." He also says that "we challenge ourselves to stay relevant, to stay fresh, to not fall into a trap of familiarity, and creativity is one of those things that sometimes people, they find that they find a lane, where there's fruit, and they just stick to it and such is the nature of creativity, it can't be contained and can't stand still."

Fallon in Minneapolis provides employees with a written document that outlines the agency philosophy and consequently becomes challenging.

Chris Foster, former CEO of Fallon says, "The challenge comes in through settings—setting the goal. So we have defined our purpose, which is a one-page document, which then sets the bar for employees, their understanding that that's where we're going. Then everyone is responsible for creating their own purpose."

TAP INTO TALENT OUTSIDE YOUR BOUNDARIES

The interviews brought to light the fact that many agencies not only encourage collaboration within the agency, but also foster an environment where employees can utilize external resources. The advertising industry and the work generated by agencies have become more complex and require the skill sets of a hugely diverse workforce. Many agency executives acknowledge that it is almost impossible to employ every skill needed in order to produce the work that is expected of them. Therefore, agencies look within their own networks, such as the branches in other places of the world, as well as to outside specialists. This ensures that the best possible skill set can be brought in to meet the challenges an agency is facing.

Several agencies represented in this book are doing even more than employing the talent of their employees. They help introduce new skills and create opportunities for their employees to get inspired or learn something they otherwise never would. Goodby Silverstein & Partners invites musicians to play concerts and comedians to do stand-up routines. Other agencies employ poets and artists to come into the office to bolster the creativity and ideas of their employees.

Creative leaders are no longer bound solely to internal resources. With many platforms available, anyone can tap into talents elsewhere, whether they are from a different country or a different discipline. This open access to talent has lead to internet platforms such as Behance, a creative network that allows people to display their creative work. Victors and Spoils, an agency created by a former executive of Crispin Porter + Bogusky, is focused on the principle of crowdsourcing. Victors and Spoils manages the creative output and talent of many individuals, not just the ones in the agency itself. They consult with clients, develop a strategy and seek outside talent in order to provide the best execution of ideas.

IGNITE THE COGNITIVE SURPLUS OF EMPLOYEES

All executives who were interviewed for this book confirmed that employees are the most crucial resource for any creative organization. Rather than trying to maximize employee productivity, it is important to balance work with fun, play and self-realization. Companies like Google have been known for allowing their employees to spend 20 percent of their time on personal projects. The daily pressures of the business and the growing demands of clients can make it challenging to have non-billable projects at an organization. However, Clay Shirky points out in his book *Cognitive Surplus* that engaging in something meaningful is a basic human need. The many examples featured in his book are proof that anyone can seek work outside of their daily jobs in order to find and engage in projects that make them feel free and challenged. Companies have to pay attention to this need so they don't lose valuable employees with excellent skills due to the fact that the employees are not provided the perfect balance of personal needs, company pressures and overall job satisfaction. Andrew Deitchman of Mother New York is very conscious that his employees need change and stimulation paired with challenge on

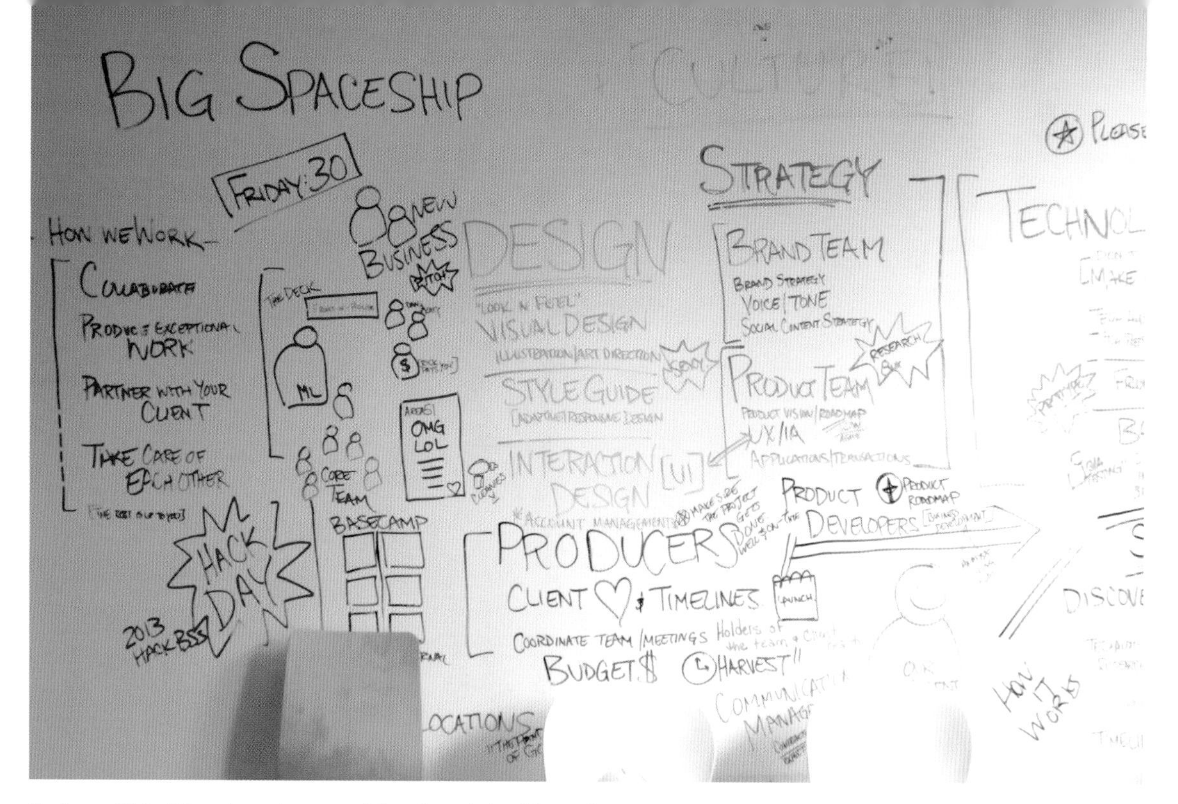

Big Spaceship's philosophy centers on collaboration, relationships and openness.

an ongoing basis. He knows that unless he provides his employees with the most interesting and challenging work, they will apply their cognitive surplus somewhere else.

"If people aren't creating and making on a creative basis and seeing their work out in the world, to have their thought out in the marketplace in a reasonable amount of time and we've resigned clients because that just wasn't working," says Deitchman. This is one of the reasons why Mother takes on a broad spectrum of interesting, diverse and challenging projects that require different skills that are typically not found in traditional agency settings. Mother considers itself not just an advertising or communication agency but a "modern creating company" that has its own design practice, organizes rock concerts, develops products and creates communication campaigns. The typical projects that Mother accepts must provide sufficient stimulus for its employees. This provides big opportunities for employees to push their own abilities further.

Deitchman described a smartphone application that his company created and will be released as an online game. People who have seen it were blown away and surprised that the app was not created by a Silicon Valley Startup. To Deitchman, this demonstrates why challenge is important and good. "When we do things like that, it just shows to people that they need to constantly challenge people to bring their A-game and also to bring ideas that they have, that don't even relate to clients, because maybe their ideas can be applied to clients or maybe not applied to clients because anything is possible. You know, when you're told 'This is your job; this is the box you are in,' and you're not shown things that go far outside of that, you're not challenged because you're basically saying, 'Well this is my job; this is what I have to do.' When you are constantly exposed to things that are really, really interesting that go way outside of the typical realm of your job, if you don't find that to be challenging and want to be a part of or create the next one, then you probably shouldn't be here."

At mediaman an old space heater was repurposed into an interactive printing device for last-minute recipes and shopping lists.

"Evolve or become extinct like Dodo bird" is part of the Martin Williams' agency philosophy.

Creative leaders must also allow employees to apply their creative talents to projects that are unrelated to their daily assignments. Michael Lebowitz of Big Spaceship has high regards for his employees and believes in their abilities to solve problems. Ever since Lebowitz established "Hack Days,"a twenty-four–hour marathon during which the agency goes offline to client work, he has been even more amazed by the output, quality, and volume of his employees. During a Hack Day, the entire agency comes together and starts an ideation process during which anything can happen. Someone might want to work on improving a specific process within the agency or to develop an idea for a business or product they have always dreamt of. These marathons are intense and focused. Different talents and skills come together and some amazing and beautiful stuff is created.

"The most recent Hack Day, I announced that I wanted to reinforce the 'company is canvas concept,' so I announced that the next Hack Day was going to be Hack the Spaceship," and they could take any aspect of this company and optimize it, improve it, make it better. They could just make something more fun, more meaningful, and it was really wide open. I didn't say how the teams had to organize; it was just however they want. We ended up with about ten teams including one team of two digital producers, and the producer team took our expense reporting process and optimized it, saving people tons of headaches. They became an expert in it, so they are now a resource to everyone, and they delivered a presentation that was unbelievably funny. So they took this very mundane, pragmatic thing and made everybody's life easier. They also really impressed people with their ability to present something that made for a very engaging subject.

"Other people did art projects; you know, here's an installation in the office based off things that are true to our culture, sort of physical computing projects. You know, if you walk through the door and have an RFID tag it plays your theme song, a lot of really beautiful things. Systems for getting more new people in the company, sort of socially acclimated and included more quickly, just beautiful things and that happens. They're not afraid to dive in and do those things. Part of the reason is I say, 'I want to see whatever you've got, so they bring what they've got,'" explains Lebowitz.

At mediaman, a digital marketing agency that I cofounded with two other partners, we have introduced similar activities during the last three years. During the "little creative project" series, a team develops ideas to promote a move into a new office location. Twenty-two employees from different disciplines, possessing diverse skills, came up with a reinterpretation of the classic arcade video game "Pong" and created "Bitball[3]", an interactive game where pedestrians in the German city Mainz became part of a life-size "Pong" game. Aspects of street soccer were added and integrated into the virtual components of "Pong" to allow participants to physically play as the two paddles returning the virtual ball back and forth and to experience the gameplay.

Another "little creative project" resulted in the creation of an on-demand recipe printer called "Dshini[4]"—that represents the German pronunciation of the helper "Genie in the Bottle." During the initial project phase, the participants identified some personal challenges they often experience when leaving the office late. Several employees mentioned that their refrigerators are often empty and that they need to go shopping after work before cooking a meal. Others mentioned the difficulty of knowing what to cook and the right ingredients to select. The team ended up developing a concept that turned an old wall heater into an interactive printer that allows users to print out a recipe with a shopping list of the ingredients.[5] The project was implemented over several weeks and now allows employees to spontaneously choose a cuisine and print recipes that come with shopping lists and time of preparation.

All companies interviewed for this book are embracing creativity and are working hard at shaping the future of the fast-changing industries of advertising, communication and marketing. Creativity has become the main tool that allows each agency to solve their clients' business challenges and to set themselves apart from their competitors. Many executives interviewed understand that their business purpose is not only producing great work and serving big clients, but also aligning their business with their employees' needs and desires. Several agencies select their clients with an eye toward providing their employees with the opportunity to engage in diverse projects and use their individual skills and talents in multiple ways. Anomaly, Droga5, Big Spaceship and Mother New York seem to be the furthest removed from the traditional advertising industry—the Mad Men era. Instead of creating new factories to churn out massive advertising messages, founders like David Droga, Andrew Deitchman, Johnny Vulkan, Michael Lebowitz and their respective partners and employees are engaging in a new kind of company that combines marketing and strategy consulting with the modern tools available to professional communicators. David Droga says that he wants to be part of that change because "No one has the answer; the industry is stuck in two levels. There are those that are pining for recovery, which I think is dangerous. I think we're trying to push it to reinvention. Not reinvention of the purpose of the industry, the mechanics of the industry; but reinvention of how we do it. I think it's an exciting time."

The creative product of those new advertising agencies or "creating companies" no longer is limited to advertising or PR efforts. Creative production literally can be anything from the traditional thirty-second commercial to the rock concert to the smartphone application to the television show to a new product, new distribution channel or even a new business. Johnny Vulkan sums up the trend: "It's the old 'to a hammer, every problem is a nail' problem. To an ad agency, every problem [needs] an ad to solve it. Looking into the future, a pyramid where advertising sits at the top and everything else has to follow sequentially to the bottom will no longer represent the industry."

CHAPTER TEN

MAINTAINING A FLEXIBLE MIND

Throughout this book we have seen that many variables influence creativity and creative thinking—and that there is not just one way to achieve these creative outputs. Human beings are born creative and can express creativity through the arts or by being flexible, creative, fluent and divergent thinkers with great problem-solving skills. A person can be both artist and problem solver by practicing creative thinking. Hopefully the 4P model of creativity has provided you with a framework and some insight into how the various dimensions can influence individual creativity as well as the creativity of the organizations where you work.

Creative skills are in demand and being knowledgeable in problem solving, idea generation and facilitation of creative processes can provide you with a competitive edge and help generate higher financial rewards. Even though your own creativity is related to the people you work with and the organizations you work in, focusing on yourself and improving your individual creativity is the easiest way to become a better creative thinker. As with many skills in life, creativity needs to be nurtured. In order to improve your creativity and to become better at utilizing and maximizing its greatest potential, you need to regularly put it into practice. Many practitioners and former students featured in this book are making an effort to practice their creativity and incorporate it into their everyday routines.

In this chapter, you will find many examples of how my former students, who learned about creativity during a formal college course, practice and hone their creativity. Additionally the creative executives interviewed in this book provide insight into how they practice their individual creative excellence and what has helped them become creativity champions in their respected industry. By no means are the examples designed to be prescriptive or directive, nor do they need to be followed in a strict way. On the contrary, they should inspire you to think about your own creativity and expand your creative practices. Keep a notebook and write down activities and routines you can do to practice and master your own creativity. You can also go to the companion website to share your ideas with other readers or featured former students.

One important takeaway that came from my many interviews with company leaders is the concept of a creative philosophy (as seen in the previous chapter). Many agency executives have developed an overarching theme or concept in order to help pull the creative energy of an agency into one, often single-minded direction. This theme can provide a foundation from which everything creative starts and from which it can expand. A creative philosophy can also guide your personal creative journey and provide a foundation or home base from which to start your daily activities.

If you have not yet developed your own creative philosophy, I recommend thinking about how you can create your own mission or ideology. Think of it as the North Star that will guide your creative life. Your own creative energy can be practiced and honed in a number of different ways, including various exercises and routines. All of these smaller components and creative activities should be connected by your bigger overarching philosophy. The concept Unlocking Creative Potential, developed by Andrew Deitchman of Mother New York, is an excellent example of how an overarching philosophy can provide a mission in order to achieve creative excellence, both individually and within an organization.

Creative Philosophy

Take a moment to write down your own overarching theme or concept that describes and guides your creativity and creative practice. If you do not have one yet, go back and review the creative philosophies discussed in chapter nine.

I also asked some of the leading creative directors from various advertising agencies to describe what truths, lessons and core values they have learned about being a creative person and how they maintain their creative mind-set. Many of them spoke about seeking inspiration outside of their line of work. Rob Schwartz of TBWA\Chiat\Day maintains a creative mind-set by absorbing things. "I love museums. I think that the internet is the best museum on the planet," says Schwartz. Marshall Ross, the chief creative officer of Cramer Krasselt expressed a similar idea: "I think that I'm a big learner. I'm a real believer in life and in trying new things." Chris Foster of Saatchi Singapore mentioned how talking to people and collaborating with others is a requisite to maintaining a creative mind: "I love sharing ideas, I love talking about ideas, I love bouncing ideas around, I love making things better."

Seeking inspiration from places outside of the business and the work space is important because doing so allows you to bring a new way of thinking and perspective to a problem. Norm Shearer says that the thing that inspires him is "stuff that [he does] outside of [his] business ... [he likes] to just stay involved in what's going on around [him] and keep record of some of that stuff. [He supposes] that's one way [he tries] to stay inspired or creative." This is especially pertinent when you are stuck on a certain problem at work, and it can be extremely helpful to take a step back and do something completely unrelated for a while in order to gain perspective and insight. Robert Sherlock says that his "whole philosophy is rather go out and have a glass of wine and think about it than bang your head against the desk and try to force it out your ear and blood." Roger Hurni draws from his personal travels and from spending time with his family. "I'm inspired by the human condition as a whole. I see it in the eyes of my children, I see it in my travels, I see it when I'm speaking to someone in a different language," he says.

Mother New York founder Andrew Deitchman's key success factors are his openness, curiosity, restlessness and his ability to stay in his own head. He does not follow the industry trends or participate in many industry panels, since those tend to make him jealous or cloud his brain. Staying your own course requires discipline and confidence. Both will come over time and need constant practice. Being an entrepreneur has helped Deitchman keep an open mind. When he looks at problems and opportunities, he always keeps a positive attitude. "I don't look at anything and think, 'Oh, we couldn't do that, that's not the business that we're in," he says. "And I think it's been about openness on a lot of levels as well. I spent the first ten years of my career at seven different companies. I was at big agencies, and I had a great time. I volunteered for any pitch. I mean, I was a workaholic, but I had a blast. I learned these are the kind of people I want to work with; these are the kind of people I don't want to work with; this is what I'm good at; this is what I'm not good at."

Taking a broad view has helped Deitchman throughout his career. "I've always been very generous with my ideas and with my time, and it's always paid back very well, whether that's the people within our company or clients or whomever else," he says. Knowing what you love is another aspect that can help build a creatively fulfilled life. "I think it's great to figure out what you're great at and what you're passionate about. There's nothing wrong with putting yourself in a box in terms of what you love doing and what you're really great at. What I never want anyone to do is put limitations on how you can apply that expertise. I think that's the way I've always thought. I've kind of had a sense of the things that I'm good at, but I've never put any limitation on what that can be applied to. That can be applied to opening a company, to starting a liquor brand. I could start a tech company; I can start a data company; I could do whatever I want with the skills that I have. And I think too often companies say, 'This is what you're good at, and this is what you can do with it', and I think that's bullshit," says Deitchman.

Margaret Johnson fuels her creativity by having a life outside of advertising. "Go to museums, go see music, go to the theater, you know, go to movies, read, look at cool sculptures and listen to opera," she says. "You have to fuel that side of you. You got in to advertising because you're a creative person; make sure to maintain that; make sure you are fueling that part of yourself, so that when you are at work and you're forced to be creative, you have things to draw on." Another contributing fact to her success is her drive and the hunger she maintains. According to Johnson, both come from hav-

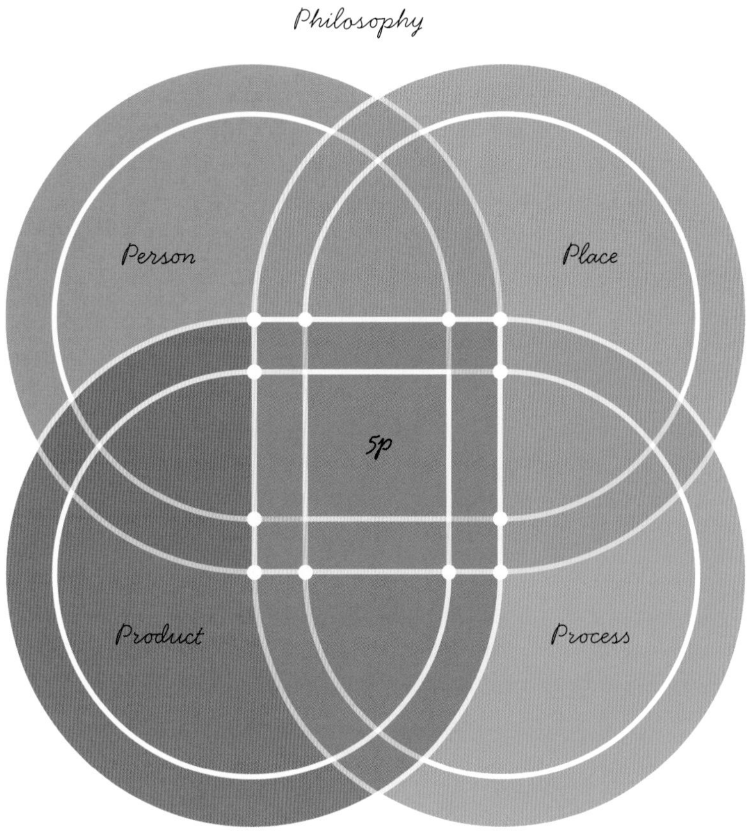

Another way of looking at creativity is through the premise of the 5Ps – by adding "philosophy" into the mix.

ing a voice inside her that constantly pushes her to be better and never allows her to get too arrogant.

David Droga is a passionate person and a hard worker, who follows what is happening in the world. He thinks that the best creativity comes from understanding, having empathy or sympathy, or whatever observations of what is going on in the real world. He attributes his success to luck and seizing opportunities when they present themselves, but also to his fascination for simple things. "There's this real love of emotions and storytelling," he says. "I grew up in a national park in Australia and most of my time was spent having to create my own entertainment with my brothers. I don't remember watching TV as a kid. We had a TV, but I don't remember watching it. I was outside playing all the time, and imagination was my entertainment. Now it's for business. But I think I've always kept it simple. Then there's this annoying competitive streak that I have which always made we want to do more and more. Not so much because I need to win or something, but I was always competitive in the sense that as a creative person you always want to feel relevant and creative and that you're a functioning creative. I don't want to be a retrospective creative. I want to feel like I'm doing, making and contributing every day, on every level. I love that. I love it. So I'm still smitten by this industry. Maybe the naiveté of that is a blessing," says Droga. To him, being a creative person is a lifetime pass to do more interesting things—and just create opportunities.

Hard work is another factor that Droga attributes to his success. "When I was younger, much younger, it was a bit like a muscle," he says. "I used to force myself to be as lateral as possible. I used

TBWA\Chiat\Day's perspective on being an advertising agency.

to—it's so painful to say—but I used to get a layout pad and draw a hundred postage stamp squares on it, and I would have to fill each one with an idea for whatever the brief was—even if I fell in love with the very first thing I did or the tenth thing. I forced myself not to fall in love with the first thing I did, and I trained my brain to be as lateral as possible. I just wanted to push myself because in our business, creativity is not like a 100-meter sprint. So I always want to give myself the best chance of having a shot at doing something great by working harder than anyone else. I believe I'm pretty talented, but I can be sure that I am working harder than anyone else," says Droga.

The various contributions by former students brought several other concepts to surface. Few are recent graduates and most have worked professionally for one to eight years in marketing agencies or in various companies. Former students, some of whom are featured in the section beginning on page 135 (also visit www.breakthroughthinking-guide.com), have taken a course in creativity and creative thinking and reflected on what they took away from the course. Surprisingly many of the preconceived notions associated with creativity still exist and were confirmed by many of the students of the Breakthrough Thinking course.

Before the beginning of the course, students were asked to rate their own creative ability. A portion of the students believed they were creative prior to the course but only because of their experience in the arts. Before the course, Cyril Urbano thought all the creativity he knew was artistic self-expression. He carried this notion throughout most of his life and had delineated the right brain from the left. But the course truly transformed the way in which students perceived creativity. They began to realize that creativity is not something utilized by artists and individuals in "artistic" lines of work only. Eric Rosati says that "being an artist and being creative were one in the same, as far as I was concerned prior to taking the course."

By employing and practicing some of the techniques and processes presented in this book, the students understood that they could be creative even though they were not artists. Beyond this, many of the students also realized that they could extend the skills they learned into other areas of their lives, both personal and professional. Brenna McCormick says the course "shattered [her] preconceived notions of what creativity was and where it could be used."

Dylan Klymenko says the "course left [him] with the belief that creativity—a seemingly mysterious gift—is something you can teach and, moreover, is something you can practice and improve upon." Similarly, Trang Phan says, "When I started the course, I was skeptical because like most people, I believed that one is either creative or they are not. What I discovered was that creativity is an innate skill that we all possess."

Usen Esiet says the course taught him that "creativity is both an attitude and a skill that can be learned and nurtured." Even though this skill is within all of us, we need to practice the right tools and guidance in order to develop it fully. In order to maximize your creative potential, you need dedication and patience to see what works best for you. Like training your muscles or practicing a sport, your early efforts may be difficult and strenuous. But with time, your skills will improve, and they will become much more second nature.

I often compare my own creative activities with rowing and yoga, two of my favorite athletic activities. Both require a baseline of skills before practicing: Basic techniques are necessary for powering the rowing shell in the water or achieving the best possible yoga pose. Every time I practice, I am provided an opportunity to apply what I have learned before as well as push a bit more and stretch my own limits. Having been a rower for all my life, I have achieved a technical level that allows me to row not only in smooth water but also in rough seas on the ocean. The ultimate goal is to maximize the physical power of my body in order to make the boat go as fast as possible. This optimal state is rarely achieved. But just like with problem solving and creativity, continuous practice, experimentation and the repeated application of technique and process, I can create a muscle memory that allows for improvisation when a situation calls for it.

Rebecca Hempen, another student who went through my course, summed this up well when she said, "Creative thinking *is* something you can learn but it is something you have to practice, and, especially in the beginning, consciously push." Getting the process started will require some time and patience but will become easier with time. However, once it becomes more routine and natural, you must continuously push yourself and try new techniques in order to become even better. When you are training for a new sport or trying to get into shape, you will see progress with a certain routine, but only up until a certain point. After a while, your muscles will become used to that routine, and progress will become much slower. That is why it is important to try new techniques and exercises in order to challenge your muscles so that they do not have time to become too comfortable with a certain routine. The same applies to creativity. By continuously pushing ourselves and taking risks, we will challenge the brain and become even more creative.

The students that went through the Breakthrough Thinking course understood and embraced this idea of challenging oneself when it comes to creativity. For example, Samantha Gutglass says that you "don't get better at your job by doing the same thing over and over. You get better by changing your routine, by looking at things differently. New perspectives lead to new ideas." By constantly switching things up, you will be able to see things in ways that you never did before, and this will lead to new and innovative ideas. Noreen Arora echoed this idea, saying, "Creativity isn't something that can be turned on and off. It's got to be flexed, stretched and challenged regularly."

There are many ways to challenge your creative potential, and they vary from person to per-

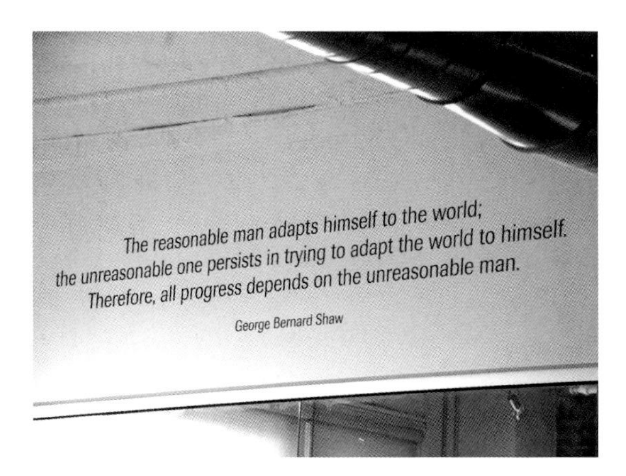

Anomaly New York finds inspiration in George Bernard Shaw.

son. For some people, the challenge involves changing up their routine. For others it may mean using new thinking techniques. Sara Wynkoop challenges her own creativity and thinking by interacting with new people. "I think the biggest challenge to practicing creative thinking and creative problem solving will be surrounding myself with people who encourage fresh and thought-provoking ideas. I am a big believer in the unplanned collaboration and open communication. I think if I can find an environment that embraces the Breakthrough Thinking philosophy, [my] creativity can only flourish." Unplanned collaborations and open communications are becoming the backbones of many of the most innovative agencies. Creative leaders are realizing that the unfiltered and spontaneous collaboration of ideas often leads to the most interesting and innovative ideas, and it is fascinating to see that my students also recognize this same notion.

Many of the students that took the course have been able to utilize, practice and sometimes further develop the course's creative thinking techniques and processes, and apply them to their professional careers. According Marissa Goldstein, "No matter what opportunities and challenges life presented, whether professionally, personally or academically, I often applied the creative philosophies and exercises that Professor Vogel championed throughout his teachings." Rebecca Hempen says that she "soon realized that creative thinking does not only apply to marketing strategies and tactics and presentations, but also to such things as spreadsheets and analyses. Letting yourself think creatively in the latter areas both makes work more fun and impresses employers." The ability to be creative in any line of work is a competitive advantage that gives you an edge in comparison to other employees.

Creative thinking techniques allow you to think in new and innovative ways and to offer ideas that may be different and that allow for breakthrough thinking. Veronica Marquez works for an innovation consulting firm in New York and acknowledges that she has been able to apply several creativity principles to her professional career. "The principles I learned in the class have been the pillars of my work: thinking expansively, discovering all the possible routes to tackle a challenge and being connected to what I love have been fundamental in my development and growth personally and professionally. A day in my office may involve participating in a brainstorming session to generate ideas or developing creative exercises to help clients think of a challenge from a fresh perspective or facilitating a qualitative research experience that will allow clients to connect with consumers in more meaningful ways. Thinking creatively and problem solving are part of my daily routine." Cyril Urbano says that "contrary to what experts say about metrics, standards and sales goals killing creativity, I have found myself applying creative thinking on how I manage my job—from the simplest act of developing a system of tracking my tasks to the most complex act of selling my idea to our stakeholders. There is always a place for creativity in business."

Matthew Fiorentino, a marketing director at Visible Measures in Boston, addresses the opportunities and need to apply creative thinking skills in our jobs every day, even if you don't work as a so-called creative. "In my work, where we distribute and measure the performance of branded video, I use creative thinking techniques frequently to create new opportunities. We are in the unique position to have the world of video literally at our fingertips and some of the smartest journalists rely on us to tell them what's happening in this world. We get questions like 'Who's more viral, cats or dogs?' from *The Los Angeles Times* (it's cats) and 'How many days did it take the biggest virals to reach 100 million views?' from *The Atlantic*. Answering these questions requires industry knowledge, a deep understanding of our platform, and video analytics, but also the ability to find the answer creatively. No one is going to give you the answer, so you need to develop a number of solutions and run with the one that is going to resonate most. When you do it right, you are rewarded for being creative, smart and timely. And, if you're lucky, you get a quote in *The New York Times*," explains Fiorentino.

Amanda Mooney, a senior manager at Edelman China in Shanghai, works as a researcher and planner helping clients with their brand strategies. Having known Amanda for more than five years, I know that she truly represents someone who lives a creative life inside and outside her professional work. Even though she might not consider herself creative, she offers an interesting perspective about the role creativity can play in one's life. Mooney argues that "creativity isn't a thing or a kind of magic or even necessarily a talent. Creativity is something that happens in the space between purpose, endurance, question after question and the fear-mixed-with-excitement blind spot at the center of what's unfamiliar. Everyone says this kind of thing but few know what it really feels like. It isn't a search for cool. It's caring about your work so much that you work through whatever it takes to try something new. It's knowing that you'll be uncomfortable and exposed and wrong most of the time and certainly always just starting out and that, whatever it is, it may never work in the end. It's bags under your eyes, hitting 'send' even if you're quite unsure, an uncomfortable conversation or even just a scary ride up a mountain road so you can see something new. It's leaving home and missing home but really trying and really searching for something."

I have presented you with a number of different techniques and processes in this book that will help you develop your own creative skills. It is beneficial to explore all of these in order to understand which of them work best for you. A theme that arose from the student interviews is that everyone had their own ways of maintaining a creative mind. Some students used the same techniques and processes but also had their own way of executing them. You may find that one technique works for you while another one may not be as successful. According to Michael Miller, his creative process "is simple as writing down the ideas as soon as I have them. If I can write the idea down, it allows me time to come back to it and think about it as I try to use it in some manner." Noreen Arora also utilizes writing for her creative process, but in a different way. "I used to be list averse, but after the Creative [Breakthrough] Thinking course, writing often (read: every single day), and in freeform, became my new normal. I had learned that the best ideas come from a strong yet nimble creative muscle." Sara Wynkoop says that divergent thinking techniques are most effective for her. "Using thinking techniques, such as word associations and reverse problem solving, I am able to provide insightful copywriting for my department and was referred to work with other departments by my supervisor." This demonstrates that for every individual creative thinking techniques will vary, and some techniques may work better than others. In order to most effectively maintain a creative mind, I recommend that you try various techniques and processes and alter them if needed in order to best fit your own thinking and working style. Also, depending on the context, some processes may be more effective than others for a given situation.

The students I interviewed provided some of their key takeaways and points of advice after taking the Breakthrough Thinking Course. The advice that they gave on how to maintain a creative mind had some prominent themes and are outlined below:

1. **If you have a good idea, write it down:**
    - Keep a journal. Write down ideas while you're on the train or bus, or before you go to sleep. Doodle. Find a way to release your creative energy every day. (Samantha Gutglass)
    - Anytime you have even a half-decent idea, make sure to write it down! (Michael Miller)
    - Keep a notepad beside your bed to write down your thoughts and ideas (Marissa Goldstein)
2. **Everyone has their own way of approaching creativity and problem solving, so take the time to discover what works for you. Not everything works for everyone. Different people will have different approaches and that is natural.**
    - Keep learning. Creativity can be developed, and learning something every day helps a great deal: a new word, a new recipe, a new fact, anything. (Milena Guzman)
    - Just like the normal function of thinking, creative thinking/ideation is a process. Discover what works for you: mental maps, brainstorming, the dictionary, Post-it Notes, etc. Create your own ideation process and continue to improve it or adjust it for your own needs and from your experience. (Milena Guzman)
    - Creative thinking is a sport that you must constantly condition for in order to be successful. Do not waste it. Practice it by going out and learning about how others stay creative, and exercise your brain with creative tasks every day. (Trang Phan)
    - Everyone is capable of increasing creativity by continuously training. Accordingly your creativity will gain muscle mass by investing time in creative assignments and activities (e.g., morning pages, artist dates, blog posts and various other creative endeavors). (Christiane Schaefer)
3. **Don't be afraid to take risks, step out of your comfort zone and trust your instincts.**
    - Be open minded. Ideas can happen anywhere, anytime. Sometimes the best ideas are the ones that initially feel like the worst ones. Taking risks is a great thing. (Samantha Gutglass)
    - Encourage wild ideas. (Noreen Arora)
    - Don't be afraid to be creative! It's not just for painters and singers; it's for everyone. Once you let go of the fear your creative energy will flow. (Sarah Hamilton)
    - Speak up. Don't be afraid to ask questions at work or to let your colleagues know that you'd like to be involved on a project. Opportunities come to those who seek them. (Samantha Gutglass)
    - Trust your instincts, and let your ideas run free. Don't settle on your first good idea because by doing so, you may have not yet arrived at that amazing idea that is sure to come. (Kristina Shigaeva)
    - At the core of creativity is permission to break the rules, to stop listening to the

outside world and take a risk on your own idea, concept or thought. Do this. (Brenna McCormick)
- Don't fall victim to the primal part of your brain that's afraid of taking risks or working outside of preconceived constraints. High risk can sometimes equal high reward. (Andrew Staub)
- Get out of your comfort zone, try new things and do not be afraid of failure (but make sure you don't make the same mistake twice). (Christiane Schaefer)

4. **Seek out inspiration from all over.**
   - Constantly expose yourself to new situations and experiences. Do something out of your comfort zone and look at things in a new way. Doing so allows for more inventive and interesting ideas. (Kristina Shigaeva)
   - You have to do things other than the things you have to do. Inspiration can come from personal experiences, events, movies, magazines, conversations or a road trip. Don't forget to take a step back and make time for your passions. (Samantha Gutglass)
   - Keep your eyes wide open: Observe and experience the environment around you but also reflect about yourself and question how you behave and think. (Christiane Schaefer)
5. **Collaborate with other people and build upon each other's ideas.**
   - Build off of the ideas of others. Never forget the key tenant of improv comedy: "Yes, and ..." (Noreen Arora)
   - Collaborate with others. Through my experience in the Breakthrough Thinking Course, I have found that some of my best ideas were often inspired by interactions and conversations with my classmates. (Kristina Shigaeva)
   - Talk about the information you gather with as many people as possible and reflect back on what they got out of your story. (Michal Shek)
6. **Realize that it takes time and dedication to come up with good ideas, so don't give up.**
   - Allow time for your ideas to sit, fester and ruminate in your brain. (Michael Miller)
   - Give yourself time. I often felt like if I were going to come up with a great idea, it would hit me right away. In reality it can take days before you come up with anything good, and it can hit you at anytime (mine usually hit me in the shower). (Sarah Hamilton)
   - Take the time to indulge your creative side (Marissa Goldstein)
   - Dedicate yourself to being a student of creativity. The learning experience is endlessly joyous and righteously difficult. It will inspire and humble you in the best way. (Brenna McCormick)
7. **Find something that you love and have fun being creative.**
   - Find what sparks your creativity. It is different for everyone so what works for a friend or colleague may not work for you. That's okay; just keep trying until you find it. (Alyse Dunn)
   - Don't be afraid to express what you love. Some interests may seem different or not mainstream, but those can be the best for honing your creative spirit. Share and be receptive. Creativity loves collaboration and expression is key to a creative euphoria. (Alyse Dunn)
   - Nurture what you love. Set aside time; it can be once a week or twice a month, to do something you love. Use this time to read, draw, sit at a café, write, etc. (Veronica Marquez)

8. **Don't be afraid of failing or of bad ideas.**
   - Don't give up after a failure. Wieden and Kennedy have a huge board in the Portland office that says, "fail harder." You can't come up with any good ideas without going through a whole lot of bad ones first. (Sarah Hamilton)
   - A bad idea can become a really good idea. In other words, there are no bad ideas. With the right peer culture, innovative thinking and trust, even something that seems silly can become a big idea. (Samantha Gutglass)
9. **Detach yourself from everything and everyone in order to be with yourself and your thoughts.**
   - Purposefully detach yourself from your busy life and allow time for actual thinking. (Michael Miller)
   - Immerse yourself in the topic but detach from the creative process. The best ideas come when you are not consciously thinking about the process, but know it so well that everything ties back to it. (Michal Shek)
10. **Be open all the time, ask questions, be open to learning new skills.**
    - Live with one foot on the comfort zone and the other on the stretch zone. Be open for new adventures and challenges. (Veronica Marquez)
    - Make a plan that includes things you think you would never do or try. Try and do one each day and let yourself discover new skills, hobbies and preferences. (Milena Guzman)
    - Take the opportunities when they are in front of you and try to actively create opportunities by asking yourself "What if ... Why not?" (Christiane Schaefer)
11. **Look at things from different angles.**
    - Be able to approach problems from multiple angles. Draw it on the board. Rearrange 100 Post-it Notes. Bring together a group of coworkers for a discussion. Rearranging the information visually is often the first step in understanding it, which ultimately leads to the solution. (Celia Nissen)
12. **Utilize creativity wherever and whenever you can.**
    - Whatever industry you work in, apply creative principles and practices when solving problems. (Marissa Goldstein)
    - Creative thinking improves your work and your play. (Rebecca Hempen)
    - No matter how you use (or plan to use) your creativity or creative thinking in your professional life, make sure to always take time to experiment and work at it in your in your personal life. (Brenna McCormick)
13. **Have fun.**
    - If you're not having fun, why are you here? (Noreen Arora)
    - Have a good time. Life's short, enjoy every second of it. (Andrew Staub)

STUDENT CASE STUDIES

BRENNA MCCORMICK

LEAD CONSULTANT, CREATIVITY AND INNOVATION

mediaman, Boston

LinkedIn: www.linkedin.com/pub/brenna-mccormick/b/830/ab3

The most important thing about studying and practicing Creative Thinking is that it gives you permission: Permission to take a chance on an idea. To do something a different way. And most important to take risks and invest in yourself—often one and the same.

In 2006, I was a student in Emerson College's Integrated Marketing Communication graduate program. I took the Creative Thinking & Problem Solving course in my final year of the program. I was not a stranger to creativity and I couldn't wait to take the course. I considered myself creative especially as I wrote prose, poetry and dabbled in mixed media artwork; but my experience working full time as a manager for a luxury paper goods company (while also going to school) taught me that, when it came to integrating creativity with the real world, creativity was always the first thing to be marginalized.

To say that studying creative thinking changed my life is not an understatement. The course that I couldn't wait to take lived up to my expectations, but more importantly, it shattered my preconceived notions of what creativity was and where it could be used. I understood my own creative habits as well as the fluid and adaptable nature of creativity, which opened the door to my understanding that I could utilize my creativity and creative thinking in all areas of my life; in other projects within the program, in my job, and even in my post-graduate job search, which was underway at the time.

Key Insights

1. At the core of creativity is permission to break the rules, to stop listening to the outside world and take a risk on your own idea, concept or thought. Do this.
2. Dedicate yourself to being a student of creativity. The learning experience is endlessly joyous and righteously difficult. It will inspire and humble you in the best way.
3. No matter how you use (or plan to use) your creativity or creative thinking in your professional life, make sure to always take time to experiment and work at it in your personal life.

I also took from the class the tools that allowed me to practice creativity, to work at it when I choose, rather than being at the whim of the Muses (of whom I still have a deep and abiding respect!). It was morning pages, written on hotel stationery during business trips that allowed me to find the courage to walk away from a dream-job-that-wasn't. And it was the foundation of exercises like visual self that helped me to create and pitch a presentation that would land me my current position as the director of client strategy for the U.S. division of an international digital marketing agency.

When you practice creativity and are aware of your creative process, the world is full of signposts showing you the way. That is, if you are open enough to see them (which you usually are) and then take the wild leap of faith that is needed to follow them.

Studying creative thinking is how I have come to teach it myself. An adjunct professor at Emerson College, I now teach the same course that I took when I was a graduate student.

While it is difficult to sideline creativity when it is the central focus of my work, I find that I rely on my creativity tools and techniques more than ever to deliver new ideas to my students and to my clients. Working at my creativity also means that I have time to express myself, and it has lead to fulfilling some of my personal dreams, such as starting my own business and exercising my writing on a blog dedicated to my passion for paper and handwritten communication.

When you love something, the proverb says, set it free. I say study it. If you are passionate about creativity, or even already consider yourself creative, then do yourself the favor of dedicating yourself to being a student of creativity and the creative process. I can say with confidence that it will change your life.

NOREEN ARORA

MARKETING COMMUNICATION LEAD
IDEO, Boston
LinkedIn: http://www.linkedin.com/in/noreenarora

Creativity cannot be turned on and off. Much like a muscle, it must be strengthened and flexed regularly. I learned this to be an absolute truth when I was fresh out of graduate school from Emerson College and trying to find my place in the working world. My situation was not unique—millions faced the same dire job market and competition from fellow applicants. But based on what I had learned from my Creative Thinking course, I knew I had the creative skills and confidence to make myself stand out.

I also knew that it would be really tough to land a dream job for a dream company and the only way to do it was to put myself out there in a way that felt authentically me. I had to be somehow bold enough, yet not corny and over the top—something that I had practiced time and time again during the Creative Thinking course. Often I felt uncomfortable and vulnerable during these creative exercises in class, but I always came out of those experiences stronger, wiser and more self-aware. During the Creative Thinking course, we were encouraged to build our creative portfolio. To be honest I had no idea how to do that, and I figured I could get by without it. But I was wrong and the many prospective job dead-ends proved it.

After months of back-and-forth correspondence, I was invited in for an informational meeting at my dream company, IDEO. The creative director asked me to bring in my creative portfolio. My first thought was, "I should have listened!" and it was followed quickly by many brainstorms that focused on how to best represent myself. The creative director knew that I wasn't a trained designer. Instead he asked me to bring in *my* version of a creative portfolio. And

if you know anything about IDEO (www.ideo.com/about), you know that the pressure was on. This creative portfolio had to be well designed, playful, thoughtful, and uniquely me. No pressure, right?

That got me thinking, what do they *need* to know about me? What's relevant and what's not? Ever the list maker, I started making all sorts of lists. I used to be list averse, but after the Creative Thinking course, writing often (read: every single day) and in free form became my new normal. I had learned that the best ideas come from a strong yet nimble creative muscle. And writing daily has helped me become more generative and confident personally and professionally.

I started building my creative portfolio by writing down the core things that are most important to me and inspire me most: my family, the culinary arts, the countries I have traveled to and lived in, and my ability to forge relationships with people from all walks of life. And then I thought, so now what? How do I showcase all of this without feeling like a child's book report? How might I design something that's effective yet simple and playful? I thought back to my daily activities and rituals. What do I do daily that allows for creativity and is something I look forward to? The idea that I kept coming back to was lunch. Whether traveling abroad or whether I am at work or at school, lunch is a daily ritual. And I look forward to the conversation, location, the company, and of course the cuisine. Yes, you read that right, I decided to showcase my creative portfolio to one of the most innovative

Key Insights

1. Build off the ideas of others. Never forget the key tenant of improv comedy: "Yes, and ..."
2. Encourage wild ideas. There's a pony in there somewhere.
3. If you're not having fun, why are you here?

companies in the world in the form of a sack lunch. As primitive as it sounds, I knew I could showcase what's most distinctive and memorable about me in the form of a sack lunch—a bound illustrative book and an actual, physical lunch.

The meeting went really well. Three years later, I write this as the marketing communication lead for IDEO's Boston studio. It's a role I grew into because of my sack lunch/creative portfolio share with the creative and marketing directors of IDEO. I was really nervous and felt quite vulnerable sharing myself in that way, but it was the only way for my now-colleagues to see me for me. Even though I only had a short time with them, it was enough for them to know they could not let me go. Because my creative confidence was unleashed, I felt completely secure in what I was sharing and how I was sharing it.

The key takeaway: Lunch sharing isn't for everybody. But there is a right way for you to share what's unique and special about what you can offer to an organization. By practicing and honing your creative thinking skills regularly, you'll surely have that breakthrough moment. I encourage you to go broad, be curious and iterative; continue to build off of your ideas—one idea built off another just might lead to that breakthrough idea you have been waiting for all along. And remember this quote from *Creative Confidence* by David and Tom Kelley of IDEO, "the real value of creativity doesn't emerge until you are brave enough to act on those ideas ... Creative confidence is the ability to come up with new ideas and the courage to try them out."

CHRISTIANE SCHAEFER

PRODUCT MARKETER

Strategy & Planning, Volkswagen Group China

Twitter: @_Christiane_S

LinkedIn: cn.linkedin.com/in/schaeferchristiane

One of my favorite sayings is "*Der Weg ist das Ziel*," a commonly used proverb in the German language, whose underlying idea is beautifully expressed in the saying of Ralph Waldo Emerson: "Life is a journey, not a destination." Especially looking back at how rewarding my personal journey into the world of creative thinking has been so far, I could not agree more with the saying.

It all goes back to my decision to apply for the Global Marketing Communication and Advertising (GMCA) Master's program at Emerson College. In one of my application essays I wrote about how it is necessary to think outside the box in order to distinguish yourself for a successful career in marketing. While being aware of the importance of creativity in my future profession, I was not familiar with the creativity concepts due to my pure business background.

Needless to say, I was especially looking forward to the innovative class *Creative Thinking and Problem Solving in a Global Environment*, which aims to enhance creativity. But entering unknown territory is challenging. During our first class we were urged to forget about grades and use the class as an opportunity to try out new things without being afraid of making mistakes. This was a scary and totally new concept for me, which I did not expect from a graduate class. Consequently, the insecurity was high; up to that point, I would not have listed creativity as one of my core strengths. On the contrary, I thought of myself as a "left brainer" who is able to think analytically and critically rather than a creative "right brainer." Luckily, the course helped me

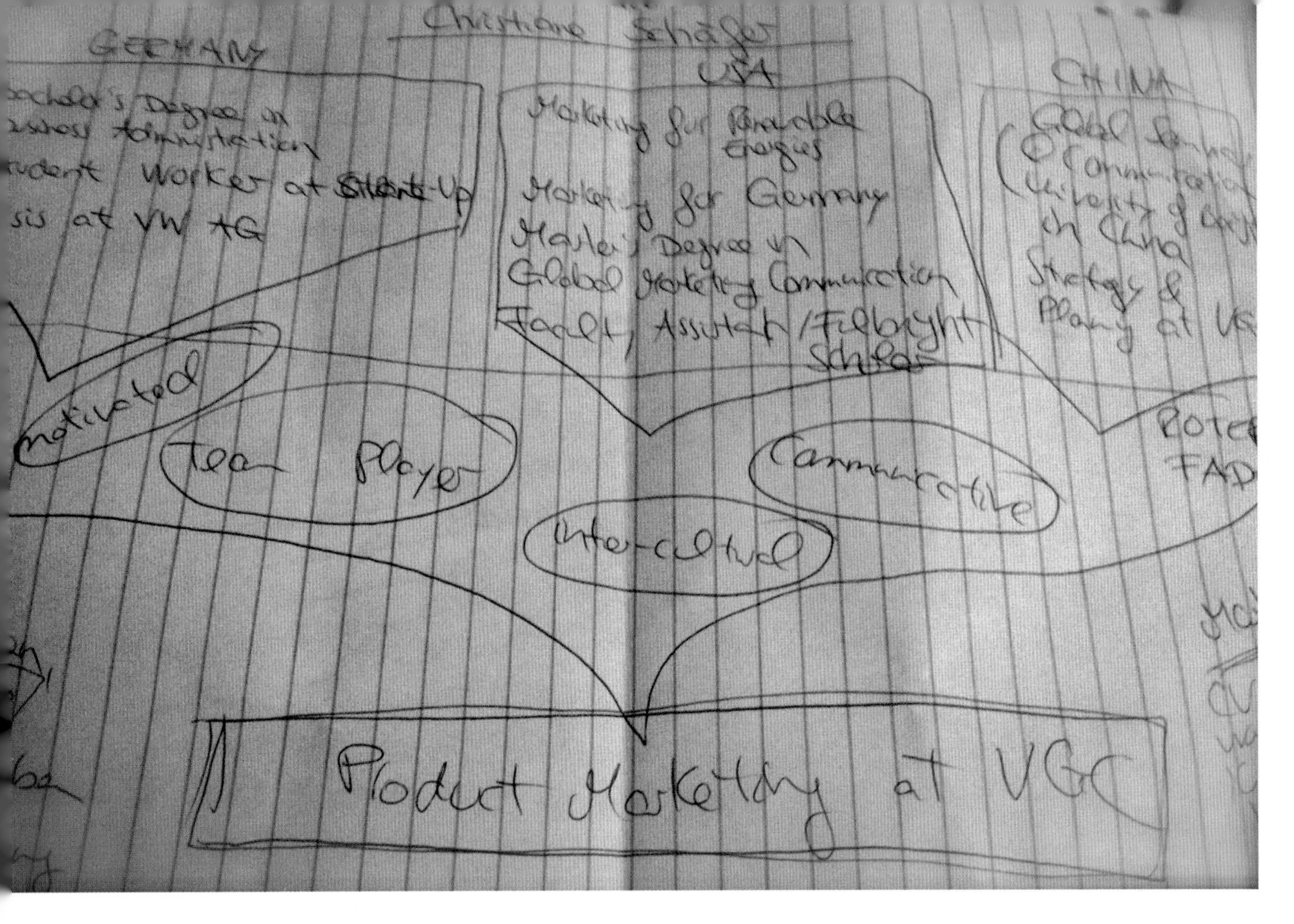

to overcome this fear of failure: One of the most memorable concepts in the class is that creativity is similar to a muscle. Against the common belief that creative thinking is a given ability, the course made it clear that everyone is capable of increasing creativity by continuous training. Accordingly, over the next four months our creativity gained muscle mass by investing time in morning pages, artist dates, blog posts and various other creative assignments. Students who thought the creativity class would require less work quickly realized this assumption was wrong.

One of the key insights that I have taken out of the class is the importance of getting out of your comfort zone in order to truly evolve and challenge yourself, as well as your established views. If someone had asked me at the beginning of my master's degree where I see myself starting my career, I never would have said in China. But with the help of the creative thinking class I learned to take a step back from my usual thinking patterns and change the perspective by asking myself "What if ... Why not?" I took the opportunity to move to China and start a job with Volkswagen Group China in Beijing despite all the concerns (lack of Chinese language skills, absence of family and friends, doubts about freedom of expression, etc.).

Moreover, the creative thinking class also helped me to prepare for my first assessment center (AC). Every candidate for a position within Volkswagen Group China has to pass an AC in order to ensure that the applicant has the appropriate skill set and fits into the company. The assignment supporting me for the AC was one I'd done in the Creative Thinking and Problem Solving class: a self-presentation with nine to twelve key visuals. It was fascinating to see how many different ways my classmates were able to present themselves —

Key Insights

1. Take the opportunities when they are in front of you, and try to actively create opportunities by asking yourself "What if ... Why not?"
2. Get out of your comfort zone, try new things and do not be afraid of failure (but make sure you don't make the same mistake twice).
3. Keep your eyes wide open: observe and experience the environment around you but also reflect about yourself and question how you behave and think.

from dough figures to cooking ingredients. Most important, I became aware of the importance of storytelling and various techniques to tell my own story. Of course, a self-presentation has to be tailored to the needs of the audience and in my case also match the key requirements of the job position I applied to. Having practiced a presentation about myself in front of my classmates and experimenting with different execution options helped me to be less nervous when one of the first tasks during the AC was a self-presentation in five minutes. I think by not just writing down my resume but instead using different colors and shapes, I was able to stand out from the other participants and leave a lasting first impression on the observers.

Nowadays, in the middle of a busy workday, it is difficult to stay creative. Some of my daily tasks do not have room for creativity, which is one of the core challenges to overcome in order to practice creative thinking after graduation. Nevertheless, I am aware of how important my creative muscle is—not only for crafting the most creative PowerPoint presentation but for problem solving as well. Fortunately, Beijing is a highly dynamic and inspiring place that offers plenty of opportunities to fuel the creative mind. By being an active part of and observing the daily life in China, I am able to keep my creative passion alive and also foster my inner artist. Riding through the city on my eBike, traveling to different parts of China, going to a wide array of events, trying new foods and studying Chinese are just a couple of ways I do that.

Looking back at my past decision, I am happy with my life's journey so far: leading from Germany to the United States and now to China, and I am excited to see where it will take me next.

ERIC ROSATI

CREATIVE DESIGN INTERN

TBWA\Chiat\Day, Los Angeles

LinkedIn: www.linkedin.com/pub/eric-rosati/59/685/4bb

I've been drawing since before I could scribble down coherent sentences in exceptionally bad handwriting. Looking back, I became interested in art one Christmas when my uncle gave me one of those "Draw Like the Pros" books on how to draw Marvel superheroes. If this meant that I could draw Spider-Man (my idol at the time), I was totally down. Whether or not you call it a hobby, an escape, or some other form of expression, drawing had peaked my interest then and continues to captivate my attention to this day. It's safe to say that aside from any personal satisfaction drawing had granted me, it had also provided me with a sense of place. By the time I was in junior high, my charcoal-caked hands and my bad attempt at growing out what I called "Led Zeppelin hair," had classified me amongst my peers as creative. Their perception of me as an artist had shaped how I saw myself.

By my angst-filled teen years, being an artist and being creative were one in the same as far as I was concerned. An artist was someone who could draw pretty damn well and shred on the guitar. The latter soon become another close passion of mine. Without hesitation, I latched onto this idea so strongly that I didn't break out of it until I got to college. If there is one universal truth about creativity that will forever be pounding away in my head, it's that drawing is so miniscule in terms of capturing what creativity and the whole creative process can achieve.

Taking a course titled Breakthrough Thinking at Emerson College helped me realize when I was using drawing as a crutch. I knew that if I put enough

time into drawing a portrait or some other image, people would respond in a relatively positive way to it. I felt so safe wrapped up in my niche that I was internally too scared to try new ideas. When presented with creative challenges, I had trouble coming up with anything that didn't involve some sort of sketch or doodle. From the get-go, I was limiting myself in terms of producing ideas that not only went beyond a pen or pencil, but the limits of physical paper. I decided that my goal from early on in the class was to think in terms of big ideas as opposed to forms of execution.

Ideas are the main source of power behind forming a connection with people. Instead of being something that's limited and tangible, ideas reside in the abstract and have the potential to take any form. As this class progressed, I found that I produced stronger results by generating more abstract ideas. Thinking in the abstract is thinking without a filter. I learned that you will have time further along in the creative process to throw your ideas against walls and poke as many holes in them as you want to. Abstract thinking does not justify a reluctance to refine and polish strong ideas. However, until you arrive at that point, you should be spontaneous with it, maybe even get a little uncomfortable.

Another great thing I discovered about abstract ideas is that they can occur at any moment. By focusing specifically on drawing, I was not introducing myself to many new experiences. I've found that trying something different allows you to focus on the present as opposed to predetermined thoughts. It is in the present where I find new, unusual connections can be made. While I found ways to incorporate drawing into some of my projects, my main ideas were spawned through alternative ways of thinking. The central themes behind a project that I did on the street artist Banksy came when I was still groggy from waking up. I had been up late the night before watching interviews and scribbling down ideas. Not only did I generate the largest amount of ideas for this project in this groggy state, I also focused on a central theme that spanned all the different executions that I chose to do.

I still love drawing, and it will always provide a creative outlet that I will find fulfilling. But now I see that focusing on one or two skills can hold you back. Putting more effort into develop-

Key Insights

1. **GET WEIRD:** There is a certain kind of uneasiness that I'm talking about. Not the "This is a bad idea" gut puncher, but rather the uneasiness that comes along with thinking whether or not your potential clients are going to think you're a nutcase. How can you push through to unknown limits if you stay stuck in what has already been done?
2. **GET UNCOMFORTABLE:** Some of my best experiences/ideas occur when I place myself in a situation that keeps me on edge. By doing this I am living in the present and not necessarily filtering in accordance to perceived future reactions or analysis of how I placed myself in the current situation. If you don't know what you're doing, you're pretty much in a corner. You have no option but to press onward and see it through.
3. **DON'T KILL YOUR BABIES (YET):** I had a teacher that once said ideas are like babies. They are going to die if you throw them at a wall when they are too young. Entertain them for a little bit no matter how weird or crazy they may be. Develop them further before you give them to the type of people who enjoy throwing them at a wall.

ing something that transcends physical execution can prove to be more rewarding than relying on an old crutch. Another effort that I am making is to continue as much as possible with the artists dates. Ideally I hope to get it to a point where they become second nature. Instead of thinking twice about doing something differently, I should just do it. This can range from deciding to get a bagel combo with guacamole on it to taking a different route home from class. In terms of being creative, I recommend trying something that's spontaneous and different. Do not filter yourself while brainstorming ideas, and think of the big ideas more so than just ways of executing them.

AMANDA MOONEY

SENIOR MANAGER,
SHANGHAI DIGITAL PRACTICE
Edelman, Shanghai City
LinkedIn: cn.linkedin.com/in/amandamooney

My phone is dead. My face is burned. My shoes are rubbed with new dirt from a new place. Seven flights in the past twenty days and I've landed here in Sarawak. I am very tired but I am very happy.

I am also three months late on an assignment to write a short piece for this book.

Tired, sunburned, very far from home and quite late, but happy.

Over the past twenty days, my office has moved from Shanghai to Kuala Lumpur, to Johor, back to Kuala Lumpur, to Penang, to Kota Kinabalu to Sarawak... from the homes of ten once-strangers-turned-friends, to the base of Mount Kinabalu at sunrise to the kampongs of Penang, to the backseat of a car driven by a kind seventy-year-old "uncle" who calls himself Gandhi, to the banks of a river discovered with an ex-sniper, and up thrilling but terrifying back roads in the mountains and jungle just before dark. Fourteen-hour days, with a crew of three, carrying more than a terabyte of footage, photos and interviews.

Eyes heavy, camera full, but happy.

My job, in title, is senior manager for Edelman China. In practice, I work with our teams and clients as a researcher and planner to help craft brand strategy. I work to help companies understand the lives, needs and complexities of the people that make up their customer bases. I work to help build or inform products, experiences and programs that help serve both corporate ambition

and customer aspiration. I work with the hope and belief that the essential connection that exists between both, if focused in the right direction, can do a tremendous amount of good in the lives and communities of customers.

Tonight my work has taken me here to Malaysia as part of a film and research project that will span at least six countries: China, Singapore, Malaysia, Vietnam, Indonesia and India, with new countries likely to follow. The project is called Words of a Generation. It's a personal window into the lives of people who have lived through rapid change in each country. It uses the emotional impact of film and the true stories of real people to help ground companies in a more personal connection with customers in these fast-moving societies. It started as a small idea I created and sent to our APACMEA (Asia Pacific, Middle East & Africa) CEO nearly a year back. Now it is an all-consuming project that will drive at least the next year and a half of my life and will result in more than thirty-five films.

Outside of this project, I have no life plan. I have no idea when I'll settle down, or where I'll settle down, or if I'll ever settle in one place, or if I'll get married or have kids or return to the United States. The only thing I know is that I've somehow landed here tonight, working on a project that I believe in and love. It is just a start, and I have so much to learn and sometimes it is very, very hard. But it is a chance very few get.

And it is a testament to a single, lasting lesson I learned in the Breakthrough Thinking class.

In class, five years back, we were asked to start taking artist dates. We had to consciously take steps to break our daily routine. We were told to walk to class using a different, slower, unfamiliar route. We were told to take the time to listen to an entire album from a genre not typical of our taste.

We were told to act often and purposefully to move outside of our place of comfort.

This simple idea pushed me to move my work to New York after graduation and then to run away on instinct, without planning or experience, to Chicago. It pushed me to plead for the chance to move anywhere outside of the United States, anywhere that felt remotely unfamiliar. It gave me the courage to say yes when a chance to move to China finally came. And it encouraged me to email a small idea—the first iteration of Words—to our CEO and then to follow that idea through with long days, unfamiliar treks, first hellos to people met in new places and an overwhelming but rewarding mountain of work.

I come from a nowhere place. A place I love, but a nowhere place nonetheless. I come from a family that has never had the chance to see the world like this. My mom just got her first passport this Christmas after I printed and filled out the application for her. And now I'm here in this hotel in Sarawak.

I have no life plan or career plan. I'm not sure what I'm really qualified to do in my work. I'm not even sure when I'll be able to get a full night's sleep. And for the next year and a half at least, I won't be in any one country for more than one month at a time.

I am quite happily lost at the moment in many respects. Five years of artists dates and I've landed only on this.

Creativity, or creative opportunity, at least — as I'm not even sure if what I'm doing would qualify as creativity-with-a-capitol-c yet — it isn't a thing, or a kind of magic, or even necessarily a talent. Creativity is something that happens in the space between purpose, endurance, question after question and the fear-mixed-with-excitement blind spot at the center of what's unfamiliar. Everyone says this kind of thing but few know what it really feels like.

It isn't a search for cool. It's caring about your work so much that you work through whatever it takes to try something new. It's knowing that you'll be uncomfortable and exposed and wrong most of the time and certainly always just starting out and that, whatever it is, it may never work in the end. It's bags under your eyes, hitting "send" even if you're quite unsure, an uncomfortable conversation or even just a scary ride up a mountain road so you can see something new. It's leaving home and missing home but really trying and really searching for something.

Tonight, for me, it's here. A long night awake in a hotel room seven flights from Shanghai—my home for now—and an assignment for this book that's three months too late. It's a first sentence on a topic too big to describe, followed by a first draft of a few hundred words. It's a start.

SIOBHAN O'SHAUGHNESSY

MARKETING MANAGER, HARVARD UNIVERSITY
Boston
LinkedIn: www.linkedin.com/in/sroshaughnessy

In the fourth grade, I was selected to participate in Odyssey of the Mind, an international problem-solving competition where students are charged to creatively solve problems ranging from building mechanical devices to presenting their own interpretation of literary classics. I was given a series of objects and scenarios and asked to quickly generate a different use or a creative solution. Everything from name a new use for this paper plate to develop a one-act play that captures the plight of average citizens of Pompeii during the eruption of Mt. Vesuvius in 79 A.D.

This was the first time the term divergent thinking had entered my vocabulary. We were encouraged to quell our inhibitions and dismiss notions of perceived absurd and outlandish thinking. In fact, there was an incentive to so-called absurdity: The more creative the solution, the more points you would receive from the judging panel. Therefore typical, safe, or vanilla answers or solutions received low scores. Odyssey of the Mind was a transformative experience for me. It offered permission to enlist my creativity when solving problems and provided me a safe zone to translate ostensibly bizarre ideas into highly potent solutions. I had found my happy place in this world.

However, all good things must come to an end. Odyssey of the Mind had ended for the season, and I moved a few months later to a different state that

Key Insights

1. Creativity is no longer a luxury. Consider creativity the currency of the future in business.
2. Time alone is vital to creative problem-solving. Group think can be inhibiting. Allow yourself time away from the group to be in your own thoughts and generate ideas. Breakaway!
3. Create an environment that encourages openness and rewards idea generation. Lose egos, barriers, norms, accepted definitions and models, and criteria. And, regardless of the author, the best idea should win every time!

did not offer the program. I had been thrown back into the rote educational system, where creativity was reserved for art class (if one were lucky). As a result, my creative muscle became atrophic.

This creative complacency continued until my first semester of graduate school, where I was enrolled in Creative Thinking and Problem Solving. I soon realized how much the course resembled the Odyssey of the Mind model. In-class exercises suddenly jogged the creative muscle that had been in a state of rest for years, forcing it to do some real heavy lifting in the early days of the course. I had not been challenged to think this way in years. However, as I progressed through the course, the muscle memory kicked in, shifting from what was once an extremely uneasy state at the beginning of the course to a well-oiled system by the end of the course. It was as if my world had been monotone for years, approaching problem-solving through safe, ordinary methods. I had become risk averse, conditioned to believe that out-of-bounds thinking would ostracize me from my peers and marginalize me from the group. The human need for belongingness is a strong one, even if it means compromising your intellectual development.

As with Odyssey of the Mind, the Creative Thinking and Problem Solving course provided me permission to be creative once again, to apply a divergent thinking lens when looking at a problem. In this course, creativity was encouraged and rewarded. I have retrained my thinking, giving myself license to exploit the unbeaten path and uncharted waters. I use the tools and tactics learned in the course in my everyday life. For example, when presented with a problem, I often deconstruct the issue by looking at it from an inverse perspective. This tactic has been enormously helpful in identifying potential pitfalls that would otherwise go unnoticed.

While the course is finite, its residual benefits are infinite. While I took away many tools and tactics, arguably the most potent lesson learned was that creativity is no longer a luxury. It is vitally important and essential to solving some of today's most complex problems. Creativity is discipline agnostic. It can be applied in everything from engineering to medicine to poverty to coding. As a born-again Creativity Evangelist, I look forward to continuing my creative journey and educating my peers about the value of unbridled creativity in their everyday lives.

LIZ GOODWIN

USER EXPERIENCE DESIGNER. MOM. RUNNER. (NOT NECESSARILY IN THAT ORDER)

Sapient Global Markets, Boston

Twitter: @LizMGoodwin

LinkedIn: www.linkedin.com/pub/liz-goodwin/1/582/b55

The first assignment I turned in for my Creative Thinking class was absolutely terrible. I sat in the back row of the classroom waiting for my turn to present my assignment, my anxiety mounting as I watched my classmates present their work. The rest of the class just seemed to get it. Their presentations were imaginative but cohesive. They were both uniquely their own, while being universally relatable. My presentation was a mess—it had no theme, no structure. I remember thinking to myself, *I am seriously outmatched here.*

The next few weeks of the class continued to be uncomfortable for me. Most of the daily homework exercises and the assignments we presented in class were well outside of my comfort zone. But as the weeks progressed and I continued to learn the building blocks of creative thinking, I began to grow more at ease and adept at taking on each new task. Instead of staring blankly at each new assignment, I had learned how to frame and approach the problem. And I was beginning to loosen up and was able to let go of the things that had been holding me back from coming up with my best ideas: self-doubt, uncertainty, fear of failure.

Key Insights

1. Dive right in. There's no better way to learn than to do.
2. Don't be afraid to make a fool out of yourself. So often we don't do something, or we don't go all out, because we're afraid of looking stupid. Ask questions and reveal what you don't know; try something new and maybe not be great at it the first time around. Give yourself permission to fail every now and then.
3. Figure out what inspires you and try to incorporate that into your day and into your workspace. Whether it's being outside or listening to music—breaking out of your typical work environment will give you new perspective.

Also, I was enjoying the work. Creative thinking requires you to dig in and reflect, and put something of yourself on the page. Which can be scary—it can be difficult to accept critique of work that's so personal to you. But, at the same time, it's an opportunity for growth and self-expression. Putting so much of yourself into your work allows you to produce work that is truly authentic and meaningful.

By the time of the final exam, I had learned to completely reframe my approach to problem solving, and I was able to take on projects that would have felt impossible to me that first week of class.

The lessons that I learned in that course have certainly stayed with me through the years. If I'm in a rut, I'll go through some of the exercises in the workbooks to spark my creativity.

But what has stayed with me the most from that course is that you don't have to be able to draw or write music to be creative. Creativity is simply about looking at things in a different way. I still consider myself to be very much a logical and analytical person. But I've learned that, while that may be my dominant nature, I can still tap into my more creative side and use those skills and qualities to find a different approach.

Like anything, though, it takes practice and nurturing. In my job as a user experience designer, I have the opportunity to develop my creativity through my work, sometimes in the form of sketching out ideas for a user interface, other times guiding users or project stakeholders—many of whom also consider themselves uncreative—through participatory design sessions and helping them discover their own inner designer.

I also try to find ways in my personal life to continue to nurture that creativity and develop those skills. I recently took a drawing class because, while my job title may be "designer," drawing does not come naturally to me at all. But it doesn't even have to be as formal as taking a class or learning a new skill. It can simply be doing the things that you love. For me, that's spending as much time as I can doing projects with my kids, or just playing with them and photographing them and our adventures together. Watching my kids reminds me that creativity isn't something that just some people are born with. It's something that we're all born with. Some of us may lose sight of it somewhere along the way, but it's always there, ready to be rediscovered.

LORELEI BANDROVSCHI

COPYWRITER

Young & Rubicam Group, New York

LinkedIn: www.linkedin.com/in/lbandrovschi

Less marketing, more making. Fed up with classes that focused on the business inner workings of advertising, that would prepare me for a career in the industry, but only at arm's length from the creative side, I jumped at the opportunity to take a marketing class with *creativity* in the title. But there was one distinction between my expectations and the class itself, a distinction that frustrated me at the time, but which, in hindsight, I could not be more grateful for.

You see, I was going to become a copywriter. This plan had been clear in my mind for years before I stepped into the classroom. It guided me as I decided to leave my home in Romania and go to a school I found by Googling "US college advertising." But things were not going according to plan. My portfolio was growing at a snail's pace. I had just found out about the existence of portfolio schools, and spending another two years (and I do mean spending—there was no way I could afford it), before I could even begin my career was not an option. I damned Google search and signed up for the class, determined to wring out of it everything that applied to advertising and hoping we wouldn't dwell too long on anything that didn't.

Writing this now, I can't help but laugh at myself and my narrow-mindedness, but at the time it seemed I had a very specific set of skills to master. Yet the things I remember most from the class, the ones I carry with me still, weren't specific to advertising at all. The brilliance of Saul Bass's title treatments, or Stefan Sagmeister's witty design, sparked in me an appetite for cre-

Key Insights

1. It's not always fun. This morning on my way to work, the flute player in the subway told me how many hours he had poured into learning to play, many of those frustrating, so now he could actually enjoy doing it. Practicing creativity feels good once you get into it, but it's okay not to love every second of the growing pains.
2. Make routine. Break routine. The opposite of creativity is inertia. Routine. Anything is creative as long as it's a break from the expected—whether it's what you do or how you do it. At the same time though, creativity is a practice, and it helps to inject it into your life in sustained habits, whether you are doodling, writing, doing social experiments, whatever. Once those become routine, hack them in some creative way.
3. Why > How.

ativity that was not confined to the realm of advertising. Before, I had thought that my singular, obsessive focus on advertising was a plus: I was not going into it as a disappointed artist forced to make ends meet, but eagerly, as my first choice. Now I felt like my blinders were coming off and my palate was expanding. I recognized the kind of thinking that had drawn me to advertising manifested in exciting new ways. I embraced it.

At the same time, the class introduced me to lateral thinking and divergent thinking, which are still key parts of my creative process. The first challenge I tackled with these new tools was my own career path. Rather than try to compete with the portfolio school students, I decided to carve out my own path. I took on a double-major that allowed me to take film and web classes. I studied script writing and made short films. I built websites, dabbled in audio production. One time, I staged an installation that people moved through in slow-motion. I practiced creativity both in ways that could give me an advantage for my future career and in ways that seemed to have no connection.

It paid off. I became a copywriter.

Surprisingly enough, all of my creative dabbling, along with the broader creative principles from class, actually served me in one of my favorite projects yet: a promotion for Showtime's hit series, *Dexter*. The task was to create a narrative so engrossing, it would keep fans engaged between two seasons, by building on the dramatic finale without giving away the next season. It was an alternate-reality game, a story that plays out as though it was real, happening everywhere from websites to phone lines to places in the real world. All this in real-time, with participants becoming characters in the narrative and influencing its course.

Through a combination of luck, sweat and insanity, I was the lead writer on the project. I had taken the role early on and was part of the four-person crew that delivered the pitch to our client. I was also the only person in the room in their twenties. Any team less ballsy would have never given me the heavy lifting of walking potential clients through the entire narrative. But I did, and we won.

Leading the *Dexter* narrative was an experience unlike anything I ever had before. An entire room was covered in story lines, lining the walls like a map, evolving as the narrative did. Plot twists were developed on the fly to react to audience participation or to unexpected glitches in our carefully constructed reality. At the end of three months, we had crafted a story that fans loved so much, they cried. It was exhausting and exhilarating.

This project was also a testament to my constant creative practice. We were not just making up the work: We were making up how we were working. Roles were blurred, teams formed around needs not titles, and everything was an experiment. We did our research and had great advisors, but in the end, we knew we wanted to do things that hadn't been done before, and we were willing to take chances.

Ever since the creative thinking class, I have put myself to task to maintain creative principles both in what I make and in how I make it. And I've kept the blinds off from my view of advertising. Early on, I made a newspaper ad into Seuss-like news of the future to make politicians see themselves as heroes for the next generation. I helped PRODUCT(RED) develop a physical store design that connected shoppers around the world with each other and with their impact in Africa. Recently I turned a street wear ad into a nineties-flavored slow jam that might just inspire sensual thoughts about fleeces. And outside of advertising, I organized a TEDx event that brought together some of New York's most exciting minds to rethink the future of cities.

I even found myself teaching. With portfolio schools offering lots of classes focused on those specific skills I was so eager to find in the creative thinking classroom, I sought to get students asking not just how they *could* make an ad (or app, or anything), but what they *should* make. Like I did back at Showtime, students present their work to clients in person. It's kind of amazing, every time.

So I hope this book finds those who think they know exactly what they want out of it. And I hope it surprises them. Or rather, helps them surprise themselves.

HARINI CHANDRASEKAR

DESIGN STRATEGIST

Twitter: @harinicsekar

LinkedIn: http://www.linkedin.com/in/harinic

"Making the simple complicated is commonplace; making the complicated simple, awesomely simple, that's creativity." — Charles Mingus

As a recent student of the Creative Thinking and Problem Solving class, I can confidently state that my perspectives have shifted over the three months of the course. I now embrace the fact that creativity can be applied to every facet of life. Coming from a design background, I walked into this course believing it was going to be a repetition of what I had previously done. This wasn't the case. At all. Through a series of applied learning practices, our cohort learned of the challenges and the triumphs of working together and that regardless of whatever professional background you came from and skills you came with, creativity is and will always be the game changer. Creative confidence grew over the course of the semester quietly but surely as the course promoted learning by doing.

Personally, I came to this class with a Masters in industrial design, feeling conflicted between my creative background and the new realm of marketing that I was stepping into. I was plagued with a heavy feeling that through this program I would be moving too far from my core skills. Prior to applying for the program, I had voiced my concerns to Professor Vogel. A great listener, he smiled and remarked that if I did join the program, the cross disciplinary creative overlaps would surprise me. Now, nearly at the end of his course, I can state with surety that it did and still does. Creative applications truly are limitless and the ability to have the vision to realize that creativ-

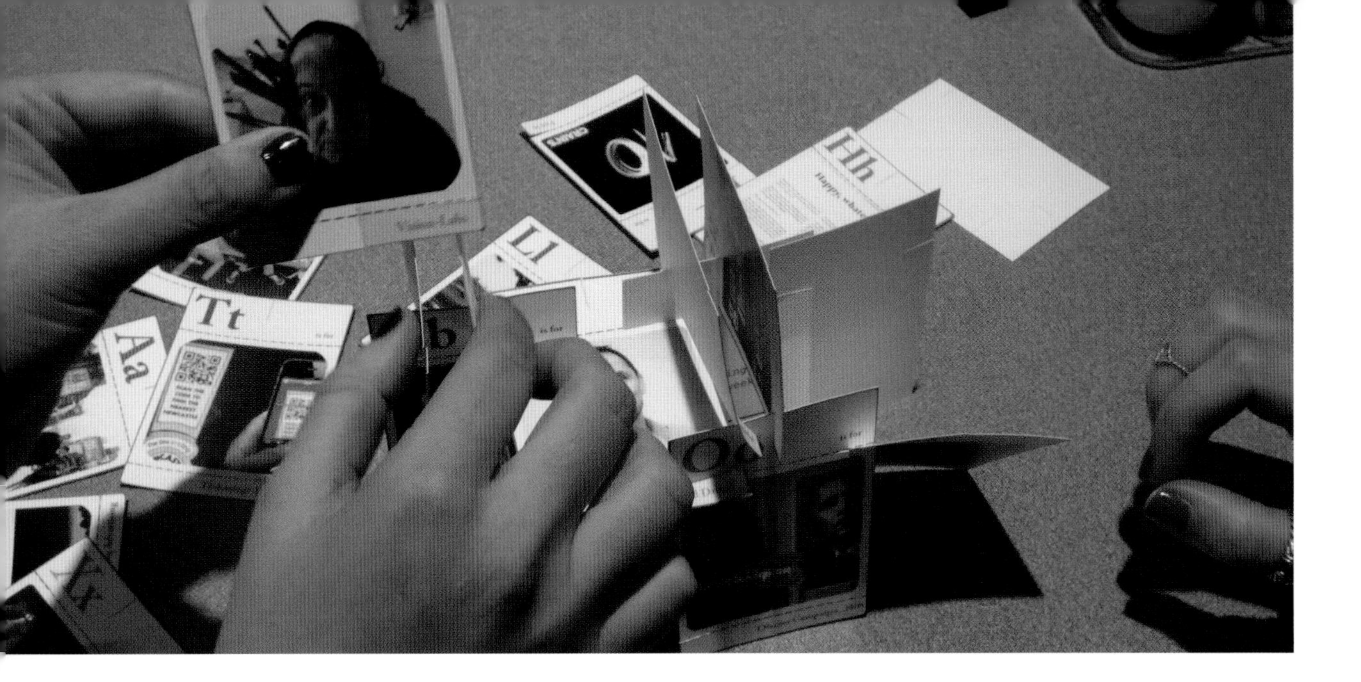

ity can be applied in everything from bio-sciences to marketing, management, engineering, law, medicine and literally everything we do is critical to staying relevant in these changing times. While art, design and advertising are fields traditionally associated with being creative, what makes Professor Vogel's course unique is the ability to apply creative thinking to fields not conventionally thought of as being creative such as marketing, management and communication. It enables people who are used to thinking in linear patterns to learn to deal with ambiguity and be innovative in new ways. This will prove a key factor in being able to differentiate oneself after graduation in competitive job markets and beyond in the real working world. Times have changed dramatically and the globe has shrunk to link people between its poles making us realize the underlying universality of things that unite us even as we celebrate the differences. Now more than ever, a course that broadens ones vision and enables us to make those critical connections through creative thinking helps keep the field relevant and dynamic.

I believe the nature of the creative thinking course is such that it is imbibed almost subconsciously. A lot of the students, including me, tend to now apply these concepts without even really thinking about it as it slowly becomes second nature and intuitive to arrive at a multiple solutions before converging on a few through creative problem solving and design thinking methods. Possibly the depth of what we have achieved in this short time will strike us months and years down the line as we use these vital insights to tackle issues at jobs that we land and projects we undertake. The sheer advantage in divergent thinking with no judgement, no matter how silly an idea, before concentrating our thoughts on ideas that we can then build on is infinite and having that knowledge, empowering.

I would like to illustrate my thoughts by sharing an example of some work done for the course in which I was assigned Droga5 as an agency to study and present. Through this journey, I realized that by looking at the commonalities between seemingly unrelated topics and bringing them together in a new way you might create something very powerful. The whole can be infinitely greater than the sum of its parts if there is synergy, creating memorable stories that stick with viewers long after a 30 second campaign.

Key Insights

1. Creative thinking can be applied to anything you do in life.
2. It isn't exclusive to a select few fortunate creative geniuses, and you don't have to be born creative. You just need to exercise that part of the brain to create new creative muscle. To this end, consistency is everything.
3. The principles of divergent, convergent thinking, brainstorm sessions, mind mapping exercises, morning pages, etc. can be applicable to everything in professional and personal journeys from decision making such as moving cities or houses, choosing option A over B, having a baby, job searches, campaigns, product development. You name it and these techniques can be used to arrive at a more well-thought out holistic solution.
4. Anybody has the ability arrive at unique, original solutions. In fact, the more diverse their background and the less exposure they might have had to these processes earlier, richer and more unique the results.

Also, the ability to engage through interactive storytelling to creatively solve problems is key. Everybody has a story to tell and most people like to share their story. Communicators, artists, designers, illustrators, advertisers all attempt to craft stories through their unique lens and transform their insights into an engaging narrative. One thought that resonated with me in the examples I saw, was that involving the consumers and giving them a platform to tell their tale can be a very convincing and empowering tool. When you give people an opportunity to engage, they all feel more involved and connected instantly

I began my project by mapping out 150 ideas of possible ways in which I could present the agency. After I was tapped out of ideas, I re-connected the ideas that had potential and built on those combining different ideas to create something new.

As the agency world was new to me, I decided to start from the basics, the A to Z of it, if you will. Connecting back to the basics and learning through known means but doing it all in a fresh way.

I wanted my audience (my classmates at Graduate school and my Professor) to feel engaged with the process as well as the company and so I developed an interactive element in which they could map their learning in a 3D Mind map forming their own connections as I presented the Droga story.

Building on the core philosophy of introducing something familiar in an unfamiliar way and compelling the audience to think for themselves in this space out of their comfort zone, I arrived upon the idea of presenting the ad agency as an interactive installation.

Through this journey, I learned that work, life, ideology, philosophy *can* converge. You just have to make it happen by creating honest and engaging conversations and keeping the communication real at every stage. Don't be afraid to be creatively bold and strategically sound to make those unlikely connections before anyone else does.

MATTHEW FIORENTINO

DIRECTOR OF MARKETING

Visible Measures, Boston

Twitter: @FiorentinoM

LinkedIn: www.linkedin.com/in/matthewfiorentino

I've been thinking quite a bit about Donald Duck recently. We've been watching and re-watching a particular episode with our daughter, where Donald tries to make waffles. The fun begins when Donald pours rubber cement into the batter instead of baking powder. The batter gets so rubbery that he can't get the spoon out of it. The rest of the episode follows his unsuccessful attempts to dislodge the spoon. My favorite bit is when he tries to stop a fast-moving crack splitting down the wall, caused by a hatchet flying into the ceiling, by opening the window to cut off its path. This gag and many others like it last for over seven minutes.

Beyond the brilliant entertainment of these jokes, I find myself thinking about the creativity needed to develop them. Being able to invent a simple premise like rubbery waffle batter is one thing, but being able to create bit after bit and sustain and build the momentum with so many variations without repetition is extraordinary.

Thinking of Donald's rubbery waffle batter brings me back to the circle exercise I did in a creativity course. The goal is to start with a circle and create a simple image—a cat's face, a baseball, the moon, etc.—and then repeat the process as many times as possible. The exercise stretches mental flexibility, the same ability needed to write multiple waffle batter jokes.

The promise of mental flexibility is simple—you can create more solutions to any problem. And to create more solutions, you need to make connections

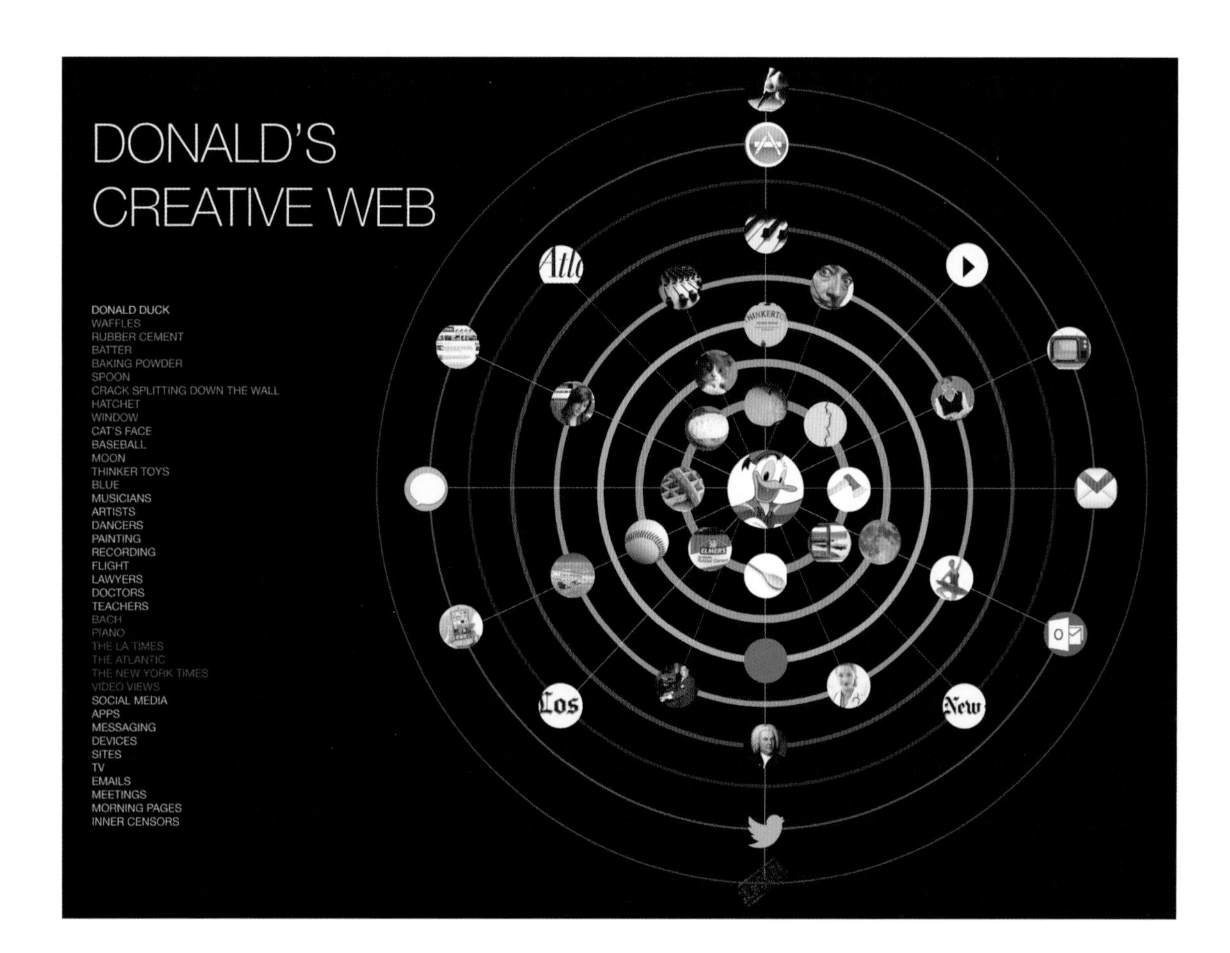

you didn't see before. This comes by shifting your perspective.

Perhaps one of the easiest ways to experience this shift in perspective is through color concentration, an exercise you can find in Michael Michalko's *Thinkertoys*. Take a moment, look around the room and search only for the color blue. Notice the patterns that emerge, the blue objects you hadn't registered before, even the absence of blue. Whatever your experience, you are now looking at your world differently and picking up signals and potential connections you hadn't before. Finding, interpreting and producing something new from a connection like this is what sits at the core of creativity.

When you think about creativity this way, it immediately becomes accessible to everyone. Which is the good news. The bad news is that most people still think creativity is the domain of musicians, artists and dancers. When I was young, I would frequently hear comments like "You're creative, you figure it out." Or, "But you're creative. I could never do that." Even in Thomas's Creativity course, the majority of the students in class didn't consider themselves creative.

Part of the reason people don't think of themselves as creative is because we rarely recognize and appreciate true creativity when we see it. This stems from the misconception that creativity equals artistry. Instead of looking for obvious creative results—a painting, recording, performance, etc.—we should appreciate mental flexibility and the quality of solutions we see. Here's a banal ex-

Key Insights

1. **ANYONE CAN BE CREATIVE:** You don't have to be an artist to be creative. Creativity is simply the ability to create a number of ideas for any situation or opportunity.
2. **MAKE A CONNECTION:** Shift your perspective and make connections you didn't see before. Finding, interpreting, and producing new connections are at the core of creativity.
3. **EMBRACE YOUR CREATIVE SELF:** Take the time to get to know your creative self and toss your inner censor. What inspires you? What are you passionate about? Being able to direct your creativity in a meaningful and effective way in real-time can make all the difference in the world.

ample: Think about the last time you had a problem with a flight. If you had a representative who was creative, they could work around the system to solve your problem and make you happy. If not, your life was terrible for a while. It makes a world of difference. It's the same with lawyers, doctors, teachers and any profession.

You could argue that we're blurring the lines between talent, expertise and creativity. But there is a difference. Look at a traditional example: musicians. There is a big difference between technical mastery of an instrument, musicality and interpretation, and creation. The giants of music flourished in all these areas. Bach would write piano inventions so quickly that he could help his transcriber finish the final copies of the originals. This is a distinct difference from a pure performer, who spends years building technical mastery, an understanding of a composer's influences and intentions, and then interprets a manuscript to re-create the composer's music.

In the advertising industry, you see these distinctions every day. There are talented people everywhere you look, across all levels of expertise. They are efficient at developing and executing media plans, eloquent when speaking with the client, skilled at creating campaign strategies and more. They all speak about the value of creativity when producing a great ad. But when it comes to the daily grind, there are precious few people who speak about creativity and creative processes. Leave creativity to the creatives, right?

But that shouldn't be the case. In my work, where we distribute and measure the performance of branded video, I use creative thinking techniques frequently to create new opportunities. We are in the unique position to have the world of video literally at our fingertips and some of the smartest journalists rely on us to tell them what's happening in this world. We get questions like "Who's more viral, cats or dogs?" from the *Los Angeles Times* (it's cats) and "How many days did it take the biggest virals to reach 100 million views?" from *The Atlantic*. Answering these questions requires industry knowledge, a deep understanding of our platform and video analytics, but also an ability to find the answer creatively. No one is going to give you the answer, so you need to develop a number of solutions and run with the one that is going to resonate most. When you do it right, you are rewarded for being creative, smart and timely. And, if you're lucky, you get a quote in *The New York Times*.

But it's hard work that requires creative dexterity to react to our always-on world. Between social media, apps, messaging, devices, sites, television, newsletters, emails, phone calls, meetings, work interruptions, personal interruptions, we have to deal with an incredible amount of information every day. While at times it can be overwhelming, this constant stream of information is an opportunity to draw inspiration in real time. The challenge is knowing and understanding your creative self—being able to direct your creativity in a meaningful and effective way and knowing what to do with inspiration when it strikes.

Much of the key concepts in the creativity course provide the foundation for unlocking the creative self. Morning pages was one of my favorite activities, one that I continued well after graduation and continue today whenever inspiration strikes. The secret of morning pages, I've found, is its ability to get beyond your inner censors. I spend a significant amount of time writing for work and when I did my morning pages my writing was dramatically more fluid. Developing this type of strength is like any other skill. The more you train, the better you get.

And as I watch Donald Duck with my daughter, I think about her creativity. I think about it flourishing as she grows and learns to do more things, but then I worry about how social influences and expectations will inhibit her creativity as she gets older. I want to help her find her creative self and get beyond her inner censors and not worry about what everyone will think of her work, or her, and ultimately, to be able to create things she will love and enjoy every day.

Even though she might not be able to appreciate the mental flexibility of Donald Duck's creators when we watch him fight waffle batter for now, I'm hopeful that with creative thinking she'll be able to add a few bits of her own one day.

CREATIVE EXECUTIVE
PROFILES

JOHNNY VULKAN

Johnny Vulkan, one of the founding partners of Anomaly believes his organization's point of differentiation is that they do not try to answer questions by focusing on the medium. "We don't think in terms of advertising or PR or digital or production innovation. We're very much grounded in a creative solution for our client's business problem."

Anomaly's creative process starts "much further back" than a traditional agency's. "We do have a process; it's called argument, and for the most part it's the friendliest version of a debate. We have a circle diagram that represents this. It puts the business problem at the center and then surrounds it with a diverse range of thinkers and disciplines, we then let the debates play out so we can interrogate the problem from every perspective." This often requires meetings of a spectrum of people, ranging from designers to digital strategists. "Everybody understands the conversation differently and applies their own biases to that," says Vulkan. "On the outset, we are looking for a range of different types of creative thinkers to engage in what has to be the broadest conversation."

It is this mentality that has allowed Anomaly to explore numerous business ventures in pursuit of the best marketing solutions for their clients. From creating a worker training program in Detroit to redesigning the outside of a freight truck, Anomaly does not limit itself.

If company leaders feel like they are unable to provide the best resources to their clients, they are not afraid to collaborate with others. In the past Vulkan and his team at Anomaly have worked with Big Spaceship, among others firms. "We're not trying to own everything," Vulkan notes, "and we think we see the other agencies as competitors as much as we see them as collaborators, because we kind of feel that there's enough business out there for all of us." Vulkan believes in what he calls the "karma of business," and judging by the success of the organization, this theory appears to be working. "If you just keep trying to do the right thing, then the business keeps coming," he says, "We very rarely pitch. Most of our client comes through recommendations from other clients and we talk ourselves into the projects."

For Vulkan and his team at Anomaly, one of the biggest challenges is the omnipresent need to have an organizational structure. "A conventional ad agency has a recognizable factory system that has a brief that goes into a defined department that spends a certain amount of defined time within that department and comes out in a certain format and is sold in familiar way." But at Anomaly, the business model is anything but traditional. "When your company's premise is 'What's the question we're even asking?', then it's very hard to formalize that process. It's much more fluid and open ended. The issue that gives us though is that there are fewer, repeatable actions."

Some of Vulkan's inspiration for this open-minded business concept stems back to his British roots. "I think in the UK, the industry thought advertising was an extension of the arts. I think that in the U.S. advertising and the communications industry thinks it's an extension of commerce, which is more grounded in what I had studied in marketing." At Anomaly, employees are expected to deliver results not awards, a philosophy Vulkan believes should be taken more seriously in the advertising industry. "Our job is not art, it's commerce; but that can be artistic," he says.

Working toward this idea of artistic commerce, the open layout at Anomaly is designed to foster optimal collaboration amongst employees. "We are nonhierarchical in how we sit, so different disciplines are dispersed throughout the company," he says. "Gradually we've seen the personal desk sizes shrinking and the amount of collaboration space is expanding." Vulkan notes that most of the work at Anomaly happens around whiteboards and sofas, but the concept of each worker having a desk is not entirely obsolete. "People like the stability of the desk, even if it is a place to charge your devices and to set up and keep your clutter and your ephemera and those kinds of things." Desk or no desk, Anomaly employees all have something unique to bring to the communal table. Coming from a wide variety of different backgrounds, from traditional business to biology, Vulkan says they all share a common thread. "I think what ties them together is really an innate sense of curiosity."

ANDREW DEITCHMAN

Andrew Deitchman of Mother New York does not claim to be a psychiatrist, but he believes people are "sad" beings, who try to find meaning and acceptance in their lives. Deitchman theorizes that different companies have ways of meeting those human needs, either through titles or perks that make one feel important, and often manifested through hierarchical business structures. "What we try to do at Mother is strip as much of that away as we possibly can," he says. Instead of creating artificial structures or handing out important titles, Deitchman focuses on the initial reasons why people like to work in the business in the first place. According to him there is a love for the creative pursuit. "Because they love the craft, they love the work, they like the thought process, it makes their brain happy, they problem solve, all that stuff."

Mother operates on a relatively flat hierarchy, but this has proved challenging. Deitchman says this is "very hard to manage." He says there is a reason hierarchal organizations are the norm. "It's more efficient; it's easier to manage, and it's a smarter way of doing things. I mean, it just is," he says. Despite the challenges Deitchman believes the structure has greatly benefited Mother. "For us, it creates more happiness, it creates more of a sense of possibility and responsibility and ownership."

At Mother, employees are given little personal recognition for their work. Instead all recognition is celebrated as a team. When the agency releases a piece of work, the credits read something like this: Art Director-Mother, Copywriter-Mother, Strategist-Mother and so on. "It's about our collective output ... It's not for everybody, and it's not an easy thing to manage," Deitchman says. This has cost the agency in the past, he admits. "We've lost good people at times because they want to go somewhere else and have a big title or have their name in lights, so to speak, relative to some of the work, and that's fine." But he would not change anything about the team-centric nature of Mother. "For us, it's simply that we're trying to foster creativity in our way," he adds.

Mother's own brand of creativity is unlike any other traditional ad agency. The New York agency has made more than great advertisements; they have unveiled numerous products, such as whiskey and an upcoming mobile application, and they have even dabbled in planning rock festivals. Deitchman attributes their success, in part, to his entrepreneurial spirit. "I don't look at anything and think 'Oh, we couldn't do that, that's not the business that we're in.'" In order be successful in all of these endeavors, Deitchman believes that Mother's flat structure is essential. "All of this is done with one core group of creators and in order for that to function, people can't have a sense of self-importance," he says. One of the biggest inhibitions to creativity at Mother, in Deitchman's mind, is having the "that's not my job" mentality. The methodology at Mother works to "break people down," allowing them to "get to their most basic reason for why they are in this business to begin with, and try to create as much joy and happiness connected to that."

Creating the right environment that brings out the best creativity and where people are happy is an important aspect. Bringing in the right combination of people is another. "When you have an agency that has a really nice reputation, attracting great talent is not your biggest issue," says Deitchman. He has learned that inspiring the best creative in people is highly correlated with two traits he and his team are looking for: kindness and openness. Deitchman adds, "People need to be able to sit around a bunch of boards from all different sorts of craft expertise and work together and have fun together."

"It's simply that we're trying to foster creativity in our way..."

The space at Mother also reflects the openness of their employees. For Deitchman, this means having a "perfectly imperfect" space. "We didn't do a lot to it and ... I think that creates a casualness and a sense that you can stick anything up on any wall and you're not going to break anything," he says. "There is nothing pristine about it." In addition, the space is constantly changing. From one day to the next, everything at Mother can change, from the contents of the office fridge to the furniture in the space. Seating arrangements are even changed every few months to prevent people from getting too comfortable. "If you're in a space that feels like it's finished, like it's done ... you don't feel like you're in a dynamic environment," Deitchman asserts.

When looking toward the future, Deitchman is optimistic. Though he does not foresee Mother ever being a thousand-person organization, he thinks the agency will become more significant over time. He wants Mother to have the well-known reputation that Goldman Sachs is known for within the financial industry. "Ten years from now, whether a kid is coming out from journalism school or film school or design school or architecture school or something involving technology, and so on and so on, he tells his mom and dad his first job is at Mother they know what that is, they are excited for them because our brand becomes this celebrated company that has very wide, very open arms to a very broad group of creators," he quips. This can only be achieved by embracing the reality that the definition of Mother as a company is far beyond that of a traditional ad agency.

DAVID DROGA

David Droga, founder of Droga5, describes the creative advertising industry as "creativity with a purpose." Somewhere in between the freedom of the arts and the discipline of business, it is a "merry dance between commerce and art." Each piece of work by Droga5 is a direct by-product of both strategic and creative thinking that considers both the client and how to maintain a competitive edge. Because of this, when building his creative team, Droga not only looks for curious, dependable and genuine creative people, but for those who can solve problems. "I look for people with disparate backgrounds and give them the canvas and the freedom to express themselves."

The environment of Droga5 is based in the collaborative—a forward-thinking place where its creative team is generous about sharing their thoughts and abilities. Although Droga fosters a certain amount of freedom, the agency is not a "free-for-all art-fest" with creativity for the sake of it. For humanitarian to pop-culture problems and everything in between, imagination and creativity is the solution. "There's purpose and intention in everything we do," says Droga.

Purpose and intention are apparent in the structure of Droga5, which is made up of defined departments. Aside from the creative core, the strategic department works on "how and where and why" the agency should say things, while the account service department builds relationships and keeps everyone on track. Daily operations and business rely on information technology and legal departments; and last but not least, there's the invaluable production department. Droga says that "the only thing worse than not having a great idea is screwing up a great idea in production."

Regardless of departmentalized responsibilities, Droga says that the creative product does not come from one department or even any particular process. One technique Droga does push, however, is exploring an idea in multiple ways before deciding on which to go with. "I try to encourage people not to fall in love with their first thoughts ... don't fle+sh it out so much that you spend all your time on one thing. Give yourself the freedom to explore multiple places."

It may come as a surprise given the industry, but Droga does not expect his employees to be experts in advertising. While an appreciation and understanding is key, too much concentration on the industry can be distracting when the overall mission and purpose of Droga5 is to move forward. In many ways, these features of the agency mirror Droga's own identity:

"I've always kept it simple. Then there's this annoying competitive streak, which has always made we want to do more and more. As a creative person, you always want to feel relevant and creative and a functioning creative. I don't want to be sort of a retrospective creative; I want to feel like I'm doing, making, and contributing every day, on every level. I love that that. Maybe the naiveté of that is a blessing. I wish I could sell out, but I just can't."

Employees at Droga5 have a unique mash up of confidence and insecurity, traits that Droga himself loves. He believes the dichotomy between the two traits creates good creative work. "It's when they wrestle each and manifest themselves in interesting ways—confident to try something new, confident enough to say something stupid. And insecure enough to sort of push on and keep on investigating and working hard," he asserts.

Droga understands that the culture of an agency is bigger, and more important, than any single department, and as a result everyone should be involved in defining the culture. At Droga5, the progress and future of the agency relies on the collaboration of all of the employees. "This collection of people are actually driving this forward, not just the people in the leadership positions," he says.

MICHAEL LEBOWITZ

From job descriptions to departments, creativity is a label commonly used in the advertising industry. But at Big Spaceship, things are done differently. As founder & CEO Michael Lebowitz explains, "We're the only agency that I know of in the world that has no creative directors." You won't see the word *creativity* in any other employee's title either. Using *creativity* in a title is a common practice that Lebowitz describes as "one of the most awful things about the industry." Big Spaceship dismisses this idea of labeling a single group of people "*the* creatives," since everyone in the agency "participates in creativity."

So with creativity as a baseline quality, what is a core characteristic that employees need to possess? According to Lebowitz, it's all about curiosity. "We look for people who want to be doing this kind of work, who think this work is really interesting," he says. "People who want to explore and aren't necessarily looking for stability and equilibrium as the defining factors for their job, but exploration and newness and discovery."

Along with trading in equilibrium for excitement, Big Spaceship employees do not follow the typical vertical management structure. Instead the agency operates on a horizontal structure, with people working on an even playing field and figuring out how to solve problems together. You won't find the typical divided departments. The open-format layout of the space reflects this feature. "One of the things that I really want is for people to think of the space itself and the company itself as a canvas, not as a structure," says Lebowitz. "Sure there are some limitations to it. I define the edges of the canvas to some level and the rules of the palette ... but really I want them to 'make' this place every day."

Although Lebowitz admits to a huge amount of humor, joking and even sometimes practical jokes (often used intentionally to promote a certain workplace comfort level), he sums up the environment at Big Spaceship as "managed chaos," a description best exemplified by knives and magnets. Read on:

"We have a magnetic knife rack in the kitchen and for many, many days someone [or maybe] many people were going in and creating patterns with the knives. And then somebody else was taking a cell phone picture of it every day, so it was [being] documented really organically. It got really elaborate and then the refrigerator poetry made its way in and then dangling spoons. I've got about thirty of these images and I show them pretty often to people. I think its one of the most important things that we've done, not because the output is important, but because of what it says about this place. All of these little moments in this little place are an opportunity for expression, of tinkering and toying and seeing what happens, everything we do is content."

"No one directs creativity."

Although everybody participates in creativity at Big Spaceship, they do have a process beyond making sure that "a lot of types of minds" are surrounding things. Lebowitz emphasizes that the agency is rigorous in their research, auditing everything that may possibly be related both informationally and behaviorally, or as he says, by answering the question, "How can we figure out what people do and what they want?" Extensive research is just one of the many steps the agency takes to succeed, as their core idea of a failure is not trying hard enough. "If we try something and it doesn't get the audience or response we want, that's not a failure as long as we tried. If we pitch a business and we lose, the question isn't 'Why did we lose?' it's 'Could we have done anything differently?'"

If it isn't obvious by now, Big Spaceship is more than open to doing things differently, and they are always looking for new insight. As Lebowitz says best, "Nothing about this place is broken, but absolutely every aspect of it is open to being improved."

ROB SCHWARTZ

Rob Schwartz of TBWA\Worldwide, fomerly of TBWA\Chiat\Day believes that creative people must have a high energy level and they must be storytellers. But these two traits are not enough to sustain a person in a creative industry like advertising. Schwartz believes that true creatives are all problem solvers. "Be they writer, art director, designer, shirt maker, cobbler, they're all solving a problem," he says.

Schwartz's creative philosophy differs from the stereotypical image of an aloof, unorganized creative. The creative magic would happen without the contribution of structure. According to Schwartz, "The more organized you are, the more liberated you can be in terms of creativity."

Schwartz likes to reference an ideology first chronicled by Benjamin Franklin to explain people's drive in the creativity industry. He says people are driven by two things: money and glory. Within a capitalist society, Schwartz says these two drivers become even more important, especially in an industry that is as high-energy as advertising. Schwartz is still hopeful, though, that many are not in it for the money or for the glory, but for the creativity.

And everyone must create in Schwartz's world. He says, "If you're the account person, you've got to create an environment where great ideas can happen. If you're the media person, you've got to create areas where consumers can see the work, connect with the work, play with the work. If you're a creative, you have to create, that one's obvious. But everyone is in service of creativity in the company." This collaboration of all parties in the realm of creativity is what makes up the heartbeat of the agency.

Sometimes the heartbeat stops when an agency loses a pitch. For Schwartz that is not the absolute sign of failure. Failure is about something more than losing, "I think that being ignored is really a failure," he says.

Another element that enhances the quality of work at TBWA\Chiat\Day is the agency's strong philosophy: to disrupt. Schwartz believes that all work should diverge from the current norm of the advertising industry. "But I still think that the process of disruption is one of the smartest ways to get to great ideas fast and consistently. And the reason why it's great is it's based on the way creatives think," he says, "It's the way ideas happen."

There is no doubt that with all the ups and downs of agency life, it is hard to continue to function and maintain your sanity. Schwartz has found the solution: "You have to give up sleep and that's what I've found I've done." But he has not done this in the way you might think. Schwartz wakes at 5 A.M. daily, allowing himself to get a head start on the day. But on most days, he tries to let go of business by 7 P.M. Though he cannot always stick to this mantra, he tries. Sticking to this helps him have a dynamic business and family life.

When asked to describe creativity, Schwartz welcomes a broad definition. "I think it's applying energy, to touch people and make them happy," he says. "There are too many things that can go wrong in life, there are too many negative things and I think making people happy is, it's a pretty good way to live." Schwartz describes the world as a "summerhouse." He says that after fixing the screen doors, one needs to paint the shutters and then the list continues. "The world always needs to be repaired somewhere, so that's kind of what creativity is, coming up with ways to do that."

SUSAN CREDLE

Susan Credle of Leo Burnett chose to enter the ad world under the impression that it was a woman- dominated industry. During the 1980s the ad industry was experiencing a cultural shift. "What's curious is that I chose it because there were so many women in it: Nancy Rice, Yvonne Smith, Mary Wells, and Charlotte Fears. They were strong, strong women that were involved with big work. And their names were endorsed." When Credle began working at BBDO, she began to understand it was really a man's world.

> "If you're not taking a little risk, I don't think you are going anywhere."

Although she was in the gender minority, Credle did not let the divide affect her. She previously spent twenty-four years in the upper west side of New York City, so she was accustomed to being in the racial minority. Instead of dwelling on the differences, she was able to embrace similarities. "I just felt like I was just in the world full of people," she says.

Regardless Credle loves the industry because she was able to combine many of her passions into one field. Coming from a theater background, she had been searching for a way to incorporate her ideals. "I was looking for someplace that I could make somewhat of a more structured living that celebrated that kind of a creativity, acting, theater and dance." She also enjoyed writing stories, so for her the fit was natural. "It looked like this was a job that really came with some structure, but I could still embrace some of the creativity that I had enjoyed doing in my personal time," Credle adds.

This love of creativity and acceptance of differences has caused Credle to learn the importance of collaboration. "If you're going to do a great creative, you can't be a creative department. You have to be a creative agency. I think that's asking every single person to do their job creatively."

Credle does not believe in a limiting perception of creativity. She says that the term is too often used to describe the fine arts, but her definition is much different. "Creativity is simply about solving problems in unique and interesting ways that stand out, that are fresh and that motivate people to do something." She believes that creativity can be incorporated into every department, not just what is typically known as the creative department.

"I want them to all embrace creativity," she says. "If we're a strategic-lead department, how does our strategic-lead department look different than anybody else? How do we create it, so that it offers something more interesting than anywhere else?"

Credle's progressive views of creativity sometimes cause her to worry about common business ideology. "We have kind of lost sight of the ability to have interesting people touch the business, because we are looking for people who can be put in front of the client, the person who can sell the work," she says. Credle does not seem to be in the advertising business just to make the sale. She cites one of her former mentors who said, "You have to careful not to sanitize your department so much that you don't have a place for these intriguing individuals to work and play." Play is important to Credle and so is risk. "I think if you're not taking a little risk, you aren't going anywhere," she says.

Her appreciation for the unadulterated creative nature of the industry is part of what has made her successful. She says there are plenty of careers that are less stressful, but for her, there are few jobs more satisfying. "I get paid to do the bad work; and I do the good work for free," she quips. As a woman, Credle has been able to stand out in the industry and let her passion, expressed through her work, speak for itself.

MARGARET JOHNSON AND RICH SILVERSTEIN

Margaret Johnson and Rich Silverstein are as alike as they are different. Together the pair runs the creative department at Goodby Silverstein & Partners in San Francisco. Johnson looks for people who are "smart, funny and driven"—what she calls the "magic trio" — while Silverstein looks for people who are aware of what is going on in the world. It is this melding of ideas that has helped GSP to be so successful.

At an agency driven by creativity, Silverstein and Johnson do their best to challenge or "squeeze the most creativity" out of their employees, although Johnson notes these employees wouldn't have been hired unless they had some inkling of creative intelligence. To Johnson, creative intelligence means, "recognizing ideas that are going to make a difference in the world, that are smart, that are innovative and have never been done before." Silverstein admits, though, that his employees focus too much on advertising alone and do not have enough life experiences for his taste. "I am extremely connected to what's going on in the arts world of America and the popular culture part of America and I don't think enough of the young people are," he says.

Silverstein and Johnson both understand that life outside of the agency is important. Johnson believes that experiencing culture, whether it be watching movies or listening to opera, fuels the creativity within. As an avid cyclist, Silverstein turns to his passion for creative fuel. His daily commutes are often decision-making journeys. "For my filtering process I would get on my bike and ride home and in that one hour I'll come up with [if the idea is] working or it's not working," he says.

Just because an idea does not work, does not mean the process of getting there is useless. Silverstein and Johnson strongly believe that failures are necessary to move forward. Learning from failures is common in the advertising world, and it's often not easy to deem whether or not something works at the start. This is where risk taking comes into play. According to Silverstein, "Any agency that wants to be relevant has to take risks." And although sometimes the risk has to be cut back when it overwhelms the client, GSP employees come into advertising because they want to take risks—and generally they are given the freedom to do so. Johnson supports the idea of risk taking but would like to know sooner when risks can become critical to the business. Lately, Johnson and her team have started coming up with many ideas very quickly early in a project. That has allowed GSP to identify good ideas from bad ones sooner.

At GSP, a specifically designed process called SPRINT allows for the incorporation of as many different perspectives as possible. "That process really helps because everyone on the team, not just the creative department, but the account team, the strategy team all have an opportunity to invest in the work that you are going to be doing moving forward, really early on," Johnson says. "And it just helps kind of shape the work in an interesting way."

Regardless of their varying perspectives, Johnson and Silverstein agree that "creativity at GSP is everything." Through creativity, GSP has developed a strong new philosophy: "Make stuff people care about." Achieving this goal requires GSP employees to be informed global citizens. For Silverstein, this idea is what has made GSP successful. "It's a love of what's going on in the world, rather than what's going on in advertising." Johnson adds, "We only want to put things out into the world that people care about. We only want to do the most innovative things. We want to affect culture. We want to be a part of pop culture."

ROGER HURNI

Roger Hurni of Off Madison Ave says his creative philosophy centers largely on employees. "Individual creativity is absolutely critical. I mean, we talk all the time about how our assets walk in and out of the door every day," says Hurni. "Without our individual employees, quite frankly, this agency doesn't exist. It is really the combination of the brainpower of everybody that really makes this place tick."

Just being creative, though, is not the most important aspect of an employee; it is only part of the equation. It's their willingness to work and develop. "I would rather have somebody who is less talented and works harder than someone who has kind of an okay work ethic and is immensely talented," says

Hurni. In addition, Hurni seeks out employees who are also interested in the world outside of their work. "Yes, I want them to be talented at their task, but it's also important for them to have talents in pursuits outside of that in order to bring those influences in the creative direction," says Hurni. In this vein he looks for potential employees who he says can "problem solve as their creative fashion."

Hurni relies partially on the physical space of Off Madison Ave to help foster a creative environment. During the construction of their office, Hurni wanted to tear down walls, literally. He also wanted to mix everyone together. The combination of these ideas has helped foster an open environment. But Hurni's passion for collaboration does not end there. Every year or so, he relocates everyone to a new space in the office. "This way, you get the opportunity to experience people, who you may work with or you get to overhear conversations about accounts you may not work on," he says.

In order to help retain creative employees within an agency structure, Hurni believes that an agency must adopt unique techniques. One way to do this is to be creative with the organizational hierarchy. "We try to keep [our organizational structure] very flat ... There's not a lot of hierarchy here as far as direct reports and, you know, there's this chain of command if you want to get an idea here's how it gets approved. We don't just have an open door policy, we have a no door policy here, which goes back to the environment," says Hurni. An open structure is not the only measure Hurni believes should be in place in order to keep employees content. Hurni believes agency workers need an immense amount of freedom in order to help them learn and progress as individuals.

With too much freedom, employees may sometimes be tempted to slack, warns Hurni. Natural human tendencies help to prevent situations from becoming too lax. "The challenge really comes a lot from peer pressure and trying to do better than everybody else and prove yourself constantly for being inventive," he says. This peer pressure drives all employees, not just the creative department. According to Hurni's philosophy "creativity doesn't happen in the creative department. Creativity happens across every department inside the agency." As a result, all employees are encouraged to contribute to the creative output of the agency.

> "Our assets walk in and out of the door every day..."

The collective nature of the agency allows for all workers to collaborate and share idea. Diversity is important in an agency, says Hurni, but he does not mean diversity in the conventional sense. Hurni places an emphasis on diversity of perspectives. But no matter how diverse, all people are fundamentally similar. In his global travels, Hurni has learned valuable lessons about human nature. "We all talk about how different we are around the world, but I see the way parents treat their children and the way we try to get along as friends and neighbors. That's universally the same. I haven't seen that different anywhere in the world. And we're a lot more alike than we're not alike, and so travel really fuels me." Ultimately Hurni finds inspiration in his travels, analyzing human behavior and learning from intercultural communications.

MARSHALL ROSS

Marshall Ross is a big believer in the adage "You are what you eat," but he isn't talking about food. As chief creative officer of Cramer Krasselt, Ross evaluates creativity both inside and outside of his agency: "If you *eat* client engagements that are unhealthy, you will perpetuate that unhealthiness." Ross believes that an agency must find clients who believe in creativity and understand its importance and power to solve business problems. Without such clients a creatively led agency might not survive

This purpose of this selectiveness is not to simply make the partnership between client and agency easier, but rather it plays a key role in the constantly changing and growing identity of Cramer Krasselt. Ross says that when the client understands the importance of creativity, the end product further illuminates his agency's future: "People outside of the organization look at [the work] and say 'I want to be a part of that.' You'll keep the quality and the caliber of your creativity within your creation high."

Ross says he is "constantly learning," a trait he also looks for in his employees. Inquisitiveness, an insatiable curiosity and life experience are far more important than textbook advertising knowledge: "I think the people who are good, or who are successful within creative organizations are people who are learning constantly from lots of different resources." According to Ross, this broad wealth of knowledge is key since the "essence of creativity is just posing items." He says that "attention-deficit syndrome is a good thing for these kind of environments," since one must take two separately familiar items and combine them to become a single new unfamiliar item.

With its open offices, chalkboards and "random tables all over" where people can gather and collaborate in a heartbeat," Cramer Krasselt strives to create an idea-sharing culture that fosters creativity. Ross believes that the next evolution within the industry will be about changing the definition of the creative team, which has historically been "a sort of sacred relationship between writer and art director." He says at this point, however, they need to learn that their output is now dependent on technology, consumer insight, contact planning and content creation activity.

In an environment that fosters so many different ideas at once, how do they decide on the right one? Cramer Krasselt's answer is the "idea-illuminating strategy," which is described by Ross as the following process: "Is the idea magnetic? Do you want to spend time with the idea? Does it feel surprising? Is it share worthy? What about it makes me tell my friend more about it—makes me want to participate?" The idea should lead to the end product, and according to Ross, "You should have a story that you want to tell about that." For him, the biggest failure is when you put in ideas, effort, time and even money, and in the very end you don't have a story you are proud to tell from the process.

CHRIS FOSTER

Chris Foster recognizes that Fallon has true Minneapolis roots. Fallon began as an independent company and was one of the first agencies to make a name for itself outside of LA or New York. According to Foster, this fact is ingrained in the culture at Fallon. "It's a sort of underdog mentality. It's kind of [like] the guys on Madison Avenue or the guys in LA, we can beat them all at the experiment on the prairie," says Foster.

Fallon's office also relates to Minneapolis's home state. "[The] space is also constructed around Minnesota, so our floors are Minnesota hickory, we have rocks and stream beds downstairs all from Minnesota lakes and Minnesota rivers, all of our conference rooms are named after places in Minnesota."

When Foster began working at Fallon, the space underwent some changes, as a result of the evolving nature of the agency. "We were in a different space; we just moved a year and a half ago. The space we were in before was designed for a much larger agency. Fallon was eight hundred people at one point, and we're now two hundred. People were rattling around in corridors. It was really cool, but it wasn't very functional."

The Minneapolis mentality of Fallon has been a slight hindrance to the creative output of the agency in the past. As a city, Minneapolis has not always attracted the diversity that Foster feels is important. "Creativity does not happen in a vacuum, and the thing that makes creativity happen is people of different cultures, different backgrounds, different perspectives all rubbing together." Foster, along with his team members, has been working to improve the amount of variety found in the staff in Fallon. "My vision is that we have somebody from every continent in play here," says Foster.

Foster understands that diversity is about more than ethnicity. "I think one of the core elements of creativity is having diverse points of view, diverse orientations, diverse thinking all brought together," he says. "You can't do that if everybody you've got is a forty-five-year-old white male who has lived in Minneapolis his entire life. You're just not going to get the kind of breakthrough creativity that [you] need." Foster strongly believes that the people are an essential part of any organization, and he has also come to understand that the lack of an extreme hierarchical structure can be detrimental to any organization, regardless of the people.

> "Creativity does not happen in a vacuum..."

When Foster got on the board at Fallon, the organizational structure was very different, so he changed it. "Fallon was structured like a big agency," he says. "It had huge sort of silos, lots of department heads, and lots of structure and process, and we had eight hundred people, and we had twenty-two department heads, and I was asking, 'What are you a department head of?' So what we did was to flatten the structure." Foster believes this changed the organization for the better.

EDWARD BOCHES

Edward Boches, professor of advertising at Boston University, and the long-term chief creative officer at Mullen, believes that advertising creatives are motivated not by sales results but by a need for personal recognition. "Just look at the award show industry if you want validation," he says.

In fact, Boches admits that a deep-rooted desire for attention sparked his interest in the business. "I think I was overly praised as a child and became somewhat addicted to it. Combine that with my love of words, film and performance and advertising became the perfect career. It takes a long time to make a movie or write a book or prepare body of work for an art exhibit. But in advertising you can generate and produce ideas far more quickly and get that immediate reaction. Of course, you also have to be tough enough to withstand the constant rejection too."

A similar intrinsic motivation drives most creatives, suggests Boches. "I can honestly say I never met a creative person who was motivated first and foremost by a desire to sell a product. More often than not he simply needs an outlet for his creativity." This isn't a knock but rather an opportunity, Boches explains. "Smart creative directors and clients must learn to take advantage of that passion for creating. It's no different than the Catholic Church hiring Michelangelo to paint a ceiling," he adds.

Boches places a huge emphasis on talent — individual and collaborative. "In this business you don't get credit for trying, you get credit for ideas and innovation," he declares. "When I'm hiring a junior person I look for people who are original and prolific in their thinking. When I hire senior talent I want people who have done something famous already."

The real challenge of Boches' job as a creative director is "casting" talent. "Not every creative person is right for every job. It's a balance of skill, passion, taste, creative judgment." He also believes that in advertising's current environment, where creative ideas are less dependent on craft and more dependent on understanding social media, technology and emerging consumer behaviors the definition of an advertising creative should extend to departments that don't have "creative" in their names. "These days, some of the best ideas come out of media, account planning, and public relations," he explains. "We should all welcome that."

Fundamentally Boches believes that everyone is creative. "They just have to exercise the right muscles and be willing to take chances," he says. "And as our industry finds itself in the business of creating experiences, apps and full-blown platforms that consumers use rather than watch or read, we need more people to be creative thinkers and contribute to those experiences."

However, Boches will quickly remind you that tools and technology are not the answer. "You can give anybody a keyboard, a camera, the full Adobe suite or an editing station. It doesn't turn them into a great writer, photographer, designer or editor," he adds.

Boches was not always in the advertising industry. He has been a journalist, a photographer and a speechwriter, among other things. "I think those experiences were helpful, especially now with all the changes in content, because it gave me a holistic view," he says.

But he was also part owner of Mullen, and even as creative director he was responsible for budgets, financial performance and people's livelihoods. "That was a great experience and certainly I'd rather work for myself than for someone else. But sometimes it forces you to compromise your purest creative standards. Do you fight for your more narrow, selfish creative idea? Or do you work to save people's jobs?"

During his 31 years at Mullen, Boches helped build a nationally recognized Ad Agency A-list agency by hiring and motivating individuals and teams of "people far more talented than me." Today he teaches creative courses at Boston University. "I think everything has changed. Technology, real time access to information, consumer control of the conversation, and hyper-connectivity present a host of new challenges for everyone working in advertising. But I also believe that nothing has changed. We still have to identify problems, develop strategies and generate ideas that attract attention and overcome indifference. Whether it's a combination of words and pictures, an interesting use of media and technology, or simply a story told in a new interactive way, we still need great creative ideas."

LYNN TEO

Lynn Teo, customer experience executive, and former chief experience officer (CXO) of McCann Erickson and AKQA, strongly believes the people within an agency are its greatest asset and differentiator. "The people are the lifeblood of the agency. They represent its point of view, how it thinks, how it expresses itself, and how it adapts in the face of rapid industry change," says Teo. When hiring, she considers candidates from a wide range of backgrounds, reaching beyond those who simply go by the obvious professional shorthand of creative, as there are too many subtleties in skillsets and strengths. Teo says they must possess other qualities, "I look a lot for curiosity, an exploratory streak, and a genuine desire to understand human behavior."

Teo believes this curiosity motivates teams and ultimately leads to solutions that are unique, relevant, and useful. According to Teo, "Creativity means being brave and going where others haven't. It's about finding opportunities or white spaces that have yet to be uncovered." In her view, this curiosity serves no purpose unless it manifests itself in some tangible way. "Creatives are driven by expression, whether through art or some other visual, narrative, or experiential means. However, my definition of true creativity is when a unique artifact — a product, service or communications piece — is conceived of that clearly meets a need in a person's life. The solution must ultimately bring emotional benefit either instantaneously or over time, through trust-building, empathy, or sheer utility. Ideally all creatives strive to make something for the consumer that is meaningful. Something that becomes part of the fabric of his or her life," she says.

"The overarching focus on creativity in an agency often overshadows its underlying raison d'etre — to help achieve business results for our clients in sustainable, measurable ways," Teo reasons. In addition, sustaining a culture of creativity and innovation internally in agencies is important and requires the right mix of personality traits, environment and collaborative relationships. "When you mention an agency and its atmosphere, what comes to mind are deadlines, a constant buzz and some quirky spaces. Sometimes it's about the pitch and the hours." The hours Teo refers to have long been a part of agency culture. Regardless of what agencies do to alter the spaces they inhabit to signify change, Teo believes that some barriers are deeper set and require more time for organizations to break through. "A lot of it has to do with how teams collaborate and how ideas are conceived of. A greater diversity of perspectives is honored in today's ideation process and those roles — be it tech, development or social — must be represented," Teo says. Related to that, the organization structure of an agency should be reviewed from time to time to see if it best reflects the way in which teams need to work. According to Teo, "The industry outside of agency walls is moving so fast that without a periodic calibration, we'll run the risk of losing some of our best people and becoming irrelevant."

"Creativity means being brave and going where others haven't."

On the topic of physical spaces and process, Teo believes that creatives tend to shy away from structured environments or frameworks that help people think through problems because "it takes the magic out of what they do." But a methodical approach, one that many creatives detest, has its benefits. "There are tremendous efficiencies and might I even add, sanity preservation benefits of distilling the understanding of a problem down to its core and applying a process of solving it. Once you've adopted a clear process, the right disciplines can come forward to add their muscle to the solution. This process serves as a firm foundation on which a range of creative ideas can flourish — ideas that solve the right problem," Teo concludes.

The physical space of an agency is often a huge draw for candidates and agency staff and sends a tacit message about its culture. At AKQA Teo explains, configurable spaces come alive during various events. Their New York office space has seen the central atrium be turned into movie night spaces, Halloween parties, bake-offs and even portfolio reviews with candidates. The spirit of change also manifests itself in the agency's seating arrangements. "We switch things up every year or so — just to keep things interesting and to see new team dynamics emerge, " Teo says.

Although the advertising industry is undergoing some significant shifts, Teo believes the fundamental truths of advertising and marketing communications are still relevant. "The reason for being hasn't gone away — we're still in the business of helping our clients engage with their consumers," she says. "The difference now is we have to engage with consumers on their terms, be it messaging or other high value utility with much more contextual knowledge, on whatever platform they may be on, and in a timeliness that ubiquitous technology has afforded us. It's exciting times. Consumers have raised their expectations, and the agencies that survive are the ones that exceed them."

TIM LEAKE

Tim Leake doesn't care about your eight month surfing expedition or the now-famous blog you wrote on your travels around the world. Although this director of growth & innovation at RPA Advertising and former creative director of Saatchi & Saatchi acknowledges a certain value to life experience, he looks for employees with sense of curiosity and a desire to keep trying. "You don't want somebody who complains a lot. You don't want somebody who is going to get frustrated really easily," says Leake. "You want them to take feedback because sometimes feedback will be harsh. Even when you don't mean it to be, it can come across harsh. And [people need to] be able to learn from that, as opposed to get frustrated by it or intimidated by it."

Leake discusses the common practice among many agencies looking to break the mold and do something that's never been done before. On the employee front, this includes a preference of hiring people with different backgrounds over advertising jobs like copywriters and art directors. "We're incentivizing people to get out of the industry because we're hiring people that don't come from it, and that's a weird thing." And according to Leake, unconventionality doesn't necessarily translate to creativity or idea generation. "Creativity itself is a funny term, because what does that mean? We tend to look at it in terms of artistic craziness or something like that, but I think what you realize is that the best term, the best trait you have as a creative person is your ability to try again."

The idea of breaking the mold does not only apply to employee selection, but it can permeate the ideation and creative process, as well as the final product. Leake says that this is usually the focus when it comes to impressing a jury for winning advertising awards. He differentiates process into two camps, the actual and the ideal. The former includes crowd sourcing and internal competition where many teams are duking it out for one big account. With a multitude of ideas, Leake says this method is great for creative directors, but rough on creatives, as it does not develop, mentor or teach them. He says the latter, ideal process would be to have fewer people who own that project and can come up with twenty great ideas. Unfortunately, in a business of increasingly demanding output, the ideation process shrinks and the method that quickly produces one hundred ideas wins out.

A big believer in learning from mistakes, Leake also says that high-demand of creative output sacrifices the opportunity to reflect on failure. "Anything that doesn't do what it was supposed to do is a failure," says Leake. "Unfortunately with the pace moving at what it is, we often talk about doing a post-mortem meeting and often don't do it. You should reflect on what went wrong, what can we learn from this, and then you do better."

Leake has many criticisms about the current culture of the industry, so it's no surprise that he views the rapidly emerging digital culture as a positive influence. "We're moving towards a culture of collaboration and openness and working together and trying to solve problems and do things right with transparency," he says. "Overall, it's more open-source, more positive. It's better to contribute to the knowledge, sharing everything we've got." In an industry where winning an award has become the incentive, and sometimes appears more important than appealing to the consumer, Leake emphasizes the importance of change. "We need to get to a place where we're constantly learning and we're constantly reflecting on what we've done, that failure is okay. We have to get there."

LANCE JENSEN

Lance Jensen, the chief creative officer of Hill Holliday and former creative director and co-founder of Modernista!, believes deeply in initiative. It's what has driven his career creating some of the most memorable advertising campaigns of the last two decades for brands like Volkswagen, Bank of America, Cadillac, Liberty Mutual, Hummer, Gap, John Hancock, MTV, (RED) and Major League Baseball. Jensen says it's also what has helped interns get jobs at the agencies he's run. He tells the story of a young intern at one agency who would always stay later than the rest, absorbing some of the evening ideation sessions, constantly looking for a way to be useful. Jensen recalls she was the only intern in her group to be hired when her internship ended. "My best advice to young people who want to work in our business is, don't wait to be told to do something," he remarks.

It's this strong point of view that has helped Jensen get where he is. "If you wait around for someone to tell you how to do your job or get ahead, you're never going to get anywhere." At Modernista!, which closed its doors in 2011, Jensen felt it was important to be restless. He reveres the anti-authoritative nature of the punk movement, which inspired a drastic cultural shift in the 1980s. Jensen notes the DIY-aesthetic of punk as an ageless mantra, which he has tried to bring to the work he does. "I think the real punks today are online; they're designing digital experiences because that's where the culture is right now. And they like disrupting things," he says.

For good creative work Jensen believes it's important to take risks. In many cases, that may be trying something you've never done before. For Jensen, the meaning of a failure is complex. "Failing is how you learn, how you get better. Failing means you took a risk, you tried something. I've always believed there should be agency awards for 'failing the best.' People who fail have conquered their fear, and that's step one in a creative career."

Jensen also believes in challenging his colleagues through honesty, particularly when assessing their work. "You need a bit of arrogance when you're young," Jensen explains. "It's such a delicate balance of being able to figure out where that line is, and it moves for every assignment, but I think we challenge our people (on an assignment) and we just say, 'I don't like it, I don't think it's good, and this is kind of boring.'" That may sound harsh, but Jensen believes it saves time, and serves the creative. "If I'm bored, I make a face, and some people can take that and say, 'oh alright, I'll go back and try again,'" he says.

On of the constant challenges a top agency faces is convincing a client why an idea is the right one. But this usually isn't easy. It's a constant negotiation and discussion, and sometimes the idea you liked doesn't win. Jensen admits that sometimes you find yourself "actually making something that you knew was never worth making in the first place, but you finally just got beat down. You get worn out," he says. But the rewards are there too. Client relationships are like any relationship. "You need honesty, open dialogue, patience, respect and sometimes you disagree, which is okay," he says.

Apathy and cynicism are the enemies of a creative career, Jensen feels. You've got to truly experience and embrace whatever product you're promoting. "Some products are easier because you can hold them in your hand, like a phone, or you can get in a car and you can feel it. But some things like banks — what is that?" he questions. This requires the agency to do what it does best: create. "That's what we're here for. Everybody wants to be a part of that," he says. "It's a lifestyle, and it's a commitment, and it's a philosophy. It makes people crazy." But Jensen wouldn't have it any other way. He's an admitted punk at heart.

Jensen left Modernista! in December 2010 and has since joined Hill Holliday as chief creative officer, where he is busy creating campaigns for clients like Bank of America, Cadillac, Dunkin' Donuts, Major League Baseball and Liberty Mutual.

BLAKE EBEL

Blake Ebel of Fear Not and formerly of Euro RSCG stresses the importance of being a dynamic worker. He feels that creativity is constantly evolving and creative professionals should be prepared to grow with the industry. "I look at our place as building creative athletes. We want people that can flex their creative muscles on digital, traditional and experiential as opposed to just print or TV. Those days are over." Aside from the ability to handle anything that comes their way, Ebel's employees must also possess a desire to learn and grow. "The type of person I'm constantly looking for is someone who's hungry," he says, "I want people that aggressively want to get better and are in my office always looking for the next great assignment. The people that disappear and try and hide in their office are the people that go away when cuts are made."

Despite the importance of being a jack-of-all-trades, Ebel does not believe that his employees' lives should only revolve around advertising. Ebel says he is a huge supporter of doing things outside of advertising. "I'm a father of two kids, a husband and a son. I bring so much of the experiences I have into my work." He expects others to do the same, "I'm the type of manager that is looking to have people not spend all night here. I know that goes against a lot of creative leaders." But there is a method behind Ebel's alternative thought process, he does not believe that good advertising has to come from working until 2 A.M. repeatedly. "I know certain agencies work like that," Ebel states, "they're sweat shops. I just don't believe in that. I believe that you should have a healthy environment." This is not only good for the output of the agency, but it is also good for the sanity of his employees, "People like working here when they have the opportunity to live outside the agency and they can bring their own life experiences into their work."

> "When you overcome fear, you own the opportunity to create change."

When Ebel came to Euro RSCG, the agency was failing. He says that one key change helped to drastically turn the organization around. "One of the things that I wanted to bring to the agency was a family environment where we cared about each other. When the going gets tough, you want the person standing next to you to be a loyal partner in crime. That does not mean that his employees do not have difficult conversations or that everything always works. "It just means that when somebody has a problem outside of work that takes priority over work," he says. This small difference began to alter employee relations in a positive way. "When people started to see and feel that they were more important and their family issues were more important than the ad we were working on, that kind of affects everything very quickly and you start to create a bond with the people that work here," Ebel notes. "I experienced creatives working harder, later and producing better work because they didn't want to let their peers down."

But ultimately, in order to create a good business, clients must be satisfied. Ebel believes, with his help Euro RSCG has flourished. "I'm all about helping my clients win through solving business problems with disruptive creative work. Today's consumers now have the power to decide how and when they engage with brands. Our job is to find consumers where they are and give them the tools they want to engage with the brands they are interested in."

Aside from great creative and a good work-life balance, Ebel believes a successful agency must eliminate fear for their clients. "I believe fear, and the missed opportunities it creates, is a frustrating barrier to big ideas, beautiful creations and valuable risks. When you overcome fear, you own the opportunity to be heard clearly and create change. In a brand. In a company and in the community."

MARK HUNTER

Mark Hunter, former creative director at Deutsch LA believes that creativity can be taught. In fact, he says he taught himself. "I was not the most naturally gifted creative. I was actually a sponge and I always tried to do things differently. I've never tried to write in the same voice twice or be the funny guy or the stylish guy, I always approached problems differently," he says.

This idea of approaching problems in a unique way is the cornerstone of the work produced by Hunter's agency. "I think the qualities that really good creatives have, natural or taught, is a kind of inclination toward original thinking. I think so many ads that you see are very familiar ads. They are quite similar to other things. They might just be a little bit different or a little bit better." But the hallmark of a good creative, in Hunter's eyes, is not just the ability to execute something that is different; he or she is also able to bring in new perspectives throughout the process. "Really great creatives solve the problem in a different way, bring a very original solution to the table," he says. Hunter thinks that good creatives are the "central component of all his agency." They are the "dominant force."

When asked to describe creatives, Hunter says they are "self-reliant," "pretty confident," but not always "wildly outspoken." He describes them as often "half there" during briefs. "I don't want to generalize but—and this is a nasty thing to say—some of them are kind of troubled in some way. I don't know, I think they're just nonconformists," Hunter adds, chiding himself for sounding clichéd.

The relaxed atmosphere at Deutsch LA helps to empower employee's creativity, something that Hunter believes is not always present in workplaces in the industry. "Let me put it this way: I've been to many places where you feel like you're walking into an art gallery, as opposed to an advertising agency," he says.

According to Hunter, having a carefree space is not the only element that should be taken into consideration when thinking about creativity. Employers must provide as much freedom as possible. This idea stems from his own needs as a creative. "I was never a big fan of the open plan. As a creative, my brain needed isolation. I needed to close a door where I could not be disturbed for an hour and I could just think. So we try to provide that." But Hunter knows that every creative has different needs. "I try to keep the department as unrigid as possible. Whatever works for you, because I think that every environment, every situation works differently for every creative." Hunter even lets employees work out of a trailer in the office parking lot. He doesn't care where his employees come up with ideas, as long as good work is being produced.

Hunter understands that employees produce the best work when they feel they are cared for, which is why there are programs at Deutsch LA to promote employees' lives outside of the agency. One of these programs is called the Side Side Project. "Anyone is able to come and pitch us their little side projects maybe they have going on but they don't really have the money, and we'll help them out with that. What happens is they'll pitch to a roomful of people, and the partners will go in and decide," he says.

When asked about work processes, Hunter is reluctant to say that his agency utilizes one, but he halfheartedly settles on one. "I'm very much about simplicity, but I don't know if that counts as a process. The more you clutter things—the more you ask of people—the less you're going to get." And judging by Deutsch's recent Super Bowl success, Hunter's theory might be spot-on.

As for philosophy, Deutsch LA focuses on a larger one that is plastered on a large billboard in the office. "It says that our mission is to invent the most original and shareable work in the world—but I don't think that counts as a philosophy," Hunter states. Instead he believes in something that is more individual. "My personal philosophy is that people want to be involved somehow in most messaging that they interact with, even if it's just seeing yourself in an ad somewhere," he says. "We talk a lot about speaking human and by that it simply means you believe in speaking to people in a way that they can relate to, that is somehow relevant to them." For Hunter, the humanness of a brand's messaging is where many fail. "A lot of brands make the mistake of just speaking about themselves, just talk about themselves all the time, and what people really want to know is that you get them, that you understand their life," he accurately notes.

DOUG SPONG

Doug Spong of Carmichael Lynch Spong in Minneapolis believes he works in a very unique place. "We're an agency of people who live and work in Minnesota and love the great outdoors," he says. People are drawn to the agency because of all the company embodies. "A part of the reason they are here is the lifestyle. They select Minneapolis not because it is the headquarters for advertising and communication." This lifestyle appreciation has been an important factor for Carmichael Lynch Spong's success.

Spong believes his employees' unique talents are a driving force behind the agency's success. He says the workers, the art and craft of what they do and this driving passion has contributed greatly to the success of the agency. If his employees were not working at the agency, he quips, "They would be off designing; they would be off doing the fine arts; they would off in the performing arts." Spong believes this concept is what defines the advertising business. "What we provide is a creative way people can monetize their passion in life, and they get a chance to come together," he says.

Carmichael Lynch Spong's office space has also created a good working atmosphere. Spong says the atmosphere encourages collaboration "We intentionally designed this space to take down traditional drywall with doors that lock people out, shut light out from the central halls," he describes, "we have close to 80,000 square feet of space here in Minneapolis that has very few walls, has very few doors and only a few conference rooms." The openness of the space further asserts Spong's collaborative ideology.

"Creativity is not limited to the twelfth floor, to our creative department. We are all expected to and encouraged to be creative in everything we do."

Behind Carmichael Lynch Spong's four walls, employees work to ensure that the client is always first. This comes from the understanding of one important but sometimes forgotten idea: "We don't manufacture the client's product. We don't retail the client's product. We don't distribute the client's product." The understanding goes into every product that Carmichael Lynch Spong produces under Spong's direction. While many of the product's details are out of the agency's realm of control, Spong is confident that the agency can still produce good, thought-provoking work, but only if they understand the fundamentals of their product. "If we've done our job and we're aware of product price and distribution strategy, the point of sale, what's going on in that retail, if we're not in tune with that, we've not done our job."

At Carmichael Lynch Spong, Spong stresses the importance of advertising knowledge. One cannot walk in and be hired because they like advertising. Instead Spong is looking for what he calls an "advertising connoisseur." This person must devour advertising news the way the best vintner enjoys a good wine. They must also be interested in lifestyle trends. "I think the more curious they are and attentive to some of those trends and ... what's going on in social fabric of America, it makes them better advertising connoisseurs."

"If you don't like change it will eat you alive..."

Staying on top of news and trends is crucial to success in the advertising field. "This is an industry [that] if you don't like change will eat you alive. Change is the name of the game. Every day is a different day."

ENDNOTES

INTRODUCTION

1. Jaafar El-Murad and Douglas C. West, The Definition and Measurement of Creativity: What Do We Know?, Journal of Advertising Research / Volume 44 / Issue 02 / June 2004, pp 188-201

CHAPTER ONE

NEW TRUTHS ABOUT CREATIVITY

1. http://dictionary.reference.com/browse/creativity retrieved on 9/14/2013 retrieved on 9/14/2013
2. Tim Brown on Creativity and Play http://www.youtube.com/watch?v=0msoKWz4MjA
3. Lange, Patricia G. and Ito, Mizuko. *Hanging Out, Messing Around, and Geeking Out, MIT Press, 2010*
4. *Robinson, Ken (2010), RSA Animate—Changing Education Paradigms.* http://www.youtube.com/watch?v=zDZFcDGpL4U&feature=youtube_gdata_player. Accessed October 20, 2010.

CHAPTER TWO

WHAT IS CREATIVITY?

1. http://www.creativeeducationfoundation.org/ and Parnes, Sidney J. (Ed.) (December 1992). Source Book for Creative Problem Solving: A Fifty Year Digest of Proven Innovation Processes. Creative Education Foundation.ISBN 978-99945-974-9-9
2. http://www.thedailybeast.com/newsweek/2010/07/10/the-creativity-crisis.html
3. *Gregory Berns, iconoclast, A neuroscientist reveals how to think differently, Harvard Business Press, 2008.*
4. http://www.fastcompany.com/1007044/neuroscience-sheds-new-light-creativity

CHAPTER THREE

CREATIVE THINKING

1. http://www.creativeemergence.com/
2. Rhodes, Terrel, ed. 2010. *Assessing Outcomes and Improving Achievement: Tips and Tools for Using Rubrics.* Washington, DC: Association of American Colleges and Universities.
3. "Can We Trust Creativity Tests?" a Review of TTCT Kyung Hee Kim JCR_2006.pdf
4. Torrance, E. Paul (1979). *The Search for Satori and Creativity.*
5. http://www.faz.net/faz-net-services/unterhaltung/gehirn-training/
6. Avner Ziv, PhD, in *Journal of Children in Contemporary Society*, Volume 20, Issue 1-2, 1989, Chapter 4: Using Humor to Develop Creative Thinking, pages 99-116
7. *Ogilvy, David. Confessions of an Advertising Man. London: Southbank Publishing, 2004.*

CHAPTER FOUR

THE CREATIVE [PROBLEM-SOLVING] PROCESS

1. Glenn Griffin, Deborah Morrison, *The Creative Process Illustrated, HOW Books, 2010.*
2. www.idea-sandbox.com
3. http://designthinkingforeducators.com/
4. http://designthinkingforeducators.com/toolkit/, Design Thinking for Educators Toolkit, Page 67

CHAPTER FIVE

CREATIVE THINKING METHODS AND TECHNIQUES

1. Creative approaches to problem solving, Scott Isaksen, 2013, page 89 and *Creative Thinking in the Decision and Management Sciences*, James R. Evans, page 38
2. http://www.fastcompany.com/3004450/alex-osborn-bob-sutton-meeting-minds-build-better-brainstorm
3. De Bono, Edward (1970). Lateral thinking: Creativity Step by Step. Harper & Row. pp. 300.
4. De Bono, Edward (1985). *Six Thinking Hats: An Essential Approach to Business Management. Little, Brown, & Company.*
5. *Harini Chandrasekar illustrates the use of a morphological analysis and how she developed numerous creative ideas to find a unique way to present the agency Droga5,* https://word.emerson.edu/gmcreativethinking-chandrasekar/2013/11/24/droga-5-a-graduate-school-project/

CHAPTER SIX

EVALUATION OF IDEAS

1. Presentation by Ted Royer, Chief Creative Officer, Droga5, on 8/19/13 in Boston
2. TED-Ads-Worth-Spreading-Report.pdf retrieved on ted.com on 2/19/2013.
3. http://www.canneslions.com/creativebravery/
4. "Why Cannes Matters", by A. Nasard, Chief Commercial Officer, provided by The Cannes Lions Team on 9/9/13.

CHAPTER SEVEN

IMPORTANCE OF COMMUNICATING IDEAS EFFECTIVELY

1. Batterson, Mark. Id: The True You. Xulon Press, 2004, Page 178.
2. *Gelb, Michael. How to Think like Leonardo da Vinci.*

CHAPTER EIGHT

CREATIVITY AND PLACE

1. White, A., & Smith, B.L (2001), "Assessing advertising creativity using the creative product semantic scale." *Journal of Advertising Research, Vol. 41, pp. 27-34.*

2. *The Art Directors Club Hall of Fame honors and recognizes highly successful innovators for their achievements in the field of visual communication and art direction, and represents the highest standard of creative excellence. See also* http://www.adcglobal.org/archive/hof/.
3. The One Club Creative Hall of Fame acknowledges and celebrates outstanding contributions of highly successful creative professionals within the advertising and communication industry. See also http://www.oneclub.org/oc/hall-of-fame/.

CHAPTER NINE

CREATIVITY AND PHILOSOPHY

1. http://www.mullen.com/about/ Retrieved on 8/5/2013.
2. http://www.houghtonmifflinbooks.com/features/cgsite/history.shtml
3. A 'making of' video can be seen at http://www.youtube.com/watch?v=CkE9C5R73fo and the gameplay in action can be seen at http://www.youtube.com/watch?v=h5KDQeMIOTM
4. A detailed description of the "Dshini" project can be found at http://blog.mediaman.de/recipe-printer-dshini/#more-261
5. A video of "Dshini" can be seen at http://www.youtube.com/watch?v=RBdZ6QyFJog#t=37.

REFERENCES:

INTRODUCTION

El-Murad, J., & West, D. C. (2004). The definition and measurement of creativity: What do we know? *Journal of Advertising Research,* 44, 188-201.

Iezzi, T. (2006, June 19). You really believe in creativity? Then stop talking and start doing. *Advertising Age.*

Koslow, S., Sasser, S. L., & Riordan, E. A. (2003). What is creative to whom and why? Perceptions in advertising agencies. *Journal of Advertising Research,* 43(1), 96-110.

Osborne, A. (1942). *How To Think Up.* New York & London: McGraw-Hill Book Company Inc.

Vogel, T. & Montepare, J. (2009). Creativity in U.S.-based Advertising Agencies: Exploring the Role of the 4 P's- Person, Place, Process and Product. *Proceedings of the American Academy of Advertising.*

White, A., & Smith, B.L. (2001). Assessing advertising creativity using the creative product emantic scale. *Journal of Advertising Research,* 41, 27-34.

CHAPTER ONE

NEW TRUTHS ABOUT CREATIVITY

Abraham, A., Pieritz, K., Thybusch, K., Rutter, B., Kröger, S., Schweckendiek, J., Stark, R.,Windmann, S., & Hermann, C. (2012). Creativity and the brain: Uncovering the neural signature of conceptual expansion. *Neuropsychologia,* 50(8), 1906–1917.

Adolphe, B. (2001). *The Origins of Creativity.* USA: Oxford UP.

Baird, B., Smallwood, J., Mrazek, M. D., Kam, J. W. Y., Franklin, M. S., & Schooler, J. W. (2012). Inspired by Distraction: Mind Wandering Facilitates Creative Incubation. *Psychological Science,* 23(10), 1117–1122.

Berdyaev, N. (1999). Salvation and Creativity (Fr. Stephen Janos, Trans.). Retrieved from http://www.berdyaev.com/berdiaev/berd_lib/1926_308.html.

Brown, R. W. (2009). "Medieval Civilization: Lecture Notes." http://www.uncp.edu/home/rwb/lecture_mid_civ.htm. Accessed July 4, 2013.

Catmull, E. (2008). How Pixar Fosters Collective Creativity. *Harvard Business Review.*

Culpepper, M. K. (2010). KEYS to Creativity and Innovation: An Adopt-A-Measure Examination. *The International Center for Studies in Creativity.* Buffalo State College. Retrieved from http://www.marykayculpepper.com/docs/keys-to-creativity.pdf.

Dworsky, D. & Köhler, V. (2011). PressPausePlay. Retrieved from http://www.presspauseplay.com/.

Hughes, G. D. (1998). Add Creativity To Your Decision Processes. Retrieved from http://www.unc.edu/-gdhughes/ARTICLES.HTM.

Ireland, C. (2013). Principles of Creativity. *Radcliffe Institute for Advanced Study at Harvard University.* Retrieved from https://www.radcliffe.harvard.edu/news/radcliffe-magazine/principles-of creativity?utm_source=SilverpopMailing&utm_medium=email&utm_campaign=08.27%20daily%20%281%29.

Johnson, S. (2010). Where Good Ideas Come From: The Natural History of Innovation. Penguin.

Kounios, J. & Beeman, M. (2009). The Aha! Moment The Cognitive Neuroscience of Insight. *Current Directions in Psychological Science* 18, no. 4 (August 1, 2009): 210–216.

Lange, P. G. & Mizuko, I. (2010). In: Hanging Out, Messing Around, and Geeking Out. MIT Press.

Lehrer, J. (2012). Groupthink. *The New Yorker,* January 30, 2012. Retrieved from http://www.newyorker.com/reporting/2012/01/30/120130fa_fact_lehrer?printable=true%C2%A4tPage=all.

Robinson, K. (2010). RSA Animate - Changing Education Paradigms. Retrieved from http://www.youtube.com/watch?v=zDZFcDGpL4U&feature=youtube_gdata_player.

Selig, T. (2011). inGenius: A Crash Course on Creativity, HarperCollins.

Smith, N. Who Says Creativity Can't Be Learned? *BusinessNewsDaily.com*. Retrieved from http://www.businessnewsdaily.com/2471-creativity-innovation-learned.html.

Takeuchi, H., Taki, Y., Hashizume, H., Sassa, Y., Nagase, T., Nouchi, R., & Kawashima, R. (2011). Failing to Deactivate: The Association Between Brain Activity During a Working Memory Task and Creativity. *NeuroImage* 55, no. 2 (March 15, 2011): 681–687.

TEDxABQ - Rex Jung, (2011). *Creativity and the Brain.* Retrieved from http://www.youtube.com/watch?v=SWIXfNEDy3g&feature=youtube_gdata_player.

TEDxAldeburgh - Vincent Walsh (2011). *Neuroscience and Creativity.* Retrieved fromhttp://www.youtube.com/watch?v=UyUAbYiEdO&feature=youtube_gdata_player.

Tippett, K. (2013). Creativity and the Everyday Brain - Transcript Rex Jung (May 2, 2013). *On Being.* Retrieved from http://www.onbeing.org/program/creativity-and-the-everyday- brain-with-rex-jung/transcript/5441.

Turak, August (2011), Can Creativity Be Taught? Retrieved from *http://www.forbes.com/sites/augustturak/2011/05/22/can-creativity-be-taught/.*

CHAPTER TWO
WHAT IS CREATIVITY?

Adams, J. L. (1986). *The Care and Feeding of Ideas: a Guide to Encouraging Creativity.* Reading, Mass.: Addison-Wesley.

Amabile, T. M. (1983). *The Social Psychology of Creativity.* New York: Springer-Verlag.

Berns, G. (2008). Iconoclast, A neuroscientist reveals how to think differently, Harvard Business Press.

Berns, G. (2008). Neuroscience Sheds New Light on Creativity. *Fast Company.* Retrieved from http://www.fastcompany.com/1007044/neuroscience-sheds-new-light-creativity.

Boehlke, S. (2008). The Politics of Creativity™: Four Domains for Inquiry and Action by Leaders in R&D1. *Creativity and Innovation Management.* 17, no. 1: 77–87.

Bruell, A. (2013). Creative Execs' Salaries Surge in Adland, Survey Finds. Retrieved from http://adage.com/article/agency-news/creative-execs-salaries-surge-adland-survey- finds/241972/.

Bronson, P. & Merryman, A. (2010). The Creativity Crisis. *Newsweek Magazine*. Retrieved from http://www.thedailybeast.com/newsweek/2010/07/10/the-creativity-crisis.html.

Cameron, J. (2002). The Artist's Way: A Spiritual Path to Higher Creativity. Penguin Putnam Inc, San Francisco, CA.

Csikszentmihalyi, M. (1996). Creativity: Flow and the Psychology of Discovery and Invention. New York: HarperCollins Publishers; New York, NY.

C2-MTL, Commerce and Creativity Conference (2013). Montreal, "Press Release 04-03-2013 | C2-MTL." Retrieved from http://www.c2mtl.com/pr04032013/.

C2-MTL, Commerce and Creativity Conference (2013), Montreal, "C2MTLbrochurecommanditeEN.pdf." Retrieved from http://www.c2mtl.com/files/C2MTLbrochurecommanditeEN.pdf.

"Creativity | Define Creativity at Dictionary.com." Retrieved from http://dictionary.reference.com/browse/creativity.

DeBono, Ed. (1992). Serious Creativity: Using the Power of Lateral Thinking to Create New Ideas; Harper Collins.

Evans, J. R. (1991). Creative Thinking in the Decision and Management Sciences. Cincinnati, OH: South-Western Publishing.

Guilford, J.P. (1950). Creativity. *American Psychologist*, Vol. 5, pp. 444-454.

Griffin, W. G. & Morrison, D. (2010). *The Creative Process Illustrated How Advertising's Big Ideas Are Born.* HOW Books, Cincinnati, Ohio.

Isaksen, S.G., Treffinger, D.J. (2004). Celebrating 50 years of reflective practice: versions of creative problem solving. *Journal of Creative Behavior*, Vol. 38, Nr. 2, pp. 75-101

Johnson, C. Y. (2010). Group IQ. Retrieved from http://www.boston.com/bostonglobe/ideas/articles/2010/12/19/group_iq/.

O'Barr, W. M. (2008). Creativity in Advertising. *Advertising & Society Review.* 8:3, pp. 1-15.

Parnes, S. J. (Ed.) (1992). Source Book for Creative Problem Solving: A Fifty Year Digest of Proven Innovation Processes. *Creative Education Foundation.*

Smith, R.E. & Yang, X. (2004). Toward a general theory of creativity in advertising: Examining the role of divergence. *Marketing Theory.* Vol. 4, Nr. 1-2, pp. 31-58.

Sternberg, R. J. (1999). Handbook of Creativity. Cambridge University Press.

Torrance, E. P. (1974). *The Torrance tests of creative thinking: Norma-technical manual.* Bensenville, IL: Scholastic Testing Service, Inc.

Torrance, E. P. (1962). *Guiding Creative Talent.* Englewood Cliffs, NJ: Prentice-Hall.

Zabelina, D. L. & Robinson, M.D. (2010). Psychology of Aesthetics, Creativity, and the Arts. *American Psychological Association.* Vol. 4, No. 1, 57–65.

CHAPTER THREE
CREATIVE THINKING

Abraham, A., Beudt, S., Ott, D. VM. & D. Yves von Cramon. (2012). Creative Cognition and Brain: Dissociations Between Frontal, Parietal–temporal and Basal Ganglia Groups. *Brain Research.*

Abraham, A., Pieritz, K., Thybusch, K., Rutter, B., Kröger, S., Schweckendiek, J., Stark, R., Windmann, S. & Hermann, C. (2012). Creativity and the Brain: Uncovering the Neural Signature of Conceptual Expansion. *Neuropsychologia.*

Adams, J. L. (1986). *The Care and Feeding of Ideas: a Guide to Encouraging Creativity.* Reading, Mass.: Addison-Wesley.

Aziz-Zadeh, L., Liew, S. & Dandekar, F. (2012). Exploring the Neural Correlates of Visual Creativity. *Social Cognitive and Affective Neuroscience.*

Berns, G. (2008). Iconoclast, A neuroscientist reveals how to think differently. *Harvard Business Press.*

Berns, G. (2008). Neuroscience Sheds New Light on Creativity. *Fast Company.* Retrieved from http://www.fastcompany.com/1007044/neuroscience-sheds-new-light-creativity.

Bonk, C. J. Creativity Tests. Accessed September 12, 2013. http://www.indiana.edu/-bobweb/r546/modules/creativity/creativity_tests.html .

Bowden, E. M., Jung-Beeman, M., Fleck, J. & Kounios, J. (2005). New approaches to demystifying insight. *TRENDS in Cognitive Sciences*. Vol.9 No.7 July 2005.

Begley, S. (2008). Eureka! How the Brain Has 'Aha' Moments. *Newsweek Magazine*, January 23, 2008. Retrieved from http://www.thedailybeast.com/newsweek/blogs/lab- notes/2008/01/22/eureka-how-the-brain-has-aha-moments.html.

Bruell, A. (2013). Creative Execs' Salaries Surge in Adland, Survey Finds. Retrieved from http://adage.com/article/agency-news/creative-execs-salaries-surge-adland-survey- finds/241972/.

Cameron, J. (2002). The Artist's Way: A Spiritual Path to Higher Creativity. Penguin Putnam Inc, San Francisco, CA.

Carey, B. (2010). Tracing the Spark of Creative Problem-Solving. Retrieved from http://www.nytimes.com/2010/12/07/science/07brain.html?pagewanted=all&_r=0.

Cressey, D. (2012). Brain Scans of Rappers Shed Light on Creativity. *Nature*.

Csikszentmihalyi, M. (1996), Creativity: Flow and the Psychology of Discovery and Invention. New York: HarperCollins.

Evans, J. R. (1991). Creative Thinking – In the decision and management sciences, South- Western.

DeBono, E. (1992). Serious Creativity: Using the Power of Lateral Thinking to Create New Ideas. Harper Collins Publishers, Inc; New York, NY.

DeBono, E. (1985). Six Thinking Hats. Back Bay Books, Boston, MA.

Guilford, J.P. (1950). Creativity. *American Psychologist*, Vol. 5, pp. 444-454.

Hébert, T. P., Cramond, B., Neumeister, S., Millar, K.L., Silvian, G., Alice F. (2002). E. Paul Torrance: His Life, Accomplishments, and Legacy. The National Research Center on the Gifted and Talented (NRC/GT), University of Connecticut, Storrs, CT, February 2002

Heid, K. (2008). Creativity and Imagination: Tools for Teaching Artistic Inquiry, Art Education, 61 no.4, July 2008. Retrieved from http://www.arts.unco.edu/ciae/resources/tools%20for%20teaching%20artistic%20inqui ry.pdf.

Huang, P., Qiu, L., Shen, L., Zhang, Y., Song, Z., Qi, Z., Gong, Q., & Xie, P. (2012). Evidence for a Left-over-right Inhibitory Mechanism During Figural Creative Thinking in Healthy Nonartists. *Human Brain Mapping*.

Isaacson, W. (2011). Steve Jobs, Simon and Schuster, New York.

Jung-Beeman, M., Bowden, E.M., Haberman J., Frymiare J.L., Arambel-Liu S., et al. (2004). Neural Activity When People Solve Verbal Problems with Insight. *PLoS Biol* 2(4): e97.

Jung-Beeman, M. (2005). Bilateral brain processes for comprehending natural language. *TRENDS in Cognitive Sciences*. Vol.9 No.11.

Kandel, E. R. (2013). What the Brain Can Tell Us About Art. *The New York Times*. April 12, 2013, sec. Opinion / Sunday Review. Retrieved from http://www.nytimes.com/2013/04/14/opinion/sunday/what-the-brain-can-tell-us- about-art.html.

Kaufman, J. C. & Sternberg, R. J. (2006). The International Handbook of Creativity. Cambridge University Press.

Kim, K. H. (2006). Can We Trust Creativity Tests? A Review of TTCT Kyung Hee Kim JCR_2006.pdf. Retrieved from http://web.mit.edu/monicaru/Public/old%20stuff/For%20Dava/Grad%20Library.Data/P DF/s15326934crj1801_2-1024782081/s15326934crj1801_2.pdf.

Lehrer, J. (2008). The Eureka Hunt: Why do good ideas come to us when they do? The New Yorker, July 28, 2008.

Lehrer, J. (2012). Imagine: How Creativity Works. 1st edition. Houghton Mifflin.

Makel, M. C. (2008). The Malleability of Implicit Beliefs of Creativity and Creative Production, page 81, ProQuest.

Miran, M. D., Miran, E. & Chen, N. (2012). Design of Living Systems in the Information Age: Brain, Creativity, and the Environment. *Origin (s) of Design in Nature,* 573–591.

Ogilvy, D., Parker, A. (2004). Confessions of an Advertising Man. Southbank Publishing, London.

Osborn, A. F. (1963). *Applied Imagination: Principles and Procedures of Creative Problem- Solving: Third Revised Edition.* 3rd Revised edition. Charles Scribner's Sons, New York.

Rhodes, T. (2010), *Assessing Outcomes and Improving Achievement: Tips and Tools for Using Rubrics.* Washington, DC: Association of American Colleges and Universities.

Ruggiero, V. R. (2012). *The Art of Thinking: a Guide to Critical and Creative Thought.* Boston: Pearson.

Sandkühler, S. & Bhattacharya, B. (2008). Deconstructing Insight: EEG Correlates of Insightful Problem Solving. *PLoS ONE* 3, no. 1.

Simonton, D. K. (2012). Quantifying Creativity: Can Measures Span the Spectrum? *Dialogues in Clinical Neuroscience.* Vol. 14, no. 1, 100.

Sperry, R. W. (1964). Problems outstanding in the evolution of brain function. James Arthur Lecture. New York: American Museum of Natural History. Retrieved from http://capone.mtsu.edu/rbombard/RB/PDFs/PHIL4500/EOI/EOI-13.pdf.

Sternberg, R. J. & Lubart, T. I. (1995). An investment perspective on creative insight. In R. J. Sternberg & J. E. Davidson (Eds.), *The nature of insight* (pp.535-558), Cambridge, MA: MIT Press.

Takeuchi, H., Taki, Y., Hashizume, H., Sassa, Y., Nagase, T., Nouchi, R. & Kawashima, R. (2012). The Association Between Resting Functional Connectivity and Creativity. *Cerebral Cortex*.

Tippett, K. (2013). Creativity and the Everyday Brain - Transcript Rex Jung. *On Being.* Retrieved from http://www.onbeing.org/program/creativity-and-the-everyday-brain-with-rex- jung/transcript/5441.

Torrance, E. P. (1974). *The Torrance tests of creative thinking: Norma-technical manual.* Bensenville, IL: Scholastic Testing Service, Inc.

Torrance, E. P. (1979). *The Search for Satori & Creativity.* Buffalo: Creative Education Foundation, Bearly.

Treffinger, D. J., Isaksen, S. G., & Firestien, R. L. (1983). Theoretical perspectives on creative learning and its facilitation: An overview. Journal of Creative Behavior, 17(1), 9-17.

Vanden Bergh, B. & Stuhlfaut, M. (2006) Is Advertising Creativity Primarily an Individual or a Social Process? Journal of Mass Communication & Society 9: 373–397.

Ziv, A. (1989). Chapter 4: Using Humor to Develop Creative Thinking. *Journal of Children in Contemporary Society* 20, no. 1–2

Wallas, G. (1926). The Art of Thought. New York: Harcourt Brace.

Wujec, T. (1995). Five Star Mind, Games & Puzzles to Stimulate Your Creativity & Imagination, Doubleday, New York.

Wynkoop, S. (2013). Exploring R/GA's Creativity, unpublished research paper, Emerson College.

CHAPTER FOUR

THE CREATIVE [PROBLEM-SOLVING] PROCESS

Adams, J. L. (1986). *The Care and Feeding of Ideas: a Guide to Encouraging Creativity.* Reading, Mass.: Addison-Wesley.

Amabile, T. M. (1983). The social psychology of creativity: A componential conceptualization. *Journal of Personality and Social Psychology,* Vol. 45, pp. 357-377.

Bengtson, T. A. (1982). Creativity's Paradoxical Character: A Postscript to James Webb Young's Technique for Producing Ideas. *Journal of Advertising.* 11, 1; ProQuest Central, pg. 3

Biondi, A. M. (1993). The Creative Process. Creative Education Foundation, Buffalo, NY.

Brown, T. (2008). Design Thinking – How to Deliver on a Great Plan. *Harvard Business Review.*

Brown, T. (2009). *Change by Design: How Design Thinking Can Transform Organizations and Inspire Innovation.* New York, NY: HarperCollins Publishers.

Brown, T. & Wyatt, J. (2010). Design Thinking for Social Innovation (SSIR). Retrieved from http://www.ssireview.org/articles/entry/design_thinking_for_social_innovation/.

DeBono, E. (1992). Serious Creativity: Using the Power of Lateral Thinking to Create New Ideas. Harper Collins Publishers, Inc; New York, NY.

DeBono, E. (1985). Six Thinking Hats. Back Bay Books, Boston, MA.

DeBono, E. (1990). Lateral Thinking for Management. Penguin Books, New York.

Dubberly, H. (2008). How do you design? A compendium of models. Retrieved from http://www.dubberly.com/articles/how-do-you-design.html.

Evans, J. R. (1991). Creative Thinking – In the decision and management sciences, South- Western.

Griffin, W. G. (2008). From Performance to Mastery: Developmental Models of the Creative Process. *Journal of Advertising*, 37 (4), 95-108.

Griffin, W. G. & Morrison, D. (2010). *The Creative Process Illustrated How Advertising's Big Ideas Are Born.* HOW Books, Cincinnati, Ohio.

Guilford, J.P. (1950). Creativity. *American Psychologist*, Vol. 5, pp. 444-454.

IDEO (2011), Design Thinking for Educators Version 1.0. Retrieved from http://designthinkingforeducators.com/.

IDEO (2012), Design Thinking for Educators Version 2.0. Retrieved from http://designthinkingforeducators.com/.

Isaksen, S.G., Treffinger, D.J. (2004). Celebrating 50 years of reflective practice: versions of creative problem solving. *Journal of Creative Behavior,* Vol. 38, Nr. 2, pp. 75-101

Isaksen, S. G., Stead-Dorval, K. B. & Treffinger, D. J. (2011). *Creative Approaches to Problem Solving: a Framework for Innovation and Change.* Los Angeles: SAGE.

Kowalik, T. F., Mitchell, W. E. (1999). CPS-Creative Problem Solving - Mitchell & Kowalik. Retrieved from http://www.roe11.k12.il.us/GES%20Stuff/Day%204/Process/Creative%20Problem%20Solving/CPS-Mitchell%20&%20Kowalik.pdf.

Osborne, A. (1942). *How To Think Up*, New York & London: McGraw-Hill Book Company, Inc.

Parnes, S. J. (Ed.) (1992). Source Book for Creative Problem Solving: A Fifty Year Digest of Proven Innovation Processes. Creative Education Foundation.

Martin, R. L. (2009). *The Design of Business: Why Design Thinking Is the Next Competitive Advantage.* Boston, Mass.: Harvard Business Press.

Runco, M. A. (2007). *Creativity Theories and Themes: Research, Development, and Practice.* Amsterdam; Boston: Elsevier Academic Press.

Sasser, S. K. (2008). Desperately Seeking Advertising Creativity: Engaging an Imaginative "3Ps" Research Agenda, Journal of Advertising, pp. 5-19

Treffinger, D. J., Isaksen, S. G., & Firestien, R. L. (1983). Theoretical Perspectives on Creative Learning and its Facilitation: An Overview. *Journal of Creative Behavior, 17*(1), 9-17.

Vanden Bergh, B. & Stuhlfaut, M. (2006). Is Advertising Creativity Primarily an Individual or a Social Process? *Journal of Mass Communication & Society.* 9: 373–397.

Venkataramani, J., Holbrook, G., Morris B. & Stern, B. B. (2001). The Role of Myth in Creative Advertising Design: Theory, Process and Outcome. *Journal of Advertising,* Vol. 30, No. 2 (Summer, 2001), pp. 1-25

Young, J. W. (2012). *A Technique for Producing Ideas.* Important Books & CreateSpace Independent Publishing Platform.

Wallas, G. (1926). The Art of Thought. New York: Harcourt Brace.

White, G. E. (1972). The X Factor in Advertising Theory. Journal of Advertising (pre-1986); 1, 000001; ProQuest Central, pg. 28

CHAPTER FIVE

CREATIVE THINKING METHODS AND TECHNIQUES

Adams, J. L. (1986). *The Care and Feeding of Ideas: a Guide to Encouraging Creativity.* Reading, Mass.: Addison-Wesley.

Cameron, J. (2002). The Artist's Way: A Spiritual Path to Higher Creativity. Penguin Putnam Inc, San Francisco, CA.

De Bono, E. (1973). Lateral Thinking: Creativity Step by Step. New York: Harper & Row.

DeBono, E. (1985). Six Thinking Hats. Back Bay Books, Boston, MA.

DeBono, E. (1990). Lateral Thinking for Management. Penguin Books, New York.

DeBono, E. (1992). Serious Creativity: Using the Power of Lateral Thinking to Create New Ideas. Harper Collins Publishers, Inc; New York, NY.

Evans, J. R. (1991). Creative Thinking – In the Decision and Management Sciences, South- Western.

Gray, D., Brown, S. & Macanufo, J. (2010). *Gamestorming: a Playbook for Innovators, Rulebreakers, and Changemakers.* O'Reilly Media, Cambridge.

Guilford, J.P. (1950). Creativity. *American Psychologist*, Vol. 5, pp. 444-454.

Isaksen, S.G., Treffinger, D.J. (2004). Celebrating 50 Years of Reflective Practice: Versions of Creative Problem Solving. *Journal of Creative Behavior.* Vol. 38, Nr. 2, pp. 75-101

Isaksen, S.G., Stead-Dorval, K. B. & Treffinger, D. J. (2011). *Creative Approaches to Problem Solving: a Framework for Innovation and Change.* Los Angeles: SAGE.

Kamenetz, A. (2013). From Alex Osborn To Bob Sutton: A Meeting Of The Minds To Build A Better Brainstorm. *Fast Company.* Retrieved from http://www.fastcompany.com/3004450/alex-osborn-bob-sutton-meeting-minds-build- better-brainstorm.

Lehrer, J. (2012). Groupthink. *The New Yorker.* Retrieved from http://www.newyorker.com/reporting/2012/01/30/120130fa_fact_lehrer?printable=true¤tPage=all.

Michalko, M. (1991). *Thinkertoys a Handbook of Creative-thinking Techniques.* Berkeley, Calif.: Ten Speed Press.

Osborne, A. (1942). *How To Think Up*, New York & London: McGraw-Hill Book Company, Inc.

Parnes, S. J. (Ed.) (1992). Source Book for Creative Problem Solving: A Fifty Year Digest of Proven Innovation Processes. Creative Education Foundation.

Vanden Bergh, B. & Stuhlfaut, M. (2006). Is Advertising Creativity Primarily an Individual or a Social Process? *Journal of Mass Communication & Society.* 9: 373–397.

Tippett, K. (2013). Creativity and the Everyday Brain - Transcript Rex Jung. *On Being.* Retrieved from http://www.onbeing.org/program/creativity-and-the-everyday-brain-with-rex- jung/transcript/5441.

Torrance, E. P. (1974). *The Torrance tests of creative thinking: Norma-technical manual.* Bensenville, IL: Scholastic Testing Service, Inc.

Wujec, T. (1995). Five Star Mind, Games & Puzzles to Stimulate Your Creativity & Imagination, Doubleday, New York.

Zwicky, F. (1969). *Discovery, Invention, Research through the Morphological Approach.* Macmillan, New York.

CHAPTER SIX
EVALUATION OF IDEAS

Achorn, G. (2003). Audi International Advertising Contest 2003 - The Decision - Fourtitude.com. *Fourtitude.com.* Retrieved from http://fourtitude.com/news/Audi_News_1/audi- international-advertising-contest-2003-the-decision/.

Aziz, P. (2011). "How One Agency Created A Brand Strategy Toolbox Inspired By The Need For Change - PSFK." *PSFK*, October 24, 2011. Retrieved from http://www.psfk.com/2011/10/humankind-a-brand-strategy-toolbox-inspired-by-the- need-for-change.html.

Bernardin, T. and Kemp-Robertson, P. (2008). Wildfire 2008: Creativity with a Human Touch. *Journal of Advertising*, vol. 37, no. 4 (Winter 2008), pp. 131–149.

Cannes Lions (2013). Case for Creative Bravery, Inspiration, Cannes Lions International Festival of Creativity. *Cannes Lions International Festival of Creativity.* Retrieved from http://www.canneslions.com/creativebravery/index.cfm.

Cannes Lions (2013). The Business Case For Creative Bravery. A special report provided by Cannes Lions management team. Retrieved from http://www.youtube.com/watch?v=YcrWl7zUMyQ&feature=youtube_gdata_player.

El-Murad, J., and West, D. C. (2004). The Definition and Measurement of Creativity: What Do We Know? *Journal of Advertising Research* 44, no. 02, pp. 188–201.

Feldhusen, J. F. and Goh, B. E. (1995). Assessing and Accessing Creativity: An Integrative Review of Theory, Research, and Development. *Creativity Research Journal*, 1995, Vol. 8, NO. 3, pp. 231-247.

Flandin, M.P., Martin, E., & Simkin, L.P. (1992). Advertising effectiveness research: A survey of agencies, clients and conflicts. *International Journal of Advertising*, Vol. 11, Nr. 3, pp. 203-214.

Glück, J., Ernst, R. & Unger, F. (2002). How Creatives define Creativity: Definitions reflect different types of creativity. *Creativity research Journal, Vol. 14, No. 1, pp. 55-67.*

Guilford, J. P. (1996). Measurement and Creativity, *Theory into Practice,* Vol. 5, No. 4, Creativity (Oct., 1966), pp. 186-189+202

Hoepfner, R. (1967). *Torrance Tests of Creative Thinking* by E. Paul Torrance, *Journal of Educational Measurement,* Vol. 4, No. 3 (Autumn, 1967), pp. 191-192

Hurman, J. (2012). The Case for Creativity. AUT Media, New Zealand. Retrieved from http://www.slideshare.net/jameshurman/the-case-for-creativity.

Gunn, D. (1998). Do Award Winning Commercial Sell? In: *How Advertising Works: The Role of Research*, by Jones, John Philip. SAGE, pp. 266-282.

Koslow, S., Sasser, S. L. & Riordan, E. A. (2003). What is creative to whom and why? Perceptions in advertising agencies. *Journal of Advertising Research*, Vol. 43, Nr. 1, pp. 96-110.

Nasard, A. (2013). Why Cannes Matters. A letter to festival attendees, provided by Cannes Lions management team. September 9, 2013.

Reid, L., King, K. & DeLorme, D. (1998). Top-level creatives look at advertising creativity then and now. *Journal of Advertising,* Vol. 27, Nr. 2, pp. 1–16.

Royer, T. (2013). An introduction to Droga5 – Case Studies. A presentation given to advertising professionals in Boston. August 19, 2013.

Smith, R.E., & Yang, X. (2004). Toward a general theory of creativity in advertising: Examining the role of divergence. *Marketing Theory,* Vol. 4, Nr. 1-2, pp. 31-58.

"TED-Ads-Worth-Spreading-Report.pdf." (2012). Retrieved from http://storage.ted.com/aws/TED-Ads-Worth-Spreading-Report.pdf.

Vanden Bergh, B. G. & Katz, H. E. (1999). *Advertising Principles: Choice, Challenge, Change.* Lincolnwood, Ill.: NTC Business Books.

White, A., & Smith, B.L (2001). Assessing advertising creativity using the creative product semantic scale. *Journal of Advertising Research,* Vol. 41, pp. 27-34.

CHAPTER SEVEN
IMPORTANCE OF COMMUNICATING IDEAS EFFECTIVELY

Batterson, M. (2004). Id: The True You. Xulon Press, Page 178.

Bernardin, T. & Kemp-Robertson, P. (2008). Wildfire 2008: Creativity with a Human Touch. *Journal of Advertising*, vol. 37, no. 4 (Winter 2008), pp. 131–149.

Catmull, E. (2008). How Pixar Fosters Collective Creativity. *Harvard Business Review.*

Csikszentmihaly, M. (1997). *Creativity: Flow & the Psychology of Discovery & Invention.* London: Harper & Row.

Berger, J. (1977). *Ways of Seeing: Based on the BBC Television Series with John Berger.* London; New York: British Broadcasting Corp. Penguin.

Berkowitz, J. (2012). Inside Volkswagen's Super Bowl XLVI Ad: Canine Cuteness Meets Star Wars. *Co.Create.* Retrieved from http://www.fastcocreate.com/1679528/inside- volkswagens-super-bowl-xlvi-ad-canine-cuteness-meets-star-wars.

Doveunitedstates. (2013). Dove Camera Shy. Retrieved from http://www.youtube.com/user/doveunitedstates?feature=watch.

Doveunitedstates. (2013). Dove Real Beauty Sketches. Retrieved from http://www.youtube.com/watch?v=litXW91UauE.

Dreier, T. (2011). Volkswagen's Mini-Darth Vader Ad: Behind the Screens - Streaming Media Magazine. *Streaming Media Magazine.* Retrieved from http://www.streamingmedia.com/Articles/ReadArticle.aspx?ArticleID=74862.

Emel, M. (2013). Five New Rules for Storytelling. Retrieved from http://www.metia.com/seattle/mandy-emel/2013/06/five-new-rules-for-storytelling/.

Gregory, R. L. (1990). *Eye and Brain: The Psychology of Seeing.* Princeton, N.J.: Princeton University Press.

Goodman, B. (1937). Sing, Sing, Sing with a Swing (written by Louis Prima). Retrieved from http://www.last.fm/listen/artist/Benny%2BGoodman/similarartists.

Gelb, M. (2000). *How to Think Like Leonardo Da Vinci: Seven Steps to Genius Every Day.* New York, N.Y.: Dell Pub.

Heath, C. & Heath, D. (2008). *Made to Stick: Why Some Ideas Survive and Others Die.* New York: Random House.

Hoffman, L. (2013). PR's Answer to the Classic Storytelling Arc. *Yahoo Small Business Advisor.* Retrieved from http://smallbusiness.yahoo.com/advisor/pr-answer-classic-storytelling- arc-171556980.html.

Minglin, P. (2011). MediaPost Publications What We Learned From VW's Super Bowl Success 02/09/2011. Retrieved from http://www.mediapost.com/publications/article/144427/#axzz2VS516LAz.

Orshan, C. (2013). WriteToShine - Class C - TUE.THURS. 8AM (721815). Retrieved from http://writetoshine.wikispaces.com/Class+C+-+TUE.THURS.+8AM+(721815).

Rapaille, C. (2007). *The Culture Code: An Ingenious Way to Understand Why People Around the World Buy and Live as They Do.* New York: Crown Business.

Scott, L. M., & Batra, R. (2003). *Persuasive Imagery a Consumer Response Perspective.* Mahwah, N.J.: Lawrence Erlbaum Associates.

Turner, T. (2013). Creativity & Attitude. *Pinterest.* Retrieved from http://www.pinterest.com/creativeleaders/creativity-attitude/.

Zaltman, G., Zaltman, L. H. (2008). Marketing Metaphoria: What Deep Metaphors Reveal About the Minds of Consumers. *Harvard Business School Publishing.*

Zeppelin, L. (1971). Black Dog. On *Headley.* England: Atlantic Music Label.

Volkswagen USA. (2011). The Force: Volkswagen Commercial. Retrieved from http://www.youtube.com/watch?v=R55e-uHQna0.

CHAPTER EIGHT
CREATIVITY AND PLACE

Amabile, T. (1996). Creativity and Innovation in Organizations. *Harvard Business School.* Case # 9-396-239.

Amabile, T., Hadley, C. N. & Kramer, S. J. (2002). Creativity Under the Gun. Special Issue on The Innovative Enterprise: Turning Ideas into Profits. *Harvard Business Review.* 80, no. 8, pp 52-61.

Amabile, T. (1983). The Social Psychology of Creativity. Springer-Verlag, New York.

Amabile, T., Hill, K. G., Hennessey, B. A. & Tighe, E. M. (1994). The Work Preference Inventory: Assessing Intrinsic and Extrinsic Motivational Orientations. *Journal of Personality and Social Psychology,* Vol. 66, pp. 950-967.

Amabile, T. (1996). *Creativity in Context: Update to the Social Psychology of Creativity.* Boulder, CO: Westview Press.

Amabile, T., Conti, R., Coon, H., Lazenby, J. & Herron, M. (1996). Assessing the Work Environment for Creativity. *The Academy of Management Journal,* Vol. 39, No. 5, pp. 1154-1184.

Amabile, T. (2001). Beyond talent: John Irving and the passionate craft of creativity. *American Psychologist,* Vol. 56, pp. 333-336.

Amabile, T. (1988). Putting creativity to work. In: *The Nature of Creativity,* R. J. Sternberg (ed.). Cambridge: Cambridge University Press.

Barron, F. (1968). *Creativity and Personal Freedom.* New York: Van Nostrand.

Bortolot, N. (2013). What is the Office of the Future? In: Entrepreneur August 2013. Retrieved from http://mobileservices.texterity.com/entrepreneur/august_2013?folio=44&linkImageSrc=http%3A%2F%2Fe-cdn.dashdigital.com%2Fentrepreneur%2Faugust_2013%2Fdata%2Fimgpages%2Fmobile_tn2%2F0046_cfaxaq.png%3Flm%3D1374603781000&lm=1374603781000#pg46. Accessed August 6, 2013.

Csikszentmihalyi, M. (1996). *Creativity: Flow and the Psychology of Discovery and Invention.* New York: HarperCollins.

Ekvall, G., Arvonen, J. & Waldenstrom-Lindblad, I. (1983). Creative Organizational Climate: Construction and Validation of a Measuring Instrument. Stockholm, Sweden.

Groysberg, B., Slind, M. (2011). Big Spaceship: Ready to Go Big? *Harvard Business Review,* 9- 409-047

Einarsen, S. (1996). Organizational climate for creativity and Innovation. *European Journal of Work and Organizational Psychology*, Vol. 5, pp. 105-123.

Fallon, P. & Senn, F. (2006). Juicing the Orange: How to Turn Creativity into a Powerful Business Advantage, Cambridge: Harvard Business School Press.

Iwerks, L. (2007). *The Pixar Story*. Documentary, Studio: Leslie Iwerks Productions. Distributed by Walt Disney Studios Motion Pictures.

Johnson, S. (2010). Where Good Ideas Come From. The Natural History of Innovation. Riverhead Books.

Kaplan T. L. & Koval, R. (2003). BANG! Getting your message heard in a noisy world, 1st ed., New York: Doubleday.

Mathisen, G. E. & Einarsen, S. (2004). A Review of Instruments Assessing Creative and Innovative Environments within Organizations." Creativity Research Journal, Vol. 16, No. 1, pp. 119-140.

Ruscio, J., Whitney, D., & Amabile, T.M. (1998). Looking inside the Fishbowl of Creativity: Ver- bal and Behavioural Predictors of Creative Performance. Creativity Research Journal, Vol. 11, Nr. 3, pp. 243-263.

Tharp, T. & Coutu, D. L. (2008). Creativity Step by Step: A Conversation with Choreographer Twyla Tharp. *Harvard Business Review*. Product Number: R0804B.

Verbeke, W., Franses, P. H., le Blanc, A. & van Ruiten, N. (2008). Findings the KEYS to Creativity in Ad Agencies: Using Climate, Dispersion, and Size to Examine Award Performance. *Journal of Advertising*, 37 (4), 121-30.

White, A., & Smith, B.L (2001). Assessing advertising creativity using the creative product semantic scale. *Journal of Advertising Research*, Vol. 41, pp. 27-34.

Zaremba, M. (2009). Agency Profile: AKQA, San Francisco | Articles. Retrieved from http://ihaveanidea.org/articles/2009/07/16/agency-profile-akqa-san-francisco/.

CHAPTER NINE

CREATIVITY AND PHILOSOPHY

Amabile, T. (1998). How to Kill Creativity. *Harvard Business Review*. Product Number: 98501.

Amabile, T., Mukti, K. (2008). Creativity and the Role of the Leader. *Harvard Business Review*. Product Number: R0810G.

Börjesson, S., & Elmquist, M. (2011). Developing Innovation Capabilities: A Longitudinal Study of a Project at Volvo Cars. *Creativity & Innovation Management*, 20, no. 3 (September): 171-184.

Chatman, J. A. & Jehn, K. A. (1994). Assessing the Relationship between Industry Characteristics and Organizational Culture: How Different can you be? *Academy of Management Journal*, *37*, 522–553.

Bick, B. M. As Told To Julie (2007). The Google Way: Give Engineers Room. *The New York Times*, October 21, 2007, sec. Job Market. Retrieved from http://www.nytimes.com/2007/10/21/jobs/21pre.html.

Eisenberg, E. M., & Riley, P. (2001). Organizational Culture. The New Handbook of Organizational Communication: Advances in Theory, Research, and Methods, Frederic M. Jablin and Linda M. Putnam, eds, Thousand Oaks, CA: Sage, 291-323.

Finegan, J. E. (2002). The Impact of Person and Organizational Values on Organizational Commitment. *Journal of occupational and organizational psychology, 73*, 149-169.

Liedtka, J. M. (1989). Value Congruence: The Interplay of Individual and Organizational Value System. *Journal of Business Ethics, 8*, 805-815.

Mediaman Mainz. (2012). BITBALL Making-Of // Vol. 1. Retrieved from http://www.youtube.com/watch?v=CkE9C5R73fo.

Mediaman Mainz. (2012). BITBALL Gameplay //. Retrieved from http://www.youtube.com/watch?v=h5KDQeMIOTM.

Meglino, B. M., Ravlin, E. C. & Adkins, C. L. (1989). A Work Value Approach to Corporate Culture: A Field Test of the Value Convergence Process and its Relationship to Individual Outcomes. *Journal of Applied Psychology, 74*(3), 424-432.

Mense, M. (2013). How To Build Your Own Recipe Dshini. *Speaking About*. Mediaman Blog. Retrieved from http://blog.mediaman.de/recipe-printer-dshini/#more-261.

Mense, M. (2013). Recipe Dshini. *TinkerDing*. Retrieved from http://www.youtube.com/watch?v=RBdZ6QyFJog#t=37.

Naranjo-Valencia, J., Jiménez-Jiménez, D. & Sanz-Valle, R. (2011). Innovation or Imitation? The Role of Organizational Culture. *Management Decision*, 49, 1, 55-72.

Nahapiet, J. & Ghoshal, S. (1998). Social Capital, Intellectual Capital and the Organizational Advantage. *Academy of Management Review*, *23*(2), 242-266.

Nyilasy, G. & Reid, L. N. (2009). Agency Practitioners Theories of How Advertising Works. *Journal of Advertising*, 38 (3), 81-96.

Oliver, J. D. & Ashley, C. (2012). Creative Leaders' Views on Managing Advertising Creativity. *Journal of Marketing Theory & Practice*, 20 (3), 335-348.

Sasser, S. K. (2008). Desperately Seeking Advertising Creativity: Engaging an Imaginative "3Ps" Research Agenda. *Journal of Advertising*, pp. 5-19.

Shirky, C. (2011). Cognitive Surplus: How Technology Makes Consumers into Collaborators. New York: Penguin Books.

Schwartz, A. (2013). How to Find out Whether You're a Good Cultural Fit at Any Company. *Co.Exist*. Retrieved from http://www.fastcoexist.com/1682632/how-to-find-out- whether-youre-a-good-cultural-fit-at-any-company.

"TBWA\CHIAT\DAY\LA." http://tbwachiatdayla.com/. Accessed July 22, 2013.

Tharp, T. & Reiter, M. (2006). The Creative Habit: Learn It and Use It for Life: a Practical Guide. New York: Simon & Schuster.

Tharp, T. & Coutu, D. L. (2008), Creativity Step by Step: A Conversation with Choreographer Twyla Tharp. *Harvard Business Review*. Product Number: R0804B.

Vogel, T., McCormick, B. & Villamil, L. (2012). Breakthrough Ideas in a Digital World. A presentation at FutureM. Retrieved from http://breakthrough.mediaman.net/.

Von Stamm, B.V. (2008). *Managing Innovation, Design and Creativity*. Wiley, Chichester.

Wilde, J. & Wilde, R. (1991). Visual Literacy: A Conceptual Approach to Graphic Problem Solving. New York: Watson-Guptill.

INDEX

abstract thinking, 145
Adams, James L., 24
Addy Awards, 68
Ads Worth Spreading, 69-70, 71
Advertising Age, 2, 24
advertising industry, creativity research and, 2
agency philosophy, 105-112
  physical work environment and, 115
  See also specific agencies and ad execs
AKQA, 18, 96, 118, 179, 180
  physical environment, 180
  See also Teo, Lynn
Amabile, Teresa, 45, 87-88, 89-90, 100, 113
  See also Amabile Process; KEYS to Creativity and Innovation instrument
Amabile Process, 42, 43, 45
American Colleges and Universities (AACU), 26-27
analysis of problems. *See* problem analysis methods
analytical thinking, 25
Anomaly New York, 63, 66, 74, 112, 123, 130, 165-166
  philosophy, 112
  physical environment, 88, 166
  See also Vulkan, Johnny
archetypes, 76
Aristotle, 8
Arnold Worldwide, 89, 96
  physical environment, 89
  See also Kay, Woody
Arora, Noreen, 129, 131, 132, 133, 134, 138-140
Artist Date exercise, 36, 47, 132, 142, 148, 149
attitude, creative, 81, 85-86
attribute listing, 59-60
Audi International Advertising Contest (AIAC), 69
awards/contests, creative, 68-72
  See also Ads Worth Spreading (TED.com); Audi International Advertising Contest (AIAC); Cannes Lions International Festival of Creativity; Leo Burnett Humankind GPC scale

Bandrovschi, Lorelei, 154-156
BBDO, 3, 54, 172
  See also Credle, Susan
Beeman, Mark, 34-35
Beethoven, Ludwig van, 10
Behance, 120
Berc, Shelley, 44, 54, 70
Berns, Gregory, 22, 35
Bhattacharya, Joydeep, 34
Biese, Lauren, 84-85
Big Spaceship, 63-64, 96, 102-104, 114, 116, 121, 122, 123, 165, 169-170
  Hack Days, 122
  philosophy, 107-108
  physical environment, 96-97, 102, 103, 116, 170
  See also Lebowitz, Michael
blurt, 10
Boches, Edward, 3, 31, 53, 62, 67, 93, 109, 115, 178-179
  See also Mullen
Botticelli, 9
Brahms, Johannes, 10
brain, creative thinking and, 32-36
brain floating, 49
brain training, 34
brainstorming, 16, 49, 50, 54, 58, 60, 92, 130, 132, 146, 159
brainwriting, 49
brand bravery, 71
brief, creative, 64, 66
Bronson, Po, 15
Brown, Tim, 49
  See also IDEO Design Thinking Process
Bruell, Alexandra, 24

Cactus Marketing Communications, 30, 53
  See also Shearer, Norm
Cameron, Julia, 10, 19, 20, 36, 47
Cannes Lions International Festival of Creativity, 68, 71, 72
  Case for Creative Bravery, 71, 72
Carmichael Lynch Spong, 31, 88, 118-119, 186-187
  physical environment, 88, 186
  See also Spong, Doug
Catmull, Ed, 100, 117
chain of associations, 49
challenges, work, 90
  freedom to take on, 118-120
Chandrasekar, Harini, 157-159
Coca Cola, 71
cognitive surplus, 118, 120-123
collaboration, 18, 89, 92-93, 96-97, 99, 103, 106, 120, 133, 172
  See also specific agencies
collective intelligence, 99-100
communication mediums, 80-86
  creative attitude, 81, 85-86
  effective idea communication and, 79-80
  environment (including scent), 81, 85
  sight or visual imagery, 80, 84-85
  sound, 81, 85
  storytelling, 80, 81-84
communication of ideas, effective, 78-81
  See also communication mediums; ideas, bringing to market
concept fan, 49
"concept of failure," 118
confidence. *See* creative confidence
conscious thinking, 26
conspiracy theory, 74, 83
convergent thinking, 15, 24, 25, 26, 27, 41, 49, 51, 113, 159
Cramer-Krasselt, 3, 36, 45-46, 61, 88, 89, 99, 110, 116, 125, 176
  philosophy, 110-111
  physical environment, 88, 89, 176
  See also Ross, Marshall
Creative and Implementation Cycle, 118
Creative Artist Agency, Los Angeles, 71
creative confidence, 21, 140, 157
Creative Education Foundation (CEF), SUNY Buffalo, 46
creative intelligence, 173

creative people, 16-18
  preconceptions about, 13, 18-21, 128-129, 142, 153, 159, 161, 162
creative philosophy, personal, 125
  See also specific ad execs
creative portfolio, 138, 139-140
Creative Problem Solving Institute (CPSI), 40
creative problem-solving process, 1, 2, 39-51, 113
  creative habits, 46
  disruption concept, 45
  idea development, 46
  idea sharing, 46
  situation analysis/research, 46
  See also Amabile Process; Five-Stage Process of Creativity, James Webb Young; IDEO Design Thinking Process; Osborn-Parnes Creative Problem-Solving Process (CPS); Wallace Four-Phase Process
creative thinking, 1-5, 11-13, 15, 18
  as skill, 2, 3-4
  brain and, 32-36
  change and, 1
  definition, 15
  environment and, 18
  learning, 11-13
  mastering skill of, 4-5
  problem solving and, 1
  See also brainstorming; creative-thinking methods and techniques; creative-thinking skills; exercises, creative-thinking; lateral thinking; random input; reversal technique; SCAMPER; Six Thinking Hats
creative-thinking methods and techniques, 54-60
creative-thinking skills, 23-25, 88
Creativity, 2
creativity, 1-3, 6-16, 37, 41, 60, 87-88
  advertising/business environment, 2, 16
  boosting, 37, 60
  creative thinking skills component, 88
  definitions, 1-3, 6-10, 14-16, 41
  diminishing individual, 13, 21
  domain expertise/special knowledge component, 87-88
  individual, 87-88
  intrinsic and extrinsic motivation component, 88
  learning, 11-13
  See also creativity, practicing personal; creative thinking; 4 Ps of Creativity
creativity, practicing personal, 21-22, 36-37, 60, 125, 129-134, 137, 140, 142, 143, 146, 151, 153, 155, 159, 162
  See also exercises, creative-thinking
Credle, Susan, 2, 66, 68-69, 111, 114, 172-173
  See also BBDO; Leo Burnett
Crispin Porter + Bogusky, 120
critical thinking, 25
crowdsourcing, 11, 23, 31, 120, 181
Csikszentmihalyi, Mihaly, 75
curiosity, creativity and, 18

da Vinci, Leonardo, 9, 84
de Bono, Edward, 7, 54, 56, 57
decision-making process, 51
deductive reasoning, 25
Deitchman, Andrew, 94-95, 104, 108-109, 117, 120-121, 123, 125, 126, 166-168
  See also Mother New York
Dentsu, 47
Design Thinking for Educators, 49, 51
Deutsch LA, 2, 30, 78, 117, 185-186
  philosophy, 186
  physical environment, 185
  Side Step Project, 185
  See also Hunter, Mark
Diageo, 71
Disney, Walt, 35
disruption, 45, 107, 171
divergent thinking, 13, 15-16, 24, 25, 26, 27, 41, 50, 51, 53, 57, 150, 151, 155, 158, 159
  exercise, 30
  skills, 48, 113, 131
diversity, employee domain knowledge/skills, 104, 175
domain knowledge, 62, 87-88
Dove "Real Beauty" campaign, 77
Draftfcb Chicago, 64
  See also Sherlock, Robert
Droga, David, 2, 17, 31, 36, 61, 65, 76, 91-92, 96, 99, 107, 115-116, 119, 123, 127-128, 168-169
  See also Droga5
Droga5, 2, 17, 31, 36, 61, 70, 91, 96, 119, 123, 158, 159, 168-169
  philosophy, 107
  physical environment, 91
  See also Droga, David
Dunn, Alyse, 31, 133
Dworsky, David, 11

Ebel, Blake, 97, 100, 114, 119, 183-184
  See also Euro RSCG Chicago; Fear Not
Eberle, Bob, 58
Edelman China, 131, 147
Edison, Thomas Alva, 7
Effie Awards, 68
Emerson College, 47, 136, 137, 138
  Breakthrough Thinking course, 128-131, 144, 148
  Creative Thinking and Problem-Solving course, 13, 21, 31, 128, 136, 151, 152, 154, 155, 156, 157, 158, 160, 161, 163
  Global Marketing Communication and Advertising (GMCA) master's program, 141
  Integrated Marketing Communication graduate program, 136
  See also Vogel, Thomas
encouragement
  organizational, 90, 101
  supervisory, 90
environment, physical, 81, 85
  See also specific agencies; Pixar Studios; workplace environment
Esiet, Usen, 129
Euro RSCG Chicago, 97, 100, 183, 184
  physical environment, 98, 114
  See also Ebel, Blake
evaluation, idea. *See* idea evaluation criteria, creative; idea evaluation processes, creative
Evans, James R., 17
exercises, creative-thinking
  Alphabet Sequence, 24
  Artist Date, 36, 47, 132, 142, 148, 149

Coffeehouse, 44, 54, 70
Creative Philosophy, 125
Divergent Thinking, 30
Enemies & Champions, 19
Hello!, 101
How Many Triangles?, 25
In My Room, 20
Insight & Intuition, 62
Know Your Audience, 53, 104
Man is Found Dead, A, 68
Map Visualization, 119
Minds at Work, 34
Morning Pages, 10, 74, 132, 137, 142, 159, 163
Musical Interpretation, 78
Musical Time Travel, 76
New Love Symbol, 58
Nine Dots, 17, 39
Personal Twist: Myth, Legend, Fairy Tale, or Fable, 74
Quick Mental, 56
Retail Environment Observation, 84
Sight, Seeing and Perception, 77
Twenty Circles, 27-28, 38, 160
Two Riders and Horses, 40
Visual Self-Presentation, 42, 137
Visualization of Concepts, 86, 92, 115
Visualize Your Personal Future, 108
World is Waiting for Something You Created, The, 80
You are a Cartoon/Comic Author, 57, 67, 79, 89

fable, 74, 83
Facebook, 70
fail faster concept, 116-117, 118
failure, fear of, 133-134, 142, 143
fairy tale, 74, 83
Fallon, 98, 114, 119-120, 177-178
philosophy, 111-112
physical environment, 114-115, 177
See also Foster, Chris
Fast Company, 2
Fear Not, 97, 183
See also Ebel, Blake
Fennell, Andy, 71-72
Fiorentino, Matthew, 85, 131, 160-163
Five Stage Process of Creativity, James Webb Young, 42, 43
Flavell, John, 39-40
Florence, Italy, 9, 10
Fogel, Alejandro, 44, 54, 70
forced relationships. *See* random input
Foster, Chris, 95-96, 111-112, 114-115, 120, 125, 177-178
See also Fallon; Saatchi & Saatchi Asia-Pacific and Greater China
4 Ps of Creativity, 4, 5, 7-8, 9, 10, 85, 89, 105, 113, 124
free association, 16
freedom, work, 90, 101, 117
to take on challenges, 118-120
See also specific agencies
Freud, Sigmund, 54

Generation Y, 11
Goldstein, Marissa, 130, 132, 133, 134
Goodby Silverstein & Partners (GSP), 24, 62, 95, 98, 113, 116, 118, 120, 173, 174
philosophy, 106-107
physical environment, 93-94
See also Johnson, Margaret; Silverstein, Rich
Goodwin, Liz, 152-153
Google, 120
Greece, creativity in ancient, 8-9
Greenberg, Bob, 99
Guilford, J.P., 24, 26, 27, 53
Gunn, Donald, 72
gut feeling, 61-62
Insight & Intuition exercise, 62
See also specific ad execs
Gutenberg, Johannes, 7, 10
Gutglass, Samantha, 129, 132, 133, 134
Guzman, Milena, 132, 134
Hamilton, Sarah, 20-21, 132, 133, 134
Haydn, Joseph, 10
Heath, Chip, 82
Heath, Dan, 82
Heineken, 72
Hempen, Rebecca, 13, 129, 130, 134
Hill Holliday, 30, 182
philosophy, 182, 183
See also Jensen, Lance
Hunter, Mark, 2-3, 30, 78, 117, 185-186
See also Deutsch LA
Hurman, James, 72
Hurni, Roger, 28, 64, 93, 97, 110, 126, 174-175
See also Off Madison Ave
Hyper Island, 17
See also Leake, Tim

iconoclasts, 35
idea development. *See specific creative problem-solving processes*; divergent thinking; ideation
idea evaluation criteria, creative, 61-72
adds value, 63
aesthetics, 67-68
brand bravery, 71
cultural compass, 70
creative wonder, 71
encourages action/interaction, 63-64
new, 65
novel, 65
relevant, 66
seminal, 67
simple, 67
social good/responsibility, 66, 71
social media transferable, 69-70
stands out, 63, 65
storytelling, 69
sustainable, 65-66
talk, 69
target market, 64
trade-offs, 66
truthful/honest, 63
ultimate user/recipient, 66-67
unexpected, 65

See also Ads Worth Spreading; Audi International Advertising Contest (AIAC); Cannes Lions International Festival of Creativity; idea evaluation processes, creative; Leo Burnett Humankind GPC scale
idea evaluation processes, creative, 61-72
ask questions upfront, 65, 66
awards/contests and, 68-72
gut feeling, 61-62
strategy and, 61
See also specific agencies; idea evaluation criteria, creative
ideas, bringing to market, 75-78
interactivity, 75, 77-78
resistance, 75-76
simplicity, 75, 76-77
ideation, 42, 43, 46, 50, 53
See also specific creative problem-solving processes; divergent thinking; judgment, ideation and; Torrance Test of Creative Thinking (TTCT)
IDEO, 49, 50, 138, 139, 140
IDEO Design Thinking Process, 42, 43, 46, 49-51
Iezzi, T., 2
impediments, organizational, 90
INC, 2
inspiration, seeking personal, 126-128, 133, 143, 153
See also exercises, creative-thinking
Instagram, 70, 84
intelligence
collective, 99-100
creative, 173
InterAd, 47
International Advertising Association (IAA), 47
internet age, creativity in, 10-13
intuition. *See specific ad execs*; gut feeling
Ito, Mizuko, 11
Iwerks, Leslie, 100

J Walter Thompson, 53, 58
Jensen, Lance, 30, 182-183
See also Hill Holliday; Modernista!
Jobs, Steve, 35, 101
Johnson, Margaret, 23-24, 62, 95, 98-99, 106, 107, 113-114, 116-117, 118, 126-127, 173-174
See also Goodby Silverstein & Partners (GSP)
judgment, ideation and, 53, 56, 59, 80
Jung, Rex E., 33
Jung v. Matt, 80, 101

Kay, Woody, 89, 96
See also Arnold Worldwide
Kelley, David, 49, 140
See also IDEO Design Thinking Process
Kelley, Tom, 140
KEYS to Creativity and Innovation instrument, 89-90, 100, 113
See also challenges, work; encouragement; freedom, work; impediments, organizational; resources, sufficient work; work group support; workload pressures
Klymenko, Dylan, 129
Köhler, Victor, 11

Lange, Patricia G., 11
lateral thinking, 15, 16, 49, 54-59, 155
main advantage, 55
techniques, 55-59
See also random input; reversal technique; SCAMPER; Six Thinking Hats
leadership, 113-123
cognitive surplus and, 120-123
constant level of critique and, 116-117
giving freedom to take on challenges, 118-120
motivation and, 114
physical work environment and, 114-116
postmortems and, 117-118
tapping outside talent, 120
See also specific ad execs and agencies
Leake, Tim, 17, 66, 97, 100, 116, 181-182
See also Hyper Island; RPA Advertising; Saatchi & Saatchi New York
Lebowitz, Michael, 63-64, 96-97, 102-104, 107-108, 114, 116, 122, 123, 169-170
See also Big Spaceship
left-brained thinking, 32-33, 34
legend, 74, 83
Leo Burnett, 2, 66, 114, 172
Global Product Committee (GPC), 68
HumanKind, 111
philosophy, 111
See also Credle, Susan; Leo Burnett Humankind GPC Scale
Leo Burnett Humankind GPC Scale, 68-69
learning organization, 100, 117
postmortems, 118
LinkedIn, 100
Lois, George, 87, 89

Mad Men era, 88, 123
Marquez, Veronica, 21, 130, 133, 134
Martin Agency, 68
Martin Williams, 30, 46, 76, 89, 92
philosophy, 110, 111, 122
physical environment, 89
See also Tom Moudry
Maslow, Abraham, 54
matrix analysis, 60
McCann Erickson, 18, 96, 179
See also Teo, Lynn
McCormick, Brenna, 82, 84, 128-129, 133, 134, 136-137
See also mediaman
media neutral ideas, 76, 77
mediaman, 122-123, 136
little creative project series, 123
See also McCormick, Brenna; Vogel, Thomas
Medici family, 9
Medieval period, creativity in, 9
mental flexibility, 124-125, 160, 161, 163
See also specific ad execs
mental maps, 132
Merryman, Ashley, 15
metacognition, 39-40
metaphors, 76
Michalko, Michael, 85, 161

Michelangelo, 9
Mildenhall, Jonathan, 71
Millennials, 11
Miller, Michael, 131, 132, 133, 134
mind mapping, 49, 159
Modernista!, 30, 182, 183
  See also Jensen, Lance
Mooney, Amanda, 131, 147-149
Morning Pages exercise, 10, 74, 132, 137, 142, 159, 163
morphological analysis, 49, 60
morphological box, 59, 60
Mother New York, 94-95, 102, 104, 108, 117, 120-121, 123, 125, 126, 166-168
  philosophy, 108-109, 125, 167
  physical environment, 94-95, 167-168
  See also Deitchman, Andrew
motivation, 88, 105-106, 114, 178, 179
Moudry, Tom, 30, 46, 76, 89, 92, 111
  See also Martin Williams
Mozart, Wolfgang Amadeus, 10
Mullen, 3, 31, 53, 62, 93, 115, 178, 179
  philosophy, 109
  physical environment, 93, 115
  See also Boches, Edward
music, 85
  Musical Interpretation exercise, 78
  Musical Time Travel exercise, 76
myth, 74, 83

Nasard, Alexis, 72
Nissen, Celia, 134
no door philosophy, 95
novel ideas, 65

O'Shaughnessy, Siobhan, 150-151
Off Madison Ave, 64, 93, 174-175
  philosophy, 110
  physical environment, 93, 175
  See also Hurni, Roger
Ogilvy and Mather, 77
open door philosophy, 95, 100
open-mindedness, creativity and, 18
organizational structure, 91-97, 103, 104
  See also specific agencies; Pixar Studios
Ortega, Tom, 53, 89
  See also Riester, physical environment of
Osborn, Alex, 3, 41, 54, 58
Osborn-Parnes Creative Problem-Solving Process (CPS), 41, 42, 43, 46-49
outside support, 98-99
  See also work group support

Parnes, Sidney, 41
persistence, creativity and, 17
Phan, Trang, 13, 129, 132
philosophy. *See specific agencies and ad execs*; agency philosophy
Picasso, Pablo, 7
pirate culture, workplace, 90-91, 106, 107
Pixar Story, The, 100-101
Pixar Studios, 100-101
  creative brain trust, 100
  daily review process, 100
  physical environment, 101
  postmortems, 117
  unplanned collisions, 101
Plato, 8
postmortems, 117-118, 182
PressPausePlay, 11
Pritchard, Marc, 71
problem analysis methods, 59-60
  See also attribute listing; matrix analysis; morphological analysis
problem solving. *See specific creative problem-solving processes*; creative problem-solving process
Procter and Gamble, 71
prototypes, 50-51, 117
proverb, 83
provocation, 49

R/GA, 36, 99
random input, 49, 57-58
rapid prototyping/testing, 117
receptivity, creativity and, 18
Renaissance, creativity during, 9-10
Renaissance Man, 10
resources, sufficient work, 90
reversal technique, 58, 131, 151
Riester, physical environment of, 89
  See also Ortega, Tom
right-brained thinking, 32-33, 34
risk taking, 132-133, 137
Rosati, Eric, 128, 144-146
Ross, Marshall, 3, 36, 45-46, 61, 75, 88, 89, 99, 110-111, 116, 125, 176
  See also Cramer-Krasselt
Royer, Ted, 70
RPA Advertising, 66, 97, 181
  See also Leake, Tim
RSA Animate, 30
Ruggiero, Vincent Ryan, 24-25

Saatchi & Saatchi, 181
Saatchi & Saatchi Asia-Pacific and Greater China, 111
  See also Foster, Chris
Saatchi & Saatchi New York, 97, 116
  physical environment, 116
  See also Leake, Tim
Saatchi & Saatchi Singapore, 125
Sapient Global Markets, Boston, 152
SCAMPER, 58-59
Schaefer, Christiane, 132, 133, 134, 141-143
Schubert, Franz, 10
Schwartz, Rob, 45, 65, 90-91, 99, 125, 171-172
  See also TBWA\Chiat\Day; TBWA\Worldwide
second product failure syndrome, 101
Seelig, Tina, 12
self-perception, creativity and, 12, 18, 20-21

Shakespeare, William, 7
Shearer, Norm, 30, 53, 126
  See also Cactus Marketing Communications
Shek, Michal, 133, 134
Sherlock, Robert, 53, 64, 65, 98, 126
  See also Draftfcb Chicago
Shigaeva, Kristina, 13, 79-80, 132, 133
Shirky, Clay, 120
Silverstein, Rich, 93-94, 99, 101-102, 106, 173, 174
  See also Goodby Silverstein & Partners (GSP)
Six Thinking Hats, 49, 55-57
Smith, R.E., 190
social media, 69-70, 78, 100
  See also Facebook; Instagram; LinkedIn; Twitter
sound, 81, 85
  See also music
Sperry, Roger W., 32-33
Spong, Doug, 31, 88, 96, 99-100, 114, 118-119, 186-187
  See also Carmichael Lynch Spong
Stanford Technology Ventures Program, 12
Staub, Andrew, 133, 134
sticky information and ideas, 74, 82, 83
storytelling, 69, 74, 80, 81-84, 85, 143
  classic structure, 83
  interactive, 159
  mediums, 83-84
  story elements, 83
  transcendent story forms, 83
structure of intellect model, 26
Subway "Jared" campaign, 82

TBWA\Chiat\Day, 45, 65, 90-91, 118, 125, 128, 144, 171
  philosophy, 107, 171
  physical environment, 90-91, 106
  pirate culture, 90-91, 106, 107
  See also disruption; Schwartz, Rob
TBWA\Worldwide, 45, 90, 118, 125, 171
  See also Schwartz, Rob
teamwork, 23, 100
  See also specific agencies
technology
  as mirror for creativity, 11
  democratization of 10-11
  See also social media
TED.com, 69
Teo, Lynn, 18, 88, 92, 96, 114, 118, 179-181
  See also AKQA; McCann Erickson
Tharp, Twyla, 117-118
thinking
  abstract, 145
  analytical, 25
  critical, 25
  lateral, 15, 16, 49, 54-59, 155
  left-brained, 32-33, 34
  right-brained, 32-33, 34
  unconscious, 26
  vertical, 26
  See also convergent thinking; creative thinking; creative-thinking methods and techniques; creative-thinking skills; divergent thinking

Torrance, E. Paul, 24, 27, 53
Torrance Test of Creative Thinking (TTCT), 15, 27-30, 41
transparency, 103-104
  See also specific agencies
Twitter, 70, 84, 100

unconscious thinking, 26
Unlocking Creative Potential, 125
unplanned collisions, 101, 114-116
urban legend, 74, 83
Urbano, Cyril, 12-13, 128, 130

Valid Assessment of Learning in Undergraduate Education (VALUE), 27
Van Gogh, Vincent, 7
vertical thinking, 26
Victors and Spoils, 120
Vienna, creativity in early 19th-century, 10
Visible Measures, 131, 160
visual imagery, 80, 84-85
visual synectics, 49
visualization
  Map Visualization exercise, 119
  Visual Self-Presentation exercise, 42, 137
  Visualization of Concepts exercise, 86, 92, 115
  Visualize Your Personal Future exercise, 108
  See also exercises, creative-thinking
Vogel, Thomas, 122, 129, 130, 131, 132, 157, 158, 161
Volkswagen Group China, 141, 142
Volkswagen "The Force" Super Bowl ad, 78
von Stamm, Bettina, 118
Vulkan, Johnny, 63, 65, 66, 74, 112, 123, 165-166
  See also Anomaly New York
Wallace, Graham, 41, 44-45
Wallace Four-Phase Process, 41-45
Wieden and Kennedy, 134
Wilde, Judith, 119
Wilde, Richard, 119
Williams, Paul, 48
word associations, 131
work group support, 90, 97
  See also outside support
workload pressures, 90
workplace environment
  collaboration and, 89
  deconstructing traditional physical, 88
  social, 88
  See also specific agencies; Pixar Studios
writing down ideas, 131, 132
Wujec, Tom, 9, 25, 38
Wynkoop, Sara, 36, 130, 131

Yammer, 100
Yang, X., 190
Young, James Webb, 42, 43
Young & Rubicam Group, New York, 154

Zwicky, Fritz, 60

PERMISSIONS

Page 17 Nine Dots Exercise used with permission. Creative Education Foundation © 2014.

Page 40 Two Riders and Horses Puzzle used with permission. Creative Education Foundation © 2014.

Page 48 Creative Problem Solving Process: Osborn & Parnes used with permission. Paul Williams, Idea Sandbox © 2014.

Page 69 Image of Leo Burnett Humankind GPC scale used with permission. Leo Burnett, Chicago. IL. © 2014.

Page 82 Visualization of Stickiness Factors used with permission. Brenna McCormick © 2014.

Page 83 Visualization of Classic Story Arch used with permission. Mandy Emel © 2014.

Page 88 Image of Anomaly New York office used with permission. Anomaly, New York, NY © 2014.

Page 91 Image of TBWA\Chiat\Day office used with permission. Thomas Vogel © 2014.

Page 94 Images and layout of Mother New York office space used with permission. Mother, New York, NY © 2014.

Pages 96, 97 Image of Big Spaceship office used with permission. Thomas Vogel © 2014.

Page 98 Image of Euro/RSCG office used with permission. Thomas Vogel © 2014.

Page 102 Image of Big Spaceship office used with permission. Thomas Vogel © 2014.

Page 106 Images of TBWA\Chiat\Day office used with permission. Bill Hornstein © 2014.

Page 110 Image of Martin Williams office "Curious Wall" used with permission. Joey Konkel & Thomas Vogel © 2014.

Page 112 Image of Anomaly office "Dead Body" used with permission. Anomaly, New York, NY © 2014.

Page 121 Image of Big Spaceship "Whiteboard" used with permission. Thomas Vogel © 2014.

Page 122 Image of mediaman office "Dshini" used with permission. mediaman & Meik Mense © 2014.

Page 122 Image of Martin Williams office "Evolve" used with permission. Thomas Vogel © 2014.

Page 128 Image of TBWA\Chiat\Day office used with permission. Bill Hornstein © 2014.

Page 130 Image of Anomaly office "Quote by George Bernard Shaw" used with permission. Anomaly, New York, NY © 2014

Page 203 About the author – Image used with permission. Photo by Tyler Guertin © 2014.

Pages 20, 22, 27, 30, 32, 44, 57, 67, 79, 81 Illustrations used with permission. Harini Chandrasekar © 2014.

Case Studies

Page 136 Brenna McCormick: all images used with permission. Brenna McCormick © 2014.

Page 138 Noreen Arora: all images used with permission. Noreen Arora © 2014.

Page 141 Christiane Schaefer: all images used with permission. Christiane Schaefer © 2014.

Page 144 Eric Rosati: all images used with permission. Eric Rosati © 2014.

Page 147 Amanda Mooney: all images used with permission. Amanda Mooney © 2014.

Page 150 Siobhan O'Shaughnessy: all images used with permission. Siobhan O'Shaughnessy © 2014.

Page 152 Liz Goodwin: all images used with permission. Liz Goodwin © 2014.

Page 154 Lorelei Bandrovschi: all images used with permission. Lorelei Bandrovschi © 2014.

Page 157 Harini Chandrasekar: all images used with permission. Harini Chandrsaekar © 2014.

Page 160 Matthew Fiorentino: all images used with permission. Matthew Fiorentino © 2014.

Companion website (additional case studies) at www.breakthroughthinkingguide.com

Veronica Marquez: all images used with permission. Veronica Marquez © 2014.

Shannon McGurrin: all images used with permission. Shannon McGurrin © 2014.

Kristina Shigaeva: all images used with permission. Kristina Shigaeva © 2014.

Marissa Goldstein: all images used with permission. Marissa Goldstein © 2014.

Samantha Gutglass: all images used with permission. Samantha Gutglass © 2014.

Kimberly Crunden: all images used with permission. Kimberly Crunden © 2014.

Usen Esiet: all images used with permission. Usen Esiet © 2014.

Summer Lambert: all images used with permission. Summer Lambert © 2014.

Andrew Staub: all images used with permission. Andrew Staub © 2014.

Alyse Dunn: all images used with permission. Alyse Dunn © 2014.

Sarah Hamilton: all images used with permission. Sarah Hamilton © 2014.

Trang Phan: all images used with permission. Trang Phan © 2014.

Rebecca Hempen: all images used with permission. Rebecca Hempen © 2014.

Cyril Urbano: all images used with permission. Cyril Urbano © 2014.

Milena Guzman: all images used with permission. Milena Guzman © 2014.

Michal Shek: all images used with permission. Michal Shek © 2014.

Dylan Klymenko: all images used with permission. Dylan Klymenko © 2014.

Sara Wynkoop: all images used with permission. Sara Wynkoop © 2014.

Creative Executive Profiles

Page 165 Profile, image and interview with Johnny Vulkan used with permission. Johnny Vulkan © 2014.

Page 166 Profile, image and interview with Andrew Deitchman used with permission. Andrew Deitchman © 2014.

Page 168 Profile, image and interview with David Droga used with permission. David Droga 2014. Photo by Steve Carty for Hermann & Audrey © 2014.

Page 169 Profile, image and interview with Michael Lebowitz used with permission. Michael Lebowitz © 2014.

Page 171 Profile, image and interview with Rob Schwartz used with permission. Rob Schwartz © 2014. Photo by Bill Hornstein © 2014.

Page 172 Profile, image and interview with Susan Credle used with permission. Susan Credle © 2014. Photo by Daniel Forbes © 2014.

Page 173 Profile, images and interviews with Margaret Johnson and Rich Silverstein used with permission. Margaret Johnson and Rich Silverstein © 2014.

Page 174 Profile, image and interview with Roger Hurni used with permission. Roger Hurni © 2014.

Page 176 Profile, image and interview with Marshall Ross used with permission. Marshall Ross © 2014.

Page 177 Profile, image and interview with Chris Foster used with permission. Chris Foster © 2014.

Page 178 Profile, image and interview with Edward Boches used with permission. Edward Boches © 2014.

Page 179 Profile, image and interview with Lynn Teo used with permission. Lynn Teo © 2014.

Page 181 Profile, image and interview with Tim Leake used with permission. Tim Leake © 2014. Photo by Gabriela Mancini © 2014.

Page 182 Profile, image and interview with Lance Jensen used with permission. Lance Jensen © 2014. Photo by Tom Peri © 2014.

Page 183 Profile, image and interview with Blake Ebel used with permission. Blake Ebel © 2014.

Page 185 Profile, image and interview with Mark Hunter used with permission. Mark Hunter © 2014.

Page 186 Profile, image and interview with Doug Spong used with permission. Doug Spong - Carmichael Lynch Spong © 2014.

Companion website (additional creative executive profiles) at www.breakthroughthinkingguide.com:

Profile, image and interview with Norm Shearer used with permission. Norm Shearer © 2014.

Profile, image and interview with Alex Bogusky used with permission. Alex Bogusky © 2014. Photo by Chad Poorman © 2014.

ABOUT THE AUTHOR

Thomas Vogel is an associate professor of marketing communication and the graduate program director for the Global Marketing Communication and Advertising Program at Emerson College. He specializes in creativity and creative thinking, as well as strategic communication, experience design and branding on the Internet. Thomas teaches courses in creativity, problem solving, creative thinking and visual communication, and has helped hundreds of students develop and master creative skills for the past twenty years. Prior to joining Emerson College he was a professor of media design at the Department of Media Management at the RheinMain University of Applied Sciences in Wiesbaden, Germany, where he served as the founding dean from 1993 - 1999.

Thomas is an active public speaker, panelist, consultant, and is involved in special projects for Internet, advertising and multi media. His creative work focuses on the strategic design and usability aspects of interactive media, developing efficient experience design and online communication. His research explores the nature of creativity, creative thinking and advertising creativity. As creativity consultant he develops educational programs and provides corporate trainings to improve and manage creativity, creative thinking and the ability to innovate. He is a founding partner of mediaman, a digital marketing agency in Germany, China and the USA. Formerly he worked as art director and creative director in New York City at Grey Advertising, Lois GGK, J. Walter Thompson and Communication House.

Thomas believes that everyone can learn and practice creativity, and become a master in creative thinking and problem solving skills. He lives with his wife and two daughters on the north shore of Boston and is an avid open water rower and yoga practitioner. If you want to reach Thomas to discuss creativity, you can find him on Twitter: @vogelthomas or at thomas_vogel@emerson.edu or at thomas.vogel@mediaman.net.

MORE GREAT TITLES FROM HOW + PRINT BOOKS

Creative Workshop

By David Sherwin

Designers often struggle to find creative inspiration because of tight deadlines and demanding workloads. *Creative Workshop* is packed with 80 unique creative thinking exercises that cover all kinds of media and time ranges (we all know how rare free time can be). Give your brain the creative workout it needs to stay sharp!

D30: Exercises for Designers

By Jim Krause

D30 is a workout book. In addition to dozens of readily applicable tips, tricks and informational tidbits, the book contains thirty exercises designed to develop and strengthen the creative powers of graphic designers, artists and photographers in a variety of intriguing and fun ways.

What will you need to begin? Not much—the majority of the book's activities make use of traditional media to illuminate creative techniques and visual strategies that can be applied to media of all sorts. Roll up your sleeves, grab some art supplies, and get busy!

Special Offer From HOW Books!

You can get 15% off your entire order at MyDesignShop.com! All you have to do is go to www.howdesign.com/howbooks-offer and sign up for our free e-newsletter on graphic design. You'll also get a free digital download of *HOW magazine*.

For more news, tips and articles, follow us at **Twitter.com/HOWbrand**

For behind-the-scenes information and special offers, become a fan at **Facebook.com/HOWmagazine**

For visual inspiration, follow us at **Pinterest.com/HOWbrand**

Find these books and many others at **MyDesignShop.com** or your local bookstore.